The Official Student Doctor Network Medical School Admissions Guide

The Official Student Doctor Network Medical School Admissions Guide

Christian Becker

Mill City Press, Inc.

Two comments offering great insight into medical training from the Student Doctor Network Forums (www.studentdoctor.net):

"One doctor gave me the most helpful advice of all. He told me to basically figure out if I could be happy doing anything else in this world, and do that instead. So, I really did look inside myself and tried my best to find something else. The truth is, I couldn't. Yes, we're all going to be working ridiculous hours, and we're all going to have to at one point in our medical careers deal with lawsuits, and, yes, we're going to have to deal with insurance companies, BUT, I know that there isn't a single career that will bring me more joy than medicine."
—Michael G. Valladares, medical student

"I'm in the middle of my third medicine month in the ninth month of my third year of medical school, and I'm feeling as though it actually is my 300th year instead. I'm tired, I'm on edge, and I'm especially bitter about almost everything. But I know it's because I'm physically exhausted. If you're talking to students, interns, residents, etc., their sour philosophy might also come from a perspective warped by post-call psychosis. I had a great career as an engineer, great income, lots of time to play, and time to sleep— absolutely no pressure from day to day. And I hated nearly every second of every day I was at work. Then I bailed at the absolute height of the dot-com era and found myself wondering whether I was crazy. Now, three years later, even though I'm stressed, tired, and continuously feeling like an idiot, I love what I'm doing, and I'm grateful I made the decision to enter medical school. I swear that nothing touches your heart like somebody saying, 'Thank you for taking care of me.' You'll get that feeling over and over again in medicine, and I assure you I never got that in engineering."
—gtb (SDN forum member)

Table of Contents

MEDICAL STUDENT ANSWERS **247**

Preface

The goal of *The Official Student Doctor Network Medical School Admission Guide* is to help you gain acceptance to medical school and succeed, making your ambition to become a physician reality. We wrote this book for the traditional, nontraditional, and even the less-than-stellar student, but keeping foremost the average applicant in mind, offering tips, strategies, and advice that apply to almost all applicants.

Only about one-third of all medical school applicants are accepted into medical school each year. In particular, two factors make it difficult to gain admission to medical school:

1. Applicants to medical school are very competitive. These are the undergraduate students who get top grades and are very driven to succeed.
2. There are more applicants to medical school than there are seats available in medical school classes.

Before you start on your journey of becoming a physician, be sure you know what you want. There are other career options available that are prestigious and well paid. Becoming a physician is a long hard road and even after training, it continues to be an intense career. As one physician put it, "Forty hours in medicine is part time."

Even most employed physicians are expected to work at least forty hours a week doing patient care (not including the extra ten to twenty hours or more per week dictating reports or taking care of paperwork). Therefore, you will find few physicians who work less than fifty hours per week.

So, make sure, before you sign up for this great journey into medicine, that you actually have an accurate picture (and expectation) of what lies ahead—both in training and in your future career.

Also, patient care is not for everyone. You see people at their worst, when they are distressed, upset, and not well—often ungrateful, cranky, and difficult. Needless to say, medicine is all about the patients and getting along with people.

In this book we will take a look at the entire premed process from A to Z and beyond.

We hope this book will be helpful in guiding you in the journey to become a physician.
Good luck in your pursuits!

Christian Becker, medical student
Lee Burnett, DO
Andrew Doan, MD, PhD

A note about the Student Doctor Network

The Student Doctor Network (SDN) is a nonprofit website (studentdoctor.net), dedicated to the pre-health and health professional student community. The SDN mission is to assist and encourage students as they traverse the challenging and complicated health professions education process. This is done by hosting an online community and meeting place, providing free and unbiased resources, and serving as a clearinghouse for associated information.

One of the unique features of SDN is the discussion forums. The SDN forums are the largest pre-health and health-student forums on the Internet. There is no cost to be a member, and our members on SDN are some of the most active on the Web, helping to make SDN nationally recognized for its vibrant and welcoming communities. Our members have even been quoted on the front page of the *New York Times*.

With over fifty thousand members and well over three million posts, the SDN forums have answers to practically any question you may have. We cover it all, from medical school, dental school, pharmacy school, podiatry school, optometry school, and veterinary school to post-baccalaureate programs, residencies, school applications, and more.

A note about the authors

Christian Becker, the lead author of this book, is a current medical student at the Medical College of Wisconsin and the creator of an SDN partner premed website, which has been providing information, hints, and unique student advice on gaining admission to medical school.

Other contributing authors are active moderators of the Student Doctor Network Forums and volunteer their time to keep the forum communities informative, fun, and safe. The SDN volunteers are medical students, residents, and senior physicians. Together, the SDN volunteers have extensive experience with applying to medical school, surviving as medical students, passing the medical boards, and practicing as physicians.

The SDN contributors to this book are:

Ai Mukai, MD, Physical Medicine and Rehabilitation Resident
Audrey Stanton, DO, MPH.
Andrew Doan, MD, PhD, Ophthalmologist
Diane L. Evans, DO, MS
KyGrlDr2B (SDN forum moderator name)
Mark Piedra, MD, Neurological Surgery Resident
Natalie J. Belle, MD
Rachel Liu, medical student, Dublin, Ireland
Robert Greenhagen, podiatry student

The efforts and hard work of all the authors/contributors are greatly appreciated. Their expertise has been invaluable in producing this book.

We also appreciate the hard work in reviewing this book done by the additional individuals who have also given valuable feedback and suggestions for improvements to produce the final polished version of this book:

Anna Peck
Brittney Becker
David P. Russo, DO, MPH, MS
Kimberli S. Cox, MD, MS, Breast Surgical Oncologist
Lee Burnett, DO, Family Medicine
Ronald W. McCune, PhD

Introduction

by Andrew Doan, MD, PhD

What does it take to be a physician?

This is a difficult question to answer. I do not think there is a standard set of characteristics that makes a good physician. Nevertheless, although physicians have diverse backgrounds and experiences, the successful physician possesses several key characteristics: a genuine desire to contribute to society, pleasure in healing the sick, self-discipline, strong work ethic, ability to be a team player, and academic endurance. Having sound business sense will also help in our current environment of financial cutbacks. Physicians of the future will likely make less income than their predecessors. Therefore, without a strong inner desire to heal the sick and dedication to a life-long endeavor of learning the art of medicine, young physicians will be discontent and burnout quickly.

How do you know that you will enjoy working as a physician? One way is to mirror physicians in practice and listen to them. Before you embark on this life-long commitment, you need to know the bad as well as the rewards of the profession. You can also spend time on the SDN forums to read posts from other students and physicians. Personally, I enjoy the science, working with patients, and being able to improve the quality of life for others. In addition, medicine provides employment stability. I enjoy my job and cannot believe that I am being paid for my services!

Advances and changes in medicine

With each new medical advancement, the field of medicine becomes more complex. We have seen a shift from generalization to specialization. While the family practice physician who does it all still exists, it is becoming exceedingly difficult to be the solo medical and surgical caregiver for our patients. Modern medicine has evolved into a team approach composed of multiple medical specialties. For example, diabetes is a multi-systemic disorder affecting the heart, brain, eyes, kidneys, nervous system, and other major organs. It is common to have patients with diabetes managed by their internist or family physician along with the ophthalmologist. If new medical issues are encountered, a nephrologist, orthopedic surgeon, or cardiologist may also manage the diabetic patient.

What does this mean for physicians in the 21st century? Medicine will encounter an explosion of technological advances in genetics and treatments. We will see the implementation of genetic therapies, novel drug delivery mechanisms, advances in microsurgery, and improvement in imaging techniques. This is an exciting time to be a physician. Because of the growth of information and technology, the medical field will need individuals with different talents and interests. Although not exclusive to the following, students with backgrounds in engineering, genetics, public health, epidemiology, computer science, and business will contribute to the advancement of patient care, biomedical research, and medical education. If you are excited to start your journey of becoming a physician, then welcome aboard. We wish you luck in your endeavor!

The outlook on physicians over the next ten to twenty years

The U.S. medical system continually evolves depending on the needs of society and the individuals who provide medical services. Due to financial pressures, our current health system is under considerable stress. It is difficult to pick up a newspaper without seeing a headline about malpractice reform, Medicare funding, or medical insurance. What does the future hold for the current generation of physicians? I am not a fortune-teller. Predicting the future of medicine is as successful as picking the hot stocks. On the other hand, similar to how older physicians must learn new medical knowledge and biomedical advances, physicians must learn to adapt to the changing financial, political, and social demands. There are no Fortune 500 companies that can remain static and survive. Successful companies develop new strategies as the market demands for their products and services shift. Likewise, in order to be successful, physicians need to adapt, change, and grow.

While the future is uncertain, medicine is an exceedingly rewarding profession, financially, personally, and socially. Medicine provides an intellectually stimulating environment. A career as a physician allows the melding of one's thirst for scientific knowledge with the ability to make a difference in other people's lives. No other career will provide this degree of responsibility and challenge. Furthermore, physicians are still one of the highest paid professions in the United States; however, I strongly believe that financial reimbursement is icing on the cake. If individuals do not enjoy their careers, then money becomes the shackle that binds them to the profession they despise.

The Path to Medicine

Brief Overview of Education and Training

General information

Becoming a physician is a long road, including, for most people, going to college for four years after high school to earn a baccalaureate degree, then attending medical school for four years, and finally completing a residency program for specialized training. Often, residency training is followed with more specialized training called a fellowship program. Residency and fellowship training combined can last about three to seven years, depending on the specialization.

The grand total of time spent for most people can be calculated as follows:

4 years undergraduate education
4 years medical school
3 to 7 years residency (and fellowship)

---

11 to 15 years of your life

Most European and other international schools only have six-year medical school programs (with some variation on the length) offered to students straight out of high school instead of after college. Overall, medical education is organized very differently in Europe and often is free, requiring no tuition. Note that there are issues with practicing medicine in the United States if you go to medical school abroad, which will be discussed later.

In the United States, medical students pay for tuition and other expenses during their undergraduate education and medical school. However, during residency, residents are paid a salary of around $40,000 or so per year, depending on location, years in residency, specialty, and other factors. For example, according to FREIDA (Fellowship and Residency Electronic Interactive Database) in 2006, internal medicine compensation at Medical College of Wisconsin for first-year residents was $43,250.[1]

Most medical students accumulate well over $100,000 in student loans while attending medical school. Some students even accumulate up to $250,000 in debt to go through medical school. A piece of good news is that most physicians have no problems paying back their loans, sometimes in just a few years after completing residency training, if they handle their finances wisely. Nearly all medical students can qualify for loans easily to cover school-related expenses.

Joint degree programs

Completion of a joint degree program such as an MD/PhD or MD/JD, or whatever it may be, adds more years to the time spent in training during medical school. For most MD/PhD combined programs, medical school takes approximately seven years instead of four years to allow enough time for completion of additional requirements and the dissertation as part of the PhD degree. Some MD/PhD programs are funded through the Medical Scientist Training Program (MSTP).[2] These funded positions include free tuition, fees, and books to the medical student making medical school essentially free, and a yearly stipend around $24,000 is paid to the student. As you might imagine, these are very coveted and competitive spots.

You can contact each medical school about the combined programs they offer. To enter a combined program, students have to be successfully admitted to both programs independently. So, you have to meet all requirements for the medical program and separately meet all the requirements for the PhD program. Usually, to be considered for the MSTP, you have to show significant research interest and/or involvement and an interest in academia.

MD/PhD programs are primarily designed to turn out academically oriented physicians, working as faculty and involved in research.

Other combined degree programs are available at most of the medical schools in the United States. Besides the MD/PhD, some other examples include the MD/JD (law), MD/MBA (business), and MD/MPH (public health). More joint degrees are available, but these are some of the most common ones.

Medical school right after high school

Some U.S. medical schools offer programs whereby individuals are admitted to medical school straight out of high school, without going to college first. This essentially allows completion of an MD degree in six to eight years total, depending on the program. For the first few years of the program, these individuals still have to complete the premed required coursework in a college-type setting that is usually not part of the medical school directly. So, the college curriculum is not really skipped, but may be condensed. The medical school usually cooperates with a local college or university to offer this program.

This option may take less time overall than completing a full college degree and then the full four years of medical school. Quite a few of these post–high school programs only accept in-state applicants. If you already know in high school that you are destined for medicine, this may be an option for you.

Also note that your high school GPA and SAT or ACT scores are used for admission rather than the MCAT and college GPA, although a minimum GPA must be maintained while completing the premed coursework to remain qualified for the program once accepted. Also, a few of the schools require that you also take the MCAT after completion of the premed coursework and that you achieve a certain minimum score to remain in the program.

Following is a list of these schools.[3]

Medical School	Length	Out-of-State Students
Albany Medical College	8 years	49%
Baylor College of Medicine	8 years	47%
Boston University School of Medicine	7 years	90%
Brown Medical School	8 years	94%
Case Western Reserve University School of Medicine	8 years	75%
Chicago Medical School at Rosalind Franklin University	8 years	
Drexel University College of Medicine	7 years	84%
East Tennessee State University James H. Quillen College of Medicine	8 years	
Eastern Virginia Medical School	8 years	17%
George Washington University School of Medicine	7 years	
Howard University College of Medicine	8 years	
Keck School of Medicine of the University of Southern California	8 years	36%
Meharry Medical College	7 years	
Michigan State University College of Human Medicine	8 years	10%
New York University School of Medicine	7 years	
Northeastern Ohio Universities College of Medicine	6 years	8%
Northwestern University, The Feinberg School	7 years	
Ohio State University College of Medicine	7 years	35%
Pennsylvania State University College of Medicine	6 years	82%
Saint Louis University School of Medicine	8 years	42%
State University of New York Downstate Medical	8 years	

State University of New York Upstate Medical	8 years	
Stony Brook University Health Sciences Center	8 years	
Temple University School of Medicine	8 years	
UMDNJ—New Jersey Medical School	7 years	
UMDNJ—Robert Wood Johnson Medical School	8 years	
University of Alabama School of Medicine	8 years	10%
University of California, San Diego School of Medicine		
University of Cincinnati College of Medicine	8 years	27%
University of Connecticut School of Medicine	8 years	14%
University of Florida College of Medicine	7 years	
University of Illinois College of Medicine	7 years	
University of Miami Leonard M. Miller School	6 years	
University of Missouri-Kansas City School of Medicine	6 years	17%
University of Rochester School of Medicine	8 years	36%
University of South Alabama College of Medicine	8 years	33%
University of Texas Medical School at San Antonio	7 years	
University of Wisconsin Medical School	7 years	
Virginia Commonwealth University School of Medicine	8 years	62%
Wayne State University School of Medicine	8 years	

Premed

Most students complete a four-year college degree before entering medical school. Typically, medical schools require a baccalaureate degree in any discipline of your choice. However, by far, most students have a science background, often in biology or something closely related. Technically, any degree will work as long as some basic course requirements are met that are required by all medical schools.

Despite being able to choose any major leading to a baccalaureate degree, in talking with many medical students, most of them highly recommend having a strong biological sciences background. Many concepts are considered prerequisites in medical school to be expanded upon and are not explained in great detail again. Those who don't have a strong background in this area seem to have a harder time during the first year and have to spend more time studying.
If you don't have a biology background, don't panic. Even without a biological science background, students seem to do well. It's just more work—but good grades are possible nonetheless.

The entire premed experience is not the easiest one in the world in and of itself. You are expected to do well in your coursework in order to be competitive for medical school admission, fulfill many extracurricular activities to bolster your application, and take some tough science courses. Ask most premed or medical students about how much fun they had with organic chemistry or physics, for example. You may wonder, "Why do I have to take this course?" Any degree in the physical or biological sciences is hard and that is what most people do for their premed work to be competitive and to be better prepared for medical school.

Medical school

Medical school is intense—much more intense than undergrad. Each semester is packed with roughly twenty-four credits of upper-division science courses including labs (no more generals or intro-type courses as in undergrad), but it is doable. It just requires lots of hard work. Many people say it is like taking a drink from a fire hydrant since the volume of information covered is overwhelming. The first two years of medical school are classroom based to study the basic sciences and the last two years are typically hospital-, clinical-, and office-based rotations devoted to clinical medicine. Combined, this results in a total of four years of medical school.

Residency

Residency is usually the final step in the training process of becoming a physician, unless you decide to pursue fellowship training, which follows residency training. Residency training is specialty specific, whereas medical school provides the basis in science knowledge as well as a foundation in clinical medicine in a more general sense. Rotations in medical school cover all major specialty areas for a short period. On the other hand, residency is spent on getting specific training in one particular specialty over a period of three to seven years, depending on the specialty, to become an expert in that area of training.

Residency is paid, so it is more like a job, but it is still considered training (postgraduate training) and is done under varying degrees of supervision. In fact, it is *the* training that turns out capable physicians with experience, who have seen it all in their respective fields before beginning to practice medicine on their own.

Note that this is usually a very intense experience, with residents routinely working up to 80 hours a week. Recent regulations, adapted just a few years ago, have imposed an 80-hour workweek limit for residents, although, historically, residents have worked up to 120 hours a week. Not all residency programs have fully committed to the 80-hour week so far, especially surgical specialties. Often, residents still work around 90 to 100 hours per week in some more intense specialties, such as surgery, whether or not they actually log those exact hours. Residents usually take call every fourth night or so, and can be in the hospital for up to 30 hours at a time, as part of their 80-hour (+) week.

Fellowships

Fellowship training is like another small residency after residency. You may complete an internal medicine residency (three years), followed by a cardiology or gastroenterology fellowship, for example. Some specialties require completion of a residency before subspecializing with a fellowship. The specialties just mentioned fall in this category because they require completion of an internal medicine residency first.

Fellowships are very common and available for almost all specialties. Orthopedic surgeons may elect to do a fellowship in hand surgery, for example. This is additional specialized training that sort of makes them hand experts within orthopedic surgery, but they are still orthopedic surgeons. They usually maintain a normal orthopedic practice that is not just focused on hand surgery, but they can limit their practice if they wish to.

Practicing Medicine

General Information

There are many different settings in which physicians practice medicine. The following is a brief discussion of a few types. Note that this is by no means an all-inclusive or comprehensive discussion, but rather an attempt to give an overview.

In 2005, of the 15,736 MD medical school graduates, 32.8 percent (or 5,161) entered academic medicine (4,752 entering clinical academic medicine and 409 entering basic science academic medicine), 35.2 percent (or 5,539) entered private practice and 8.1 percent (or 1,274) took salaried clinical positions (976 hospital employed, 62 HMO employed, and 236 state or federal employment).[4]

Group practice

Most private practice physicians today join existing group practices rather than starting their own. Of the 5,539 graduates who entered private practice in 2005, only 314 (5.6 percent) started their own practice, 535 (9.6 percent) entered a practice with a partner, and 4,690 (84.7 percent) joined practices with three or more physicians.[4]

There are several benefits to joining an existing practice, including lower or no start-up costs and shared call schedules, among others. Several physicians sharing call (say five physicians, each taking every fifth week of call for all of the patients seen in the practice) can be a huge plus in a group setting. Often, in solo practice, a physician is responsible for all of his or her own patients all of the time, taking calls essentially every night, unless other arrangements are made with other physicians of the same specialty.

Financially, when finishing residency, most residents are not exactly wealthy, but instead may owe from $100,000 to $250,000 or so in student loans. In 2005, the average indebtedness for graduates who attended public MD medical schools was $110,000 and for those who attended private MD medical schools was $138,093.[5]

Additional practice start-up costs and the potential of having to build up a practice for several years may not be very appealing or even possible for some new physicians just out of residency.

Most often, already established practices are looking for physicians to recruit and pay a yearly salary or some other financial package based on performance. In other group practice settings, physicians get together to jointly finance a building and share office staff and other expenses, but each physician bills patients separately and remains more independent.

As already mentioned, some physicians are employed by HMOs and other large healthcare companies or hospitals, drawing a fixed paycheck or performance-based pay.

Other financial concerns are the costs to maintain an office, collections, malpractice costs, etc., that may make employment much more appealing than maintaining a solo practice.

Solo practice

Solo physicians often have arrangements to share call with other physicians of their specialty, despite the fact that they are not sharing part of the same practice. Solo practice is becoming less common, but exists, and some physicians still seem to prefer this type of setting, especially if they are more entrepreneurial. Also, depending on geographical location in the United States, the number of solo physicians seems to vary. In some areas, it is harder to compete in solo practice due to patient demographics and health care reimbursements, and group practice seems to be the more attractive option.

Academic medicine and hospital-based medicine

Another type of setting is in the hospital as an employee or an individually billing physician who spends his or her entire time in the hospital setting. An example of this is an anesthesiologist or an intensivist who works in the intensive care unit of a hospital and does not have any other patients other than those who are referred to him or her for specialized care from other physicians.

In academic medicine, working as clinical faculty associated with a medical school or residency program presents a unique type of environment centered on the hospital setting. These types of physicians, in all specialties, draw a regular paycheck from the university and do not have to worry about collecting on bills, staffing issues, malpractice insurance, etc., as many other physicians do. They are typically surrounded by residents and medical students who do a lot of the daily routine work for them. They teach and are part of the educational program for medical students and residents. Academic physicians can also be involved in basic science teaching at a medical school.

Many academic physicians dedicate three to four days a week to patient care, one day to teaching, and one day to research, but there seems to be some variation in how much time different individuals spend on each activity. Many academic physicians also maintain their own private practices on the side.

Subspecialties that are very highly specialized are typically only found in larger teaching hospital and academic settings. Smaller hospitals do not supply enough patient cases to sustain a specialist who is highly specialized; therefore, these physicians often work in university/academic hospitals.

Some of the children's hospitals around the country are examples of this type of setting and are most often associated with medical schools. Most average hospitals do not have physicians who are trained in the more subspecialized pediatric surgical specialties, pediatric intensive care, or other pediatric subspecialties, for example.

Military medicine

The military offers scholarships (Health Professions Scholarship Program (HPSP), for example) that pay for all medical school expenses, including tuition, fees and books, and a monthly stipend. In return, graduates owe them years of service in the military as payback. There are also certain residency stipulations.

Some physicians decide to remain in the service until military retirement and then enter private practice. Others only put in the minimum time required to fulfill the payback.

Attending the Uniformed Services University of the Health Sciences (medical school) is another way to enter the military while in medical school and receive officer's pay instead of a stipend with all education expenses paid in full. The payback is longer for this option, but you earn full officer's pay while in school as well.

Whether just paying back the minimum time or staying in longer, military medicine simplifies many aspects of medicine such as billing, malpractice, etc. Benefits or drawbacks, depending on the viewpoint, are potential international moves and more frequent relocations as well as potential deployments to war zones or crisis areas. Some physicians enjoy military medicine and the officer benefits as well as seeing the world; others prefer to avoid the military option for the same reasons.

Work Hard or Coast in Medical School?

One saying you always hear or have probably heard at least once is:

Pass = Doctor.

As long as you pass all of your courses in medical school and the board exams, you will be a physician in the end. Nobody will ever ask you about your grades or board scores once you are practicing medicine. So, some students may set their goal to pass their classes, rather than achieving honors or being in the top 10 percent of their class.

In reality, it is probably not possible to just coast in medical school. Just passing your courses and the boards takes a lot of effort and hard work. Passing classes and boards with higher scores and grades above pass takes even more effort and hard work.

Passing may work just fine if you are less concerned about obtaining a top-rated residency spot or a residency in one of the very competitive specialties such as dermatology, orthopedic surgery, plastic surgery, ENT (ear-nose-throat), radiation oncology, or neurosurgery, to name just a few.

These and other very competitive specialty choices are almost inaccessible with average grades and board scores. Internal medicine, pediatrics, family medicine, psychiatry, and others are examples of specialties that are easier to get into, and there is a great need for additional practitioners in these fields. Therefore, there are many more residency spots available in these specialties and they are less competitive as a result. They typically do not require top grades and board scores either, unless you are interested in the top residency programs in the country for those specific specialties, in which case these are also very competitive.

For example, according to a report on the 2005 NRMP match results,[6] the average board score for Dermatology was a 233; 49 percent were in Alpha Omega Alpha Honor Society ("AOA" for short, in which membership is primarily based on grades achieved in medical school; students usually have to be in the top 10 percent or so of their class to qualify); 95 percent of applicants had participated in research; and 80 percent had research publications. Overall, 546 graduates (366 U.S. MD graduates and 180 U.S. DO graduates or international graduates) had applied for 316 available training spots in 2005. That comes to about 1.73 applicants per available position.

The average board score for family medicine was 210, 6 percent were in AOA, 67 percent of applicants had participated in research, and 37 percent had research publications. Overall, 2,667 graduates (1,110 U.S. MD graduates and 1,557 U.S. DO graduates or international graduates) had applied for 2,761 available training spots in 2005. That comes to about 0.97 applicants per available position.

How hard you work in medical school, as reflected by grades (e.g., honors) and high board scores, is important in some residency considerations. Some medical schools are on a straight pass/fail system that, obviously, makes actual grades less important and board scores even more important. Also, as these numbers show, research during medical school and other factors can also be very important in your ultimate quest to become a physician.

Chapter References

1.   FREIDA, http://www.ama-assn.org/ama/pub/
        category/2997.html

2.   Medical Scientist Training Program Overview,
        http://www.nigms.nih.gov/Training/Mechanisms/
        NRSA/InstPredoc/
        PredocOverview-MSTP.htm

3.   Information on Combined College/MD Programs for
        High School Students, Medical School Admission
        Requirements (MSAR), 2007–2008, pages 59–62

4.   U.S. Medical School Graduates by Race and
        Ethnicity, AAMC Data Book 2006, page 27, First
        Choice of Career Activity by Percent for Graduating
        U.S. Medical Students, AAMC Data Book 2006,
        page 35

5.   Educational Indebtedness of U.S. Medical School
        Graduates, AAMC Data Book 2006, page 58

6.   Charting Outcomes in the Match: Characteristics
        of Applicants Who Matched to Their Preferred
        Specialty in the 2005 NRMP Main Residency
        Match, https://services.aamc.org/Publications/
        index.cfm?fuseaction=Product.displayForm&prd_
        id=159&prv_id=189

The Premed Requirements

Premed Requirements

Almost all medical schools require taking the MCAT, specific course work, and obtaining a degree. There are also many extracurricular activities that may not be required or spelled out anywhere per se, but are absolutely necessary to be a competitive applicant. Some schools will not only consider you a weak applicant if you cannot show some of the activities on your application, but also will deny an interview if they don't see enough of it.

What medical school admissions committees look for

Most premed advisors will probably agree that maybe 70 to 80 percent of the admissions decision depends on your GPA and MCAT scores alone (since these are given much emphasis). However, there is more to the admissions decision. The weight placed on different aspects of your overall application varies by school. Some medical schools place very heavy emphasis on the MCAT and don't consider much else, while other schools almost completely ignore MCAT scores unless they are very low. Instead, they may place all their emphasis on extracurricular activities and a well-rounded application.

Generally, the following are the main areas used by admissions committees to evaluate candidates:

1. GPA
2. MCAT scores
3. Application material
4. Recommendation letters
5. Personal interview

Note that recommendation letters are written by people (usually faculty, physicians, or managers) who have interacted with you in extracurricular activities or in the classroom. Therefore, these really reflect how you did in the activities that you listed on your application and what type of person you are.

The personal statement of your application, the personal interview, and recommendation letters all have one thing in common: They allow the admission committee to get a glimpse into your personality, your character, and give them an overall impression about you. Numbers on a page are meaningless by themselves. Most applicants have a good GPA and at least a decent MCAT score, so some of these other factors are just as important, or even more, than your scores and grades.

Your application, scores, grades, and recommendation letters will get you the interview. Your personality, character, and the overall impression you leave at the interview will get you the spot in the class.

Most medical schools will not seriously consider you if you have never been in a clinical setting. How would you know what physicians do or that you like what physicians do?
Also, some schools have an absolute requirement that you do some sort of research—without it, they will not consider your application, either. Other schools may not care about research at all. Therefore, a lot depends on the specific medical schools you are interested in.

Generally speaking, it is best to prepare as if you needed to cover all of the areas mentioned next. This makes you a very strong applicant no matter where you end up applying in the end.

Specific school requirements

Some schools are more specific than others in specifying what activities are required or are just good to have to make your application stand out from the pack. The list of requirements or recommendations should look about the same for most medical schools. Some research powerhouses may have larger research requirements than your average schools. There may even be various lists available from different schools, but most don't spell out their requirements very well.

For this discussion, I will use a list provided by the University of Utah School of Medicine. The list is useful because it does not just list what activities are recommended, but it also details very specifically what must be done to meet each goal on the list. These numbers were compiled by averaging what previous years' applicants actually did who applied to their school. So, it may provide a look at what the average applicant has done in the past and it allows you to set some specific goals that you can meet, or better yet, exceed. Therefore, generally speaking, following these guidelines should make you a better candidate for admission to most medical schools.

In order to qualify for an interview, a candidate has to meet at least the average values in five of the eight categories and the minimum value in the other three. The average reflects the true average for all of their applicants each year. At the University of Utah, performing below the minimum in any one category automatically disqualifies applicants from receiving interview invitations. The statistics for 2004 are:[1]

Category	Minimum	Average
GPA*	3.0	3.7
MCAT*	21	30
Shadowing	1 day	3 days
Volunteer/Service	3 hrs/week for 3 months	4 hrs/week for 4 years (no typo)
Clinical Exposure	4 hrs/week for 2 months	4 hrs/week for 3 months
Research	4 hrs/week for 2 months	4 hrs/week for 3 months
Leadership Positions	1 in past 3 yrs	3 for 3 months each in past 4 yrs
Multitasking		20 hours per week

* *Values for matriculants, all other values in this table for applicants.*

Time spent in these areas can overlap. For example, volunteer tutoring hours would be considered leadership and volunteer time. Time spent in a volunteer clinic would count as volunteer/service time and clinical exposure.

The weaker your MCAT score and GPA, the more important are all the other areas to strengthen your overall application. If your MCAT or GPA are average or below average, you will need to make your application stand out in other areas. This allows you to prove to the admissions committee that you have something to offer that is not reflected by your MCAT score and GPA alone.

The goal of all of this

Your goal is to score well on the criteria the admission committee uses to evaluate you and gain admission to the school. Having spent plenty of time in each of these areas makes you a much stronger applicant and shows the school that you are serious about medicine.

The importance of recommendation letters is to show the admissions committee how you did in different activities, but even more importantly, what type of person you are.

Again: Why should you do all of these?

1. To make you a better applicant
2. To make you stand out from the pack of applicants
3. To show them you are serious about medicine

So, your MCAT and GPA are average? (If you don't know your score yet, prepare as if it were average and you cannot go wrong with your preparation.) Is there anything else you can show the admissions office that they should choose you over someone with a higher GPA and MCAT score than you? You bet! All kinds of hours spent in extracurricular activities demonstrate your commitment.

All these extra activities look good on your application and may make it stand out from the rest. Perhaps you could also argue that most everyone does those things, so you really can't stand out. Reverse that thought: all the more reason to do them so you are not behind your competitors.

Also, not all applicants do these, so you have a chance to stand out.

You can pick one area that you really like and spend much more time there to stand out. If you love research, try to invest years there instead of months. If you love shadowing, put in hundreds of hours instead of twenty hours only. If you can't stand out everywhere, pick one area in which to do it. I personally think you can beat the averages listed in the table previously in all categories fairly easily.

Required Premed Courses and Degree

Course work

All medical schools pretty much require the following premed course work:

Course	Length
General Chemistry with Lab	2 semesters
Organic Chemistry with Lab	2 semesters
General Physics with Lab	2 semesters
General Biology with Lab	2 semesters
English	2 semesters
Calculus	1 semester

Note that some medical schools require courses such as biochemistry or additional calculus, for example. Other special non-science courses may also be required by some medical schools. A few examples: The University of Nevada in Reno requires one upper-division behavioral science class or something like it (and they are very specific about which ones will cover this requirement) and the University of Utah requires a diversities class such as women's studies, gender studies, or some sort of minority studies. Harvard requires two semesters of calculus instead of just one.

A baccalaureate degree

Most medical schools require a completed baccalaureate degree, but not all schools do. Some schools only require completion of the prerequisite courses and at least ninety-two completed credits (you are a senior at that point). Overall, most U.S. MD and DO medical schools require the four-year degree, but most U.S. Podiatry and Caribbean schools only require the ninety-two credits.

Having completed a Master's Degree or PhD is advantageous for admissions and may give you an edge by making you stand out from your peers, but is not required by any medical school for admission. These degrees are especially helpful when applying to some of the more prestigious medical schools.

It is important to find out all the details about course prerequisites and degree requirements for the schools you are interested in. A few schools have some odd requirements and at a few schools, you may have to take additional courses in the social sciences, humanities, psychology, or in math, for example.

The importance of your undergraduate college or university

Generally speaking, the better your undergraduate institution is, the better it is for you and your pursuit of getting into medical school. So, graduating from a highly ranked and well-known school with your baccalaureate degree will make things easier for you than graduating from some small unknown state university. This still holds true even if you get a lower GPA at the top school than you would at the unknown college.

Admission committees look at the school you attended and consider this when they analyze your GPA. Someone who graduated from Harvard may only have a 3.2 GPA and someone at an unknown college may have a 3.9 GPA, but they may have about equal chances for admission to a certain medical school when looking at their GPA alone since most schools factor in the difference in school difficulty and quality of education obtained. Obviously, this is also just comparing the extremes here. Most schools fall in between these extremes.

Realize that you will see some people in medical school who have only attended small, unknown colleges or state schools rather than Ivy League or top undergrad schools. Like everything that is part of your application, the school you attend can help you. Also note that your undergrad school may be more important if you are trying to go to medical school at one of the top schools in the country.

According to some premed advisors, your undergraduate institution is of extreme importance; but this is somewhat overrated, unless you are trying to get into one of the most prestigious medical schools, as already mentioned.

Nonetheless, the best advice is probably to try to get into the best undergraduate school you can. It will only help you, but realize that it is not going to be the end of the world if you attend a less well-known school. The rest of your application may have to be a little stronger in that case, but you should still be able to get into medical school.

If you have a choice, try to choose an undergraduate institution that has successfully graduated students (more than just a couple) who were able to gain admission to medical school. Ideally, your school should have a premed advisor and committee as well as a strong premed or biology program. Of course, attending a smaller college can be a disadvantage because they typically don't have strong programs of this type. This is more important than how well known the school is. Try to stay away from schools that have no track record or a bad track record of getting premed students admitted to medical school. It will make things harder for you, but still not impossible.

Post-bac (post-baccalaureate) premed programs

Post-bac premed programs can be useful for two types of individuals in particular:

1. An individual who completed his or her baccalaureate degree, took the MCAT, applied to medical school, and did not get in.

> These programs can help improve an applicant's chances for admission for several reasons:
>
> **a.** They improve the student's science background, increasing chances for better MCAT performance and increasing the student's GPA directly.
> **b.** They show that the student is serious about getting into medical school.
> **c.** They prepare the student for medical school and are typically more intense than undergrad, showing that the applicant can handle a more rigorous course load just fine. Some of these programs already teach a number of courses found in medical school itself for that reason—demonstrating that the applicant can handle it.

2. An individual who has already completed a baccalaureate degree in a non-science field, or, it has been a long time since graduation and would like to prepare for medical school now.

This option should be weighed against just returning to a regular college or university to take the required courses needed for medical school admissions and MCAT preparation. Technically, it's not necessary to go to a post-bac premed program per se. You could just as well enroll at any college or university for two years to take two semesters of physics, two semesters of general biology, and two semesters of general chemistry followed by two semesters of organic chemistry. On the other hand, some students are successfully admitted to medical school after completing one of these programs when they were previously unable to gain admission several times through the normal route. These programs seem to be able to make a difference for some applicants.

Post-bac programs vary from organized programs to individually planned studies that are tailored to the individual. Some even lead to a master's degree. Check out the available programs to make sure they meet your schedule, needs, and budget before choosing one. For the most part, you want a program that will boost your competitiveness for admission to medical school.

Some useful courses to have beyond the requirements

As you might expect, taking only two semesters each of general biology, physics, general chemistry, and organic chemistry does not really prepare you all too well for the actual medical school curriculum. But these are really all the science courses required for you to take the MCAT and to gain admission to medical school in most cases. These courses really just give you the very basics in understanding, especially in biology. Therefore, additional courses in biology can be very beneficial.

To make your medical school life a little easier, it is also beneficial, if you still have some room in your undergraduate elective schedule, to take some of the following courses. They will help you be better prepared for medical school, but realize that they are not typically required.

Highly recommended:
Biochemistry
Anatomy
Physiology
Genetics

Also recommended:
Histology
Microbiology
Immunology
Statistics
Embryology
Neuroscience
Pathophysiology

Pharmacology
Calculus

If you look closely at the course list for the first two years of medical school in the *Taste of Med School* section of this book, you will see all of these topics. So, any prior knowledge or experience in any of these will be useful to you and give you a better background. Don't stress out about covering all of these. If you have a choice to add electives to your schedule, or you can take some of these courses to fulfill your degree requirements, that is all the better.

Where to find specific medical school requirements

To find out more about medical school requirements, you should order the publications covering the medical school admission requirements for both allopathic (MD) and osteopathic (DO) schools. You could also check medical school websites directly for this information, but these books contain the information for all the schools, which saves you a lot of work in gathering the information.

The Medical School Admission Requirements (MSAR) for MD schools is available for $25.00 at: https://services.aamc.org/publications/ (*Get it!*).

The Osteopathic Medical School Information Book (DO) is available for free at: www.aacom.org/data/cib/ (*Get it!*). You can browse through the guide online or order a free copy to be sent to you.

Note that these guides will not elaborate on the extracurricular requirements as discussed here, but list cost of tuition, course requirements, and the like. The MD school guide also included numerous statistics such as how many people applied in state and out of state, how many of those were interviewed and were admitted, etc. These publications are very useful tools.

GPA and MCAT
Contributions to this section by KyGrlDr2B (SDN moderator name)

The GPA

Obviously, the higher your GPA, the better. Generally, anything above a 3.5 GPA is considered very good and very competitive. Jumping from a 3.0 to a 3.5 GPA will make a huge difference in someone's application, whereas jumping from a 3.5 to a 4.0 GPA will not be quite as dramatic (although it is obviously an advantage to have a 4.0 versus a 3.5 GPA).

The GPA really reflects how seriously an applicant has taken his or her undergraduate studies. A high GPA is a reflection of strong study habits and work ethics and medical schools look at an applicant's GPA for that very reason—to evaluate if the applicant is likely to work hard in medical school. The GPA has been found to be a very good predictor of success and the likelihood that someone will drop out of school or keep going.

It is also worth pointing out that a high GPA can compensate somewhat for a lower MCAT score. The GPA usually does carry a lot of weight in the admission decision. If both MCAT and GPA are lower, admission to medical school becomes much harder. However, having said that, there is more to the overall application than the MCAT and GPA alone. An otherwise stellar application can also overcome a lower GPA and MCAT score—to a point.

The 3.0 GPA is a cutoff for most medical schools. However, some applicants are accepted every year who have a lower GPA, so this value is by no means absolute. Again, it all depends on the strength of the overall application...and the MCAT score.

For example, for the 2005 school year, 155 applicants were accepted to allopathic medical schools (out of 17,978 total accepted that year) with a GPA that was lower than a 2.75.[2] So, it is possible to gain admission with a low GPA, but you can see from these numbers that this is very rare. Also, these individuals most likely had stellar applications otherwise.

For most of the allopathic (MD) medical schools, an average GPA of 3.0 is the minimum they will consider for extending interview invitations, regardless of what the rest of your application looks like, but there are a few exceptions.

The dreaded MCAT

The MCAT (or Medical College Admission Test) is one of the most dreaded parts of medical school preparation and is required by all U.S. medical schools, including all allopathic (MD) and osteopathic (DO) schools. Note that most Caribbean and international medical schools do not require the MCAT.

As of 2007, the test is administered twenty-two times per year in a computerized format from January until September. Before 2007, it was only given twice a year as a paper test—once in April and once in August. With the changes in 2007, the MCAT has also been modified in length. The time has been nearly cut in half to four and a half hours and the test has 30 percent fewer questions, which were removed equally from all sections.

If possible, you should try to take the MCAT early so you receive your scores back by the time you submit your medical school application (AMCAS for allopathic schools and AACOMAS for DO schools). Before 2007, it took sixty days to grade the MCAT and release your scores, so taking the April MCAT around April 15 gave you the best possible timing for submitting your applications early (around June 15). The earliest date applications can be submitted is June 1, but you needed to wait for your MCAT scores to submit your application. So, in reality, your earliest day for submitting your application before 2007 was around June 15. With the 2007 changes, scores are now returned within thirty days (and supposedly the eventual goal is a fourteen-day turnaround at some point). To submit your applications on the earliest day possible, you should therefore plan to submit your applications June 1 and take the MCAT no later than thirty days before this date (May 1). Submitting your applications early gives you a huge advantage in the admissions game.

The MCAT is still pretty much an all-day event and takes five hours to complete, including breaks. All sections, except the writing sample, which is essay, are multiple choice. Students are typically given a section of text to read and then asked questions about the section. Some general knowledge questions are also part of the exam, but they are far less frequent than the passage-related questions.

Overall, there is not much time to read the passages and answer questions, so you have to work at a pretty fast pace, as you can see in the following table. Considering the fact that you have to first read a passage before answering questions, you may actually have less than one minute to answer each question. The questions are not easy and often require some intense thinking, reasoning, and interpretation.

These are the sections on the MCAT:

Section	Questions	Time (minutes)
Optional Tutorial		5
1. Physical Sciences (Physics & General Chemistry)	**52**	**70**
Optional Break		10
2. Verbal Reasoning	**40**	**60**
Optional Break		10
3. Writing Sample (2 essays)	**2**	**60**
Optional Break		10
4. Biological Sciences (Biology & Organic Chemistry)	**52**	**70**
Survey		5

On test day, make sure you have had a good night's rest the night before, a good breakfast so you don't get hungry, be at the testing center early, and take a sweater with you in case the room is colder than expected. You'll be expected to bring photo ID and your admission ticket with a photo attached. So make sure you don't forget those, either.

It is also very important during the test to pace yourself, so bring a watch. That is one reason why you should take plenty of practice exams—to get used to timing and pacing yourself, so you know how much time you can spend on each question.

You may want to skip questions or passages that are too hard or complicated and then return and finish them later. Many expert test takers also recommend reading the questions first, then reading the passage, so you can already look for answers specifically as you read the passage the first time. However, make sure that you don't leave any questions unanswered because you are not penalized for guessing wrong.

MCAT sections and questions

All of the MCAT sections, except the writing sample, are in multiple-choice format. The science sections test both your science knowledge and your ability to reason through problems in subjects required as prerequisites to medical school. The biological science section encompasses questions from organic chemistry and general biology. The physical science section contains questions from general chemistry and general physics.

In general, these sections contain two question formats. The first are stand-alone questions that are purely testing your knowledge base of the subject. These questions are interspersed throughout the section in small groups of two or three questions. The vast majority of the section, however, consists of longer passages followed by sets of questions directly related to and involving each passage. The passages are a few paragraphs long and may contain graphs, charts, diagrams, and other types of data. The questions that follow, usually ranging from five to nine questions, require you to make inferences on the information presented, may require calculations, or may test your knowledge on the subject. These questions are more difficult to answer and test your ability to reason and apply concepts rather than just recall memorized information (although you need to know your science information thoroughly).

The verbal reasoning section contains some questions that may simply ask you to recall concepts or information based on the passage you just read, or ask you about tone or mood of the passage or what the author meant with certain statements. The subjects of these passages are diverse and may include any the following topics: psychology, history, art, science, philosophy, and a number of other subjects. Fortunately, this section does not require any former knowledge of the subject presented in a passage. You are tested on your ability to quickly read and comprehend a passage and think through some answers.

The writing sample consists of two prompts (scenarios/statements) for which you must thoroughly answer a few questions. This section does not require knowledge of a particular subject, but instead requires you to write from both sides of an argument. Your writing should include a brief intro, an organized treatment of the subject with a few paragraphs, and a closing statement. It is not easy and you should practice writing a couple of these so you get organized and know how you will tackle this task on the real exam. For medical school application purposes, most medical schools place the least amount of weight on this section, but an extremely low score may hamper your ability to be accepted.

The MCAT score

Each of the three multiple-choice sections is worth 15 points for a total of 45 points, but it is nearly impossible to achieve a perfect score. The average MCAT score each year is somewhere around a 24 (eight in each section).

A good score that is competitive at most MD schools is around 30 and a stellar score is somewhere above a 34 to 36, which is competitive at the top medical schools in the country. A score of 36 or better would put you in the top 2 percent of the country. The writing sample is scored with a letter system from J (lowest) to T (highest), but is much less important than the number score. You never hear anyone mention the letter score. All you ever hear people talk about is the number, although some people insist that the letter score is also considered in the admissions process somehow.

To give you an extreme example that the MCAT is not the only measurement that is important, 60 applicants were admitted to allopathic medical schools in 2005 who had an MCAT score that was less than 17.[3] Keep in mind that there are a few allopathic medical schools in Puerto Rico, for example, that have very low MCAT averages (20.1, 21.3, and 23). These schools could be responsible for many of these numbers. Again, this sort of low score is a rare exception. Essentially, an MCAT score below 25 will make it almost impossible for you to gain admission to allopathic (MD) medical schools. You will still be competitive for osteopathic medical schools, podiatry schools, and Caribbean medical schools.

For most of the allopathic (MD) medical schools, an average MCAT score of 21 is the minimum they will consider for extending interview invitations, regardless of what the rest of your application looks like, but there are a few exceptions. For some of the more prestigious medical schools in the country, the minimum MCAT score is around 30 to 32, below which you will not make it past any screening for interviews, regardless of how strong the rest of your application is.

The more applications a medical school receives every year, the more the school tends to eliminate applicants by MCAT scores and GPA alone when screening applicants. It is the easiest and most cost-effective way to limit the search for competitive applicants— and especially the more popular and prestigious medical schools use these criteria more heavily. These are typically the medical schools that receive the most applications.

Medical schools like to use the MCAT as a way of screening and comparing applicants since it is the most objective measurement. Your GPA varies with the difficulty of the courses you take and the type of college or university you attend for undergrad. The MCAT provides one way to compare everyone at the same level. It becomes even more important in validating your GPA so if your GPA is significantly lower or higher than what your MCAT score indicates, you know it may raise some questions.

The MCAT score is a reflection of your ability to reason, think, and interpret charts and data. It has less to do with your work ethic or your ability to memorize, which are two factors reflected more by your GPA.

MCAT preparation

The MCAT test is intended to test material presented in general biology, general chemistry, organic chemistry, and general physics. For review, it is important to stress the most important concepts and information in each of these areas. Generally, it is better to know the basic concepts very well than to know a lot of information superficially. Having said that, most of the questions on the MCAT are very difficult, and often it feels like they are testing concepts you have never heard of. Some additional course work can be helpful, but is not required. Although it is not necessary to memorize every formula in physics, chemistry, and the other courses covered, you should know some of the bread-and-butter formulas of each subject, particularly in physics. Don't focus on all the derivative formulas. Memorize some of the main ones—you will need them.

They may ask a question like "If I throw a ball out of a window 25 m above the ground, at an initial velocity of 15 m/s, how long will it take until it hits the ground? How far does it travel vertically until it hits the ground?" So, you will need to know your formulas to figure out these questions.

You will need to decide what type of person you are and what you will need for preparation.

Some students swear by commercially available review courses such as offered by Kaplan, Princeton Review, Columbia Review, Cambridge, and Lippincott Williams and Wilkins. They are rather expensive, with a price tag up to $1,500, but many physicians and other successful applicants strongly suggest you take a review course, particularly the Kaplan course (Kaplan is considered the leader of the pack).

Review courses provide a classroom type setting with lecture format to review pertinent topics in all the MCAT prerequisites. You still have to study the extensive review material that comes with the course as you would in any class.

You could say that you still have to put effort into the class like any other class you have taken before. Just attending the prep course may not help you out much, although they do cover a lot of test-taking strategies, which are helpful for test taking in general and not dependant on how much material you learned. Also note that these courses work only for review. If you have not had physics or organic chemistry before, you cannot learn the material in the prep course. These are review courses.

They also offer practice tests throughout the course and provide hints and tricks, do all kinds of analysis of what was on previous tests, and help you with time management techniques and other topics. This type of review may be very well worth it if you are the type of person who is a procrastinator or needs a structured program that is already set up and scheduled.

For those who are able and willing to work through self-study, there are many good review books, including a Kaplan Comprehensive MCAT review book for about $50. They contain the same basic material used in the course, but you are on your own. So, you have to set aside a certain number of hours per week for a few months to review and work through the materials on your own. Expect to prepare for three to four months before the test.

I would highly recommend purchasing the real paper or Web practice MCATs online, preferably the Web versions since the MCAT is now computerized. They are the real deal, made available by the AAMC (Association of American Medical Colleges), the makers of the MCAT and not some version made up by Kaplan, Princeton Review, or other test-prep companies. These practice tests are well worth the money and you can take them under real testing conditions. Set aside a few Saturdays at your library in a quiet corner, or at home—undisturbed. You get the actual test booklets and multiple-choice answer sheets, or access to the online equivalent, and you can grade yourself at the end to see how you did. You can purchase these paper practice tests online (https://services.aamc.org/publications).

The MCAT is really a thinking test. You will need to know the sciences to do well, but many of the questions do not directly test knowledge. They may ask you to interpret some data or extract some answers from a passage. It has been said that you cannot really cram for the MCAT.

You can find more information about the MCAT on the official MCAT website (www.aamc.org/students/mcat/).

Average GPA and MCAT scores

Note that the two following tables give average GPA and MCAT scores for both allopathic (MD) and osteopathic (DO) school matriculants (accepted applicants) for a few years.

Data for allopathic (MD) schools[4]

Entering Year	Overall GPA	MCAT (Verbal)	MCAT (Phys)	MCAT (Bio)	MCAT (Essay)	MCAT Total
2005	3.63	9.7	10.1	10.4	P	30.2 P
2004	3.62	9.7	9.9	10.3	P	29.9 P
2003	3.62	9.5	9.9	10.2	P	29.6 P
2002	3.61	9.5	10.0	10.2	P	29.7 P
2001	3.60	9.5	10.0	10.1	P	29.6 P
2000	3.60	9.5	10.0	10.2	P	29.7 P

Data for osteopathic (DO) schools[5]

Entering Year	Science GPA	MCAT (Verbal)	MCAT (Phys)	MCAT (Bio)	MCAT (Essay)	MCAT Total
2004	3.36	8.24	7.89	8.53	-	24.66
2003	3.45	8.07	7.99	8.51	-	24.57
2002	3.44	8.06	7.97	8.50	-	24.53
2001	3.43	8.10	8.08	8.54	-	24.72
2000	3.43	8.11	8.18	8.69	-	24.98

Note that it is easier to get into osteopathic (DO) schools than allopathic schools (MD) by roughly 5 points on the MCAT and something like 0.15 points on the GPA.

Regarding GPA calculation, MD schools count every course grade earned even if you have retaken a course. If you earned a "C" in organic chemistry the first time, retook the course and earned an "A" later, they will count both grades for calculating your GPA. DO schools only count the retake grade ("A" in this example) and not the lower grade you earned the first time.

The average MCAT score for MD schools is around 30 and GPA lies around 3.6. For DO schools, the average MCAT score is around 25 and GPA around 3.4. Especially if your MCAT score and GPA are below these values, your extracurricular activities weigh heavier in the admissions decision and can make the difference between getting an interview and no interview.

Also note that as of January 2007, most podiatry schools will require the MCAT. Caribbean medical schools typically do not have any MCAT requirements with few exceptions. Both, however, will accept lower GPA and MCAT scores than MD and DO medical schools.

Retaking the MCAT

If you score low on the MCAT, it may be a good idea to retake it. However, you absolutely have to show improvement. I know some students who increased their scores a good three to five points and it made all the difference. If you score the same or lower than your original MCAT score, retaking the MCAT only hurts you because you have just demonstrated that you really cannot do it, even if you have another chance.

Often, it is advisable to take a prep course, if you haven't already done so, to prepare for retaking the MCAT, especially if you didn't take the exam seriously enough the first time. You have to be willing to put a lot of hard work into preparation before retaking the exam again; just retaking it will buy you nothing.

Sometimes, if the MCAT score is not very high but still acceptable, it might be better to work on extracurricular activities to increase the overall strength of the application to compensate. However, a lower MCAT can limit some of your medical school choices. Certain medical schools may not consider you at all. Generally, DO, Podiatry, and Caribbean medical schools have lower MCAT requirements. There is also quite a bit of variation between various MD schools.

The decision to retake the MCAT may depend on your goals overall and not necessarily on the score you received the first time. Also, keep in mind that it is very hard to increase your MCAT score, especially if you were prepared for the test the first time and there is not much else you can do to prepare. Increasing a score from a 24 to a 28 is probably much easier than raising a score from a 30 to a 34.

Important Note: A premedical advisor should be consulted to help you decide whether you should retake the MCAT and what strategies are appropriate for you to maximize the effectiveness of additional preparation. Only an experienced premed advisor who knows you personally and knows something about the MCAT can tailor advice to fit your specific circumstances. This is a big and important decision. You may retake the MCAT up to three times, which can be all in the same year if you wish. However, retaking the MCAT for the fourth time, and every time thereafter, you have to jump through some hoops to be able to take the MCAT again. The AAMC requires a letter proving that you are really applying to medical school and not just taking the MCAT for other reasons (maybe you are teaching MCAT prep courses on the side and you can teach it better by taking the MCAT yourself every year).

Shadowing

Overview

Shadowing, in my personal opinion, besides hands-on participation in an actual clinical setting, is one of the best extracurricular activities because it provides you with clinical exposure and stories to talk about in the interview. Also, you can see what medicine and a physician's life are like. You will also quickly discover if medicine is really for you.

For myself, I can emphatically state that I know that I want to be a physician due to my shadowing experiences. I was asked about my shadowing in the admission interviews and was able to easily answer the question "Why medicine?" due to my shadowing. I was also able to share some of the things I had seen and experienced during shadowing with my interviewers and use them in my personal statement. Shadowing is what convinced me that I wanted to be a physician.

If you are still worried about answering "Why medicine?", I would suggest doing more shadowing. I would recommend spending a good amount of time to really get to know the physician, the specialty, and medicine. Also, if you only spend a few hours shadowing here and there, you really miss part of the experience. So, be sure to spend enough hours shadowing the same physician. Don't forget to enjoy this opportunity to be immersed in a clinical setting while working through the premed course work.

Setting up shadowing

Realize that you can set up your shadowing however you like. Some people like to shadow a few hours every week for several weeks or months. I personally preferred spending time with one physician for an entire week in one stretch, Monday through Friday, 8:00 a.m. to 5:00 p.m., to get a better idea of what it is really like. I did my shadowing during the summer when I was out of school for a few weeks, so I could do it this way.

To schedule your shadowing, just open the local Yellow Pages, pick the specialty you are interested in shadowing, and call any physician's office. Tell the office person that you are a premed student at the XYZ University, planning on going to medical school next year (or whenever). Ask them if Dr. Smith allows students to come into the office to shadow him or her. Typically, they have done this before with other premed students and the physician has no problems with this. Tell them what dates you would prefer to shadow. Usually, the office help will take down your phone number and then call you back later, after asking the physician or office manager.

To follow a surgeon into the operating room, you may have to call the hospital or surgery facility as well. The physician's office would be able to give you this information. Tell the office staff at the physician's office you would like to follow the surgeon in the office, in the operating room, and on rounds if possible. They usually know if there are hoops to jump through on your part. For example, I had to watch a video on the "Aseptic Technique" before they would let me into the OR at the local hospital. Some hospitals and facilities have special rules and regulations and may require you to sign some paperwork.

However, when in doubt, remember that the physician you are shadowing is the key to getting you into the OR and on the hospital floors. The physician will typically let everyone know that you are with him or her. Most of the time, that is enough justification for your presence.

When shadowing

This may be obvious, but make sure you are dressed and groomed professionally when shadowing. If in doubt, overdress for the first day until you can get a feeling for what is acceptable in the office or the physician tells you it is okay to dress down. For men, that should be dress pants, shirt, and tie and for women, dresses or professional business attire.

Most of the time, you pretty much just stand back and observe what the physician does without doing anything yourself. Try not to get in the way. After all, that is what shadowing is. Some physicians may involve you to some degree, may let you look in ears, for example, or be part of what they do in some fashion. If so, great, but don't expect too much.

Actively ask questions between patients or when appropriate. Right during a patient visit may be a bad time to quench your own thirst for knowledge. You want plenty of interaction with the physician so the physician can get to know you and see that you are interested in medicine, in patient care, etc. Make sure you ask the physician for a great recommendation letter. Don't underestimate the letter and do it right, because there is a right and a wrong way to ask for a letter. Check the *recommendation letter* section for more information.

Volunteer Work and Service

You may wonder why this is important, but after all, physicians are in the business of helping people. You say you want to help people? Can you show that you mean it or is this just talk?

Volunteering and participating in service opportunities are some ways to demonstrate your commitment to help others. Volunteer tutoring, summer camps, soup kitchen, hospital or clinical volunteer work, shoveling snow off driveways, church service, missions, etc., all work to show that you care about helping people during your premed preparation. Ideally, you participate in more than one type of activity.

Do whatever is interesting to you or get involved in a cause that you can personally gain satisfaction from. You may be asked in your interview why you got involved in what you chose.

Many people have already begun giving back to the community and are involved in specific projects involving the poor, elderly, underprivileged, sick, or children and adolescents who are in great need and in danger of slipping through the cracks in society. If you are already involved, then continue with what you are doing.

If you are extremely short on time, you may want to try to find activities that will help you participate in volunteer or service opportunities while at the same time gaining valuable exposure to a clinical setting. For example, try to volunteer in a clinic or hospital. Your hours spent are considered clinical exposure time and volunteer time when it comes to your application; especially if your time is limited, this is a great way to go.

Medical missions and other service or relief projects are also a great way to get involved in very intense service. For most students, these are life-changing opportunities, being exposed to extreme poverty, different cultures, and customs. You may or may not be able to participate in providing medical care, but rather be involved in the project in various ways. Medical missions and various other relief projects are often organized by student or professional groups at universities. There are also different religious and nonreligious groups that organize service missions and medical missions. Most often, you have to pay your own way, but frequently these organizations also provide some assistance to help you find a sponsor for your trip. Overall, these can be very fulfilling and humbling experiences.

Clinical Exposure

See the note in the "Volunteer and Service" section of this book and appreciate the fact that your volunteer service in a clinical setting (anything with patients around) also counts as clinical exposure. Also, shadowing time counts toward clinical exposure. In fact, it is a great way to immerse yourself in clinical settings and gain clinical exposure.

However you do it—volunteer, paid, or by shadowing, make sure that you do enough of it. Talking about your experiences drawn from clinical exposure are guaranteed interview topics. They also provided you with reasons and excitement for choosing medicine. You will have specific situations, patients, etc., to talk about (without disclosing private information) in your interviews.

These experiences and their impact on you, the things that make you tick, are the things that interviewers are interested in because it gives them a view into your thoughts and feelings about medicine.

Research

Most medical schools want to see some research experience, generally, the more the better.

It really depends on the school you apply to, though. Some medical schools don't care at all whether you have done research. However, most medical schools prefer to see some research experience on your application and yet other schools absolutely require it and will not consider you if you have done little or no research. Some minimal exposure, such as working in a research lab for a semester, is okay for most schools.

Some schools will want to see major research involvement, perhaps that you have done your very own project, and may prefer published work. This is especially true if applying to research powerhouses and top medical schools.

Some professors help undergraduate students set up their very own research projects that lead to publication of their work in the end. Others involve students in ongoing projects or use them as grunt workers to care for animals or have them clean their labs. Try to avoid the latter two. You need research experience or involvement.

To strengthen your application for most medical schools, the goal here is to:

1. Be involved in hypothesis-driven research.
2. Be able to explain what the goals of the project were.
3. Show what you did to contribute and what your responsibilities were.
4. Be able to give some background and detail in your interview.

Again, schools that are big into research will probably put more focus on research than other medical schools. Make sure you prepare appropriately. Find out if the medical schools you are interested in have specific requirements or a reputation for requiring research or expecting research of students—and how much of it.

Spending just a few minimal hours every week for one semester may work out well and may be sufficient for many of the schools you want to apply to.

Leadership and Multitasking

Leadership

Leadership is an area that includes things like tutoring, student government positions, supervisory positions at work or elsewhere, church or other teaching assignments and positions, military service, or anything like it. It is beneficial to be able to show these on your application.

For example, at the University of Utah School of Medicine you have to show a specific number of positions you have held over the years to be considered. However, most medical schools may not be as stringent on this requirement, but rather consider these good experiences that will strengthen your application.

Multitasking

Medical school is tough. You are enrolled in courses totaling about 24 credits per semester of upper-division science courses and labs to go with them. If you have only taken 12 credits per semester during undergrad, you need to be able to show that you have kept an otherwise busy schedule, indicating that you could handle 24 credits per semester if you had to. If 12 credits per semester took all of your time and maxed you out, medical school could be a bit much or at least the admissions committee may think so.

Showing that you worked 20 to 40 hours a week, took 12 credits, and did various other activities for some number of hours each week shows that you can handle it and that you can multitask. Balancing family responsibilities (if you have kids) also counts as time spent multitasking and is justification for having taken a less-intense class load during undergrad.

The bottom line is that you don't have to take 24 credits during undergrad in any one semester, but be sure to demonstrate that you can handle a busy schedule in your life.

Other extracurricular activities

Most of the discussion about extracurricular activities has focused on premed specifically or activities (volunteer, shadow, do research, etc.), which can directly benefit your application by involving you in some aspect of medicine. There are certainly many other activities, including athletics, getting involved in politics, or participating in other clubs and organizations that may have nothing to do with medicine at all.

These are also worthwhile extracurricular activities. All of these activities take a lot of time out of your busy schedule and show commitment to a cause. They also make you unique and set you apart from other applicants. They show that you also have other interests besides medicine, which is important. It is not good if you cannot show much else on your application besides studying at the library.

However, another important point to keep in mind: Don't sacrifice your good GPA for too many extracurricular activities. You still want to maintain a good GPA.

Recommendation Letters

Overview

Recommendation letters are one of the criteria admission committees use in the admissions process and are, therefore, one important part of your application. To get good letters, participation in extracurricular activities and positive interactions with faculty are important since both provide you with great recommendation letters written on your behalf.

Admissions Committees see on the application what activities you have listed, but recommendation letters tell them about how you interact with people in activities and (hopefully) stress your good qualities.

Bad letters

"He was dressed nice and followed me in my office for a week... and I think he will be a great physician...I strongly recommend this individual..." This is pretty much worthless as a recommendation letter and won't do you any good. Letters that merely state you were present are worthless. A doctor's opinion that you would be a great physician without any stated supporting evidence is also worthless. Letters that don't stress your personal strengths and qualities are worthless.

You really don't want worthless letters. Indeed, you need great letters!

Great letters

What will help you are descriptions that show what type of person you are so that the admissions office can see who you are and what you are like. In a great letter, you should be able to find strong positive descriptions of your personal characteristics and your attitude toward medicine that will make you a great physician.

You should see statements that explain to the admissions people why you would be a great addition to the medical community.

The letter writer has to support the recommendation he or she is making in your behalf with evidence, writing about your qualities rather than just stating that you will be a fine physician or that you spent so many hours shadowing.

"He was punctual, eager to learn, very interested, asked questions, was very attentive, well mannered and friendly, and interacted well with patients. I enjoyed discussing things with him, etc. He eagerly watched surgeries and was very inquisitive, professional, and respectful. He interacted well with patients and responded well to them. He was enjoyable to work and interacted with..." You get the idea.

The best letters are from people you have spent some time with so they could get to know you. That is why it is important to shadow physicians for more than just a few hours. One physician really opened up to me on day three and we developed a relationship. His letter was also great.

Faculty letters

For faculty letters, make sure that the faculty member gets to know you by name. If he or she cannot greet you by name in the hallway, you should find someone else to write a letter for you or do everything you can to get to know him or her.

You can do this by visiting with the faculty member in his or her office to discuss prior assignments, for example:
"What can I do better?"
"Could you explain the details of this problem because I would have chosen a different way to solve this?"

Ask questions about homework, assignments, readings, or how you are doing in class. Here are some more specific suggestions.

In physics and organic chemistry, homework or assignments can be intense. You may only have to turn in very little or none of your homework or assigned problems for grading but may have plenty of assigned material to work through on your own. When one of the problems doesn't make sense or presents an opportunity to ask your professor something, use them as an excuse to interact with your professor instead of just bypassing them.

What a wasted opportunity if you just bypass them! You need excuses to get to know your professor for a good letter, so use them. Go to your professor and ask him or her about the problem, even if you understand it.

Another example: In your biology course, if you are learning about a topic, find some extra info in your text, maybe something that was not directly assigned reading or something that is difficult to understand (maybe you understand it, but you can ask for some clarification). You can ask about something that is related or still to be covered, but hasn't been covered yet in lecture.

What you will gain from this:

1. The faculty member will get to know you if you do this several times during the semester.
2. It indicates you are interested in the material enough to ask.
3. It shows you work hard, especially since you are doing extra work besides the minimum required to turn in.
4. It gives you opportunity to mention you are going to med school and other topics to build a relationship.

If you don't talk to your professor, you will only be an unknown student to him or her in the class and the result is a very impersonal letter, which is worthless. Focus on a couple of faculty members in the sciences to do this with (preferably in the sciences, but any will do). Pick someone you can connect with or just someone who seems nice and easy going.

How to ask for a recommendation letter

Physicians

Once you get to the end of your shadowing time, ask the physician: "Would you be able to write me a positive letter of recommendation for my med school application?" Or: "Do you have any reservations writing a positive letter of recommendation for me?"

Make sure you ask for a positive letter. Also, be sure to ask if he or she can honestly give you a good letter. If he or she cannot, thank him or her and ask someone else. Most letter writers are not cruel enough to say they would write you a positive letter and then write a bad one. Usually, if you ask, they will be honest and tell you that they can give you a great recommendation or tell you that they will not be able to, for whatever reason (it does happen).

Faculty

Same story: Ask for a positive letter and get their guarantee that they can write a great one. If not, don't have them write it! You need a great letter, nothing less.

If they have any hesitation or concerns about writing a great letter, thank them and ask someone else. You have to be firm on this. Don't be shy. Make sure you ask. They will usually be up front and tell you if they cannot give you a stellar letter. You want the best and you can only be assured of that by asking for one bluntly.

What a letter writer may want from you

Often, the letter writer may request a resume or curriculum vitae, listing your major accomplishments, schooling, etc. You may be asked to provide some additional biographical information about yourself or why you are interested in medicine. So, be prepared to provide this information if necessary. You may even consider providing this information without being asked for it to allow the letter writer to personalize the letter even more. Most likely, you will be asked for this information anyway, so be ready for it.

What to do with letters

Most premed advising offices or student affairs offices at colleges and universities will give you a choice between having an open or a closed student file in which they collect all documents pertinent to your medical school application, including recommendation letters written on your behalf. You usually have to sign a statement and decide at the beginning, when your file is first created, if you want your file to be open or closed. If you ask medical schools which type of file is best to choose, some will tell you that they don't care. Don't believe them! Some medical schools will only consider recommendation letters that were kept in a closed file and by far all schools prefer closed files to open files. What's the difference?

Open or closed file for your recommendation letters

Open file: You, as the student, have full access to all documents placed in your file. After a recommendation letter or any other document is received, you have full access to it and can look at anything in your file at any time. Most faculty members and others writing recommendation letters for you want to know in advance if your file is open or closed. If it is open, they are less likely to write negatively about you. When it is closed, they have nothing to fear and write frankly. Therefore, medical schools prefer (and some outright require) that you have a closed file to ensure a more unbiased appraisal. *You must have a closed file* in my opinion and some advisors will tell you the same thing. That is why it is so important to ask letter writers frankly if they are able to write a very good letter without reservations up front. You won't be able to see it once it is in your file.

Faculty members usually know the drill and you won't see the letter they write for you. With physicians, many don't know about your file and they may either send their letter directly to the premed office or hand you a sealed envelope to deliver yourself. I'd recommend asking them for a second copy of the letter for your own records. Some premed offices require the physician to mail a letter directly to them or notify the physician that your file is closed. If the physician, therefore, does not provide a copy for you, I would still recommend asking for a personal copy for your own records a few weeks or months later, letting the physician know you'd appreciate a copy if possible, but that he or she is not required to give you one. Or, if the physician would prefer to keep the letter confident without showing it to you, you'd understand and have no problem with that. Most physicians should not have a problem with your request.

Who should write letters for you

The following people should write letters of recommendation for you:

1.   Physicians you spent time with
2.   Managers of places you volunteered/worked at in clinical settings
3.   Faculty who taught you
4.   Faculty/mentors you did research with

NO personal friends, family, colleagues, or others should write letters for you!

Getting your personal copy of the letters

You should be able to get a personal copy from everyone with the exception of faculty, maybe, since they may be hesitant and most likely familiar with the closed file (and are happy about the arrangement). If you have more letters than medical schools require, you can then choose the best ones to send to them. Most medical schools specify what types of letters and how many they want (usually one to four) when you get your secondary application materials from the medical school.

Most medical schools only want one physician letter sent to them. If you have a letter from several physicians, you can decide which is better and instruct your premed office to send that letter only.

Similarly, if you have four or five faculty letters and the medical school only requires two, you can choose which two to have the office send. If you really don't know which to choose, go by your gut feeling. Some premed offices may not let students choose which letters to send anyway.

Letter timing

Recommendation letters are sent directly to medical schools from either your undergrad premed office or from the letter writers. You will have to tell your premed office or committee (or the letter writer) which letters to send from your file and which schools to send them to. Typically, when you receive your secondary application materials from the medical school, they provide you with information about what kind of letters they want from you (e.g., two faculty and one physician letter or one premed committee letter, one physician letter, and one faculty letter, or whatever) and where to send them.

Letter types

Most medical schools require a premed committee letter to be sent and an additional one to three other letters written by faculty or physicians in your behalf. Only submit what they ask for. If you have more letters or different letters than what they want, don't send the additional letters—they just clutter your file and your best letters may not get read at all. It is recommended that you don't send any school more than three or four letters total.

Chapter References

1.   Required Activities, Office of Admissions, University of Utah, http://uuhsc.utah.edu/som/admissions/frame_mainS.htm

2.   Undergraduate Grade Point Average, Medical School Admission Requirements (MSAR), 2007–2008, page 29

3.   Performance on the MCAT, Medical School Admission Requirements (MSAR), 2007–2008, page 27

4.   Mean Medical College Admission Test (MCAT) Scores and Grade Point Averages of U.S. Medical School Applicants and Matriculants, AAMC Data Book, 2006, page 38

5.   Grade Point Averages and Mean Medical College Admission Test (MCAT) Scores for Entering Students, Osteopathic Medical College Information Book, 2007 Entering Class, page 8

School Considerations

School Considerations

Note before we start this discussion: Many students are very passionate about school choice and why they chose a specific school or school type. These overviews and comparisons of different schools are very brief and much more could be said about each school type. Moreover, many people differ widely in opinion about which school type is most preferable for their very own reasons.

Some of your decision about school choice may depend on how competitive your overall application is, but other factors such as location or prestige of a school may also weigh in.

Quick overview (MD, DO, DPM, Caribbean, International)

For most applicants, allopathic (MD) schools are the most desirable option if they can gain admission. Generally, people consider schools to be in the following order from most desirable, prestigious, and competitive to less desirable, prestigious, and competitive.

1. Allopathic (MD) schools in the U.S.
    a. Hardest to get into, considered most desirable
    b. Competitive atmosphere, most prestigious
    c. Highest MCAT and GPA requirements
    d. USMLE1 passrate: 92%, USMLE2: 93%, USMLE3: 94% (2005 NBME Report[1])

2. Osteopathic (DO) schools in the U.S.
    a. You learn some unique skills beyond those taught at MD schools
    b. Equal to MD for all practical purposes
    c. Slightly easier admissions due to lower MCAT and GPA requirements
    d. USMLE1 passrate: 72%, USMLE2: 85%, USMLE3: 95% (2005 NBME Report[1])

    e. Most students take the COMLEX board exams instead of the USMLE exams

3. Caribbean and other international schools (non-U.S.)
   a. Easiest admissions, harder to get U.S. residency of your choice
   b. Least prestigious, some not accredited, some practice limitations
   c. Low (or no) MCAT and GPA requirements
   d. USMLE1 pass rate: 59%, USMLE2: 71%, USMLE3: 68% (2005 NBME Report[1])

4. Podiatry schools in the U.S. are another path worth mentioning.
   a. Easy admissions in comparison to MD and DO schools
   b. Practice is limited to treatment of the foot and ankle
   c. Low MCAT and GPA requirements
   d. Residencies and surgical careers available

Allopathic (MD) Medical Schools

General information

There are currently 125 Allopathic schools in the United States and 16 in Canada. Successful completion of the medical school curriculum leads to the MD degree. Admission to MD school generally is the hardest, but the MD is also the most recognized by people. The MD is also internationally recognized, which means that you can practice in other countries outside the United States.

MD schools are typically more research oriented with faculty involved in research and the school receiving significant research funding. Faculty is responsible for teaching and research. The education is centered on the classic basic sciences for two years, followed by hospital-based and non-hospital-based rotations for two years.

MD students take the USMLE board exams and enter the residency match for allopathic residencies. Application for MD schools is handled through the AMCAS (www.aamc.org/audienceamcas. htm) or American Medical College Application Service for most schools with only a few exceptions that require direct application to the schools. General historical MCAT and GPA info for MD schools can be found in the "GPA and MCAT" section of this book.

Residency

As far as residency choice is concerned, MD graduates are considered by all allopathic residency programs. Some residency programs will only accept MD graduates (sometimes only from U.S. medical schools) and may not consider DO or foreign graduates (International Medical Graduates, IMGs for short). MD graduates are often preferred over DO graduates or IMGs at allopathic residencies, all other factors of the residency application being equal. However, in recent years, the school attended for the four-year medical education is supposedly losing in importance and board scores are gaining in importance. Some residency programs are still biased and may even have policies that only allow consideration of U.S.-trained MD applicants, though.

Also note that there are special residency considerations if participating in a military scholarship that apply to both MD and DO graduates. Military residencies consider both MD and DO graduates completely equally. Students involved with the military arc required to go through a military residency match instead of the civilian residency match in most cases.

Combined degree programs

Many schools also offer MD/PhD or other combined degree programs. Some of the MD/PhD spots are often supported by the Medical Scientist Training Program (MSTP). This MSTP program pays all of your tuition and a stipend.

The MD/PhD is primarily designed for those who wish to enter academic medicine and/or be involved in major research. Other combined degrees, particularly the MD/JD (law), MD/MBA (business), and MD/MPH (public health) are often available.

Osteopathic (DO) Medical Schools
Contributions to this section by Diane L. Evans, DO, MS

General information

There are currently twenty-three osteopathic schools in the United States. The DO is slightly less well known than the MD, but if you look around, you will actually notice quite a few osteopathic physicians in practice, if you haven't already.

In medical practice, DOs are in all aspects equal to MDs, with all the same rights and privileges to practice medicine, surgery or any other specialty, and to prescribe medications. DO physicians are found in all specialties and practicing in all fifty of the United States.

Osteopathic (DO) medical schools are somewhat easier to get into than allopathic (MD) medical schools due to lower average GPA and MCAT requirements. However, admission to osteopathic medical schools is still competitive.

There are some limits on international practice rights for DO graduates that don't apply to MD graduates. You can read the full text about international practice rights on the Michigan State University College of Osteopathic Medicine website.[2] In short, the DO degree may not be recognized in all countries around the world, although the number of countries that do recognize the degree is increasing.

For most students, this won't be an issue since they are planning on practicing in the United States anyway, but if you are specifically interested in practicing abroad, you may want to check out your international options and specific countries to make sure this path will meet your needs.

Faculty is generally research oriented, but often the general school mission is more clinically oriented. Also, generally speaking, most osteopathic schools do not have large local teaching hospitals affiliated with them. In fact, in some cases, the required core third and fourth year rotations are not locally offered at all.

DO students normally take the COMLEX (Comprehensive Osteopathic Medical Licensing Examination) board exams and may take the USMLE board exams, in addition to the COMLEX, if planning to apply to MD Residency Programs as well. Many osteopathic graduates apply to MD residencies due to a shortage of DO (American Osteopathic Association/AOA approved) residency spots in many competitive specialties.

Application to osteopathic medical schools is handled through the AACOMAS application, which can be found at https://aacomas. aacom.org/.

The osteopathic approach

What distinguishes osteopathic (DO) medical schools slightly from allopathic (MD) medical schools is the osteopathic philosophy or approach to medicine. Besides the normal basic science and clinical curriculum, DO students also learn Osteopathic Manipulative Medicine (referred to as OMM most of the time), which comes close to a cross between physical therapy and chiropractic. It is really neither, because it is unique in its own right, but can address some of the same type of musculoskeletal problems as the two professions mentioned.

These OMM techniques are quite useful for treating back pain, headaches, and address many other problems related to the musculoskeletal system and are extra skills that MD graduates don't have.

Some osteopathic physicians and current osteopathic medical students choose the DO path over the MD path for the additional OMM training. However, most osteopathic physicians either do not or rarely use their extra skills once in practice.

Residency

DO graduates can apply for both osteopathic (DO) residencies and allopathic (MD) residencies in all specialties but may find it slightly harder to compete with MD graduates for allopathic (MD) residencies. Some very competitive MD residency programs are virtually impossible for osteopathic graduates to get into.

Osteopathic graduates participate in the osteopathic residency match and can participate in the MD match as independent applicants. Many osteopathic medical schools were originally set up to produce primary care specialists (family medicine, pediatrics, internal medicine, ob-gyn) and most DO physicians still enter primary care specialties. Currently, there are approximately 50,500 practicing osteopathic (DO) physicians in the United States.[3] While this number only represents 6 percent of the country's physicians, osteopathic physicians handle approximately 10 percent of all primary care visits. Although 60 percent of graduating DO physicians choose to practice primary care in family practice, general internal medicine, and pediatrics, 40 percent pursue a wide range of other medical specialties.[2]

As previously noted, there are special residency considerations if participating in a military scholarship that apply to both MD and DO graduates. Military residencies consider both MD and DO graduates completely equally.

Combined degree programs

Some schools also offer DO/PhD or other combined degree programs including DO/Bioethics, DO/MPH (Master's in Public Health) or a DO degree with some other master's degree.

International Medical Schools (Including Caribbean Schools)
Contributions to this section by Rachel Liu

This chapter mainly addresses issues pertaining to American students attending medical school abroad. However, information in this chapter may also apply to international students interested in practicing medicine in the United States. In general, it is always best to study in the country where you intend to practice (usually your home country) because of immigration requirements, familiarization with regional practice standards, technology, and social awareness as well as ease of access to training and accreditation issues.

First a warning: Approach international schools with caution. Even if a school is WHO (World Health Organization) listed, locally accredited, and confers a medical degree, graduates from certain schools may not be allowed to enter residency programs in the United States or practice in certain (or all) U.S. states. Not all schools are reputable and not all schools grant valid degrees. If you decide on this path, you MUST do your homework by researching your schools of interest thoroughly. Otherwise, you risk losing time, money, and a lot of sanity in the process. You do not want to be stuck with a worthless MD degree. Your goal is to practice medicine in the United States in the end and you don't want to be severely restricted on which states you can practice in. There have been cases in the past in which medical students at foreign schools have reached their final year of medical training only to discover that their programs were not certified and their degrees worthless. They were unable to practice medicine in their home countries and carried many thousands of dollars of debt. Please don't let this happen to you!

According to a report by the American Medical Association (AMA), about 23 percent of physicians working in the United States are internationally trained.[4] Note that this means they attended at least medical school somewhere outside of the United States. However, to practice medicine in the United States, residency training must be completed in the United States. This even applies to fully trained physicians who have already completed medical school and residency training in a foreign country and may even have worked as practicing physicians for many years.

Since your ultimate goal is to practice medicine in the United States, you will have to meet the following requirements if you graduate from a foreign medical school:

1.   Complete at least four years of medical training (any three-year "accelerated" program leading to an MD will not work)
2.   Graduate with an MD or equivalent degree (e.g., MBBS)
3.   Graduate from a medical school listed in the International Medical Education Directory
4.   Pass the USMLE1 and USMLE2 board exams
5.   Become ECFMG certified
6.   Complete a U.S. residency program
7.   Complete the USMLE3 for board certification and the ability to practice medicine on your own.

Again, notice that passing the USMLE (United States Medical Licensing Examination) series and completing a U.S. residency are absolute requirements for practicing medicine in the United States, not limited to international medical graduates.

Graduates from international medical schools (including Caribbean medical schools) are usually referred to as IMGs (international medical graduates) or FMGs (foreign medical graduates). United States citizens studying in foreign countries are known as U.S. IMGs. IMGs are represented in all specialties in the United States. However, most of the IMGs practice in primary care or other nonsurgical, less specialized fields. Most of these fields are in less demand than other specialties, making residency training spots less competitive to enter, and thus easier for IMGs to gain access to. As a result, there is a greater willingness and tendency for IMGs to fill spots in these specialties that would otherwise be understaffed.

The three paths to residency training in the United States for IMGs

The only paths to obtain a residency training position in the United States are:

1. ECFMG Certification (most accessible)
2. Fifth Pathway Program (limited spots)
3. Transfer to U.S. medical school (almost impossible)

Most international students enter residency training via the ECFMG route. A few medical schools allow their students to enter the Fifth Pathway Program and even fewer students transfer from a foreign medical school to a medical school in the United States. The first two options are explained in more detail in the following sections.

The last path involves transferring from a foreign medical school to a medical school in the United States sometime after the pre-clinical years, usually right before third-year rotations begin. Note that this path is very, very limited. Most medical schools in the United States only have very few openings (or none at all) for transfer students. Typically, a spot may open up if someone in the class drops out, which is rare since 97 percent of medical students in U.S. medical schools graduate. Also, you have to have very good USMLE1 board scores to be considered for a transfer, so the U.S. medical schools are typically very picky in whom they will accept for transfer. If you are interested in this option, you should identify the program(s) you would like to transfer to and review their eligibility requirements for transferring, as well as speak to the schools' admissions representatives.

ECFMG

The ECFMG (Educational Commission for Foreign Medical Graduates) was established by the American Medical Association and other similar organizations in the United States to evaluate the qualifications of IMGs who are trying to obtain residency positions or practice medicine in the United States. It acts as the centralizing base of operations for processing IMG application materials for residency programs as well as the USMLE exams, certifies IMGs' credentials, and grants eligibility to practice medicine in the United States.

The most important requirement for IMGs to achieve residency placement is ECFMG certification. Without it, IMGs cannot participate in the residency match or become licensed physicians in the United States. Requirements for ECFMG certification include passing the USMLE1 and USMLE2, including the clinical skills evaluation (USMLE2 CS). Note that the current USMLE CS replaces the prior need for IMGs to take the clinical skills assessment (CSA) and the TOEFL English exam because it evaluates English proficiency along with clinical acumen.

Check the ECFMG website frequently (www.ecfmg.org) for more details regarding requirements for licensure, the USMLE exams, and other IMG-related issues. It is a good idea to check the ECFMG bulletin as well as sign up for their email list to receive updates and notices.

Fifth Pathway Program

Another less available avenue for IMGs to qualify for residency positions in the United States after graduating from a foreign medical school is the Fifth Pathway Program. In this case, no ECFMG certification is required. This program applies only to graduates of foreign medical schools that require one additional year of clinical work or social service after completion of the four-year medical school curriculum in order to graduate from the foreign school. Medical schools in Mexico fall into this category, for example.

There are a few requirements in order to qualify for this program:

1. Students must be U.S. citizens or legal permanent residents of the United States.
2. Students must have completed their four-year under-graduate degree in the United States.
3. The foreign medical school must be listed in the World Health Organization's World Directory of Medical Schools.
4. All requirements for graduation from the foreign medical school must be met, with exception of the one year of clinical work or social service.
5. Students must have passed the USMLE1.

Note that this is different from being an IMG/FMG, because students who go through the Fifth Pathway Program actually never graduate from the foreign medical school, nor do they graduate from any of the medical schools in the United States that sponsor this program. They are given a certificate of completion that is accepted by most U.S. states for physician licensing, being able to enter residency training and practicing medicine.

Essentially, IMGs in this program have to complete a fifth year of medical school rotations in the United States after graduating from the foreign medical school.

Additional information about the Fifth Pathway Program can be found at:
www.ama-assn.org/ama/pub/category/9306.html#pway4
www.mssm.edu/medschool/fifth_pathway/
www.nymc.edu/depthome/fifth.asp

Licensing and other issues

It is important to note that not all international medical schools (and especially Caribbean medical schools) are equal when it comes to being able to secure U.S. licensure, residencies, or electives. Some residency programs will not accept IMGs and a few states will not allow IMGs to complete rotations or residencies.

Quoting from *Iserson's Getting Into a Residency*, Galen Press, 7th edition, page 392:

> "There are thousands of IMGs in the United States who have not been able to obtain a license to practice medicine. In many cases, this is because residency programs will not accept them for training: all jurisdictions in the United States require at least one year of postgraduate training in the U.S. or Canada for licensure... In addition, 25 licensing boards....maintain lists of state-approved foreign medical schools whose graduates are eligible for a medical license."

When considering a foreign medical school, the first step to take is to ensure that the school is listed by the World Health Organization (WHO) Directory of Medical Schools (www.who.int/hrh/wdms/en/) and also in the International Medical Education Directory (IMED), which can be found at http://imed.ecfmg.org.

Accreditation of a school is the responsibility of each individual government. A country's government compiles a list of medical schools that they deem suitable to train physicians, and submits that list to the WHO. WHO enters them into their directory, but as of yet, no universal standardization of education exists. U.S. state medical boards often use the WHO list to determine which schools have "safe" programs, assuming that no country would allow their citizens to be subjected to unqualified physicians. Being listed reduces but does not completely absolve the likelihood of the school being a sham, so be careful and do your research!

Next, it is important to check with the medical board of the U.S. state(s) you are interested in practicing to determine their eligibility criteria for licensure. Certain states have requirements about the type of medical school they recognize, and may even have blacklisted schools that should be avoided if you intend to work in that state. They may have additional criteria besides ECFMG certification to fulfill, and consider graduates on a case-by-case basis. The Federation of State Medical Boards (FSMB, www.fsmb.org) has the contact information and medical board websites for all states.

At the time of this writing, the following jurisdictions were maintaining lists of approved medical schools:

Alabama	Idaho	New Mexico
Arkansas	Indiana	North Dakota
California	Kentucky	Oklahoma
Colorado	Louisiana	Oregon
Connecticut	Minnesota	Puerto Rico
District of Columbia	Mississippi	Rhode Island
Georgia	Missouri	South Dakota
Guam	Montana	Tennessee
		Vermont

Just to make sure you will be able to practice in the states of your choice after attending a specific foreign medical school, you should also check with the state medical licensing boards of states not on this list because rules, laws, and regulations may change over the years and it's better to be safe than sorry.

In a few instances, certain international medical schools have made misleading statements and false claims about the hospitals, clinical facilities, or government programs they were supposedly affiliated. To be sure, contact the hospitals directly that the school claims it is affiliated with to verify the claim. If you find inconsistencies, stay away from that medical school. Also, be wary of all the advertising, literature, and website information thrown at you.

You can assess the legitimacy of a school in other ways. Ask students familiar with that location or current students of the school what their experiences have been. Call administration and admissions offices directly to ask questions, and "feel out" their responses. Visit online resources like the Student Doctor Network forums frequently to ask about schools, life, experiences or hardships, and success of graduates in securing U.S. residencies. If you hear multiple bad rumors or warnings about a school's practices, it may be best to heed them.

Checking residency match lists for international medical schools you are interested in is also a good way to get a feel for how well students are doing in getting into U.S. residencies. Finally, stay away from any foreign medical schools offering medical degrees in less than four years, or you will not be able to enter a U.S. residency because you will not qualify for ECFMG certification.

Residency challenges for IMGs

Many U.S. residency programs will not consider you if you haven't spent at least a few rotations (the more the better) of your clinical rotations in the U.S. hospital and clinical setting. You will need strong recommendation letters from these rotations. This is especially important for U.S. IMGs and thus becomes an unwritten requirement. Non-U.S. IMGs can get by without U.S. rotations, but may be required to do observerships before acceptance into residency programs, so it never hurts to have a few U.S. clinical rotations under your belt anyway.

This places an additional demand on fulfilling the requirements of your own medical program, because you will have to spend extra time setting up and completing U.S. electives. Be prepared to give up a portion, if not all, of your holidays. Most successful IMGs advise completion of two to three U.S. electives and if you know which field you want to enter, at least two electives in your chosen specialty.

Even then, some U.S. residency programs will not consider IMGs, or will place them last on their list to review. Getting into competitive residencies is hardest for international medical school graduates. About 55.6 percent (1,143) of U.S. IMGs and 55.8 percent (3,087) of non-U.S. IMGs matched in 2005, compared to 97.3 percent (13,798) of U.S. graduates.[5] This does not take into account those entering internship outside the match; those who matched into the PGY-2 year instead of the PGY-1 year (internship); or other factors limiting success on the exams (i.e., English proficiency).

In short, if you definitely know you want to practice in a highly populated or competitive location or enter a very competitive residency, you might want to rethink becoming an IMG. Having said that, it is not impossible to fulfill your ambitions as an IMG, but it just might be harder to do. If you acknowledge and accept these risks before going abroad, your time overseas will be much happier and well spent.

Despite the challenges IMGs face, IMGs can be found in all specialties including the very competitive ones. Fantastic board scores (easier said than done) and a mature, amiable personal demeanor eliminate many disadvantages. However, realize that many residency directors will prefer U.S. medical school graduates to fill the residency spots in their programs and often consider IMGs last (or not at all in rare cases). Therefore, you should strive to make your application stand out with higher board scores than those of most of the U.S. applicants and substantial extracurricular work such as research and involvement in unique organizations and in the community. Some of these extra requirements can be challenging to meet if you are attending a foreign medical school that does not have a strong research commitment, for example, as seen with some of the Caribbean medical schools.

Financial aid issues

Many of the international medical schools are not eligible for U.S. government loan programs. If students attending a particular international medical school are eligible for U.S. government loan programs, this is a good sign that the school is reputable and stable with an established track record. Students of qualified medical schools are eligible for Federal Stafford loans after submitting an FAFSA application, which is discussed more fully in the financial aid chapter. Canadian students may qualify for the CanHelp and Canada Student Loan programs.

If a school claims that you will be able to qualify for U.S. federal government loans, ask for the school's "Federal School Code," which is maintained by the United States Department of Education for every school that qualifies for its loans. The medical school has to have this number available for you to qualify for its loans. You can use the number the school gives you to inquire at the student loan office of any major bank in the United States to verify that the number is indeed valid and you will qualify for these loans if you attend that particular medical school.

Otherwise, you are completely dependent on private loans. Any medical school pursuit is very expensive. Even if receiving assistance through the Stafford Loan program, students often need to supplement their expenses using additional private loans. You can easily spend over $100,000 in tuition alone, although many international schools are less expensive than their U.S. counterparts.

It is very rare for any medical school to offer scholarships. However, some countries provide free (or nearly free) education (Germany) with marginal costs, while others charge tuition at varying rates ($15,000 to $25,000). However, cheaper tuition will be offset by plane flights to and from home, and living expenses may be more expensive (i.e., United Kingdom or Ireland). At the time of writing, other currencies are quite strong against the dollar, which pushes up the costs as well.

Why go abroad?

Now that we've spent the previous few pages outlining the hardships IMGs may face, what makes applicants choose to study overseas, knowing that the road toward returning to the United States as practicing physicians is often a harder one?

In the past and as the case may be today, one of the main reasons for studying elsewhere is to pursue an alternative route toward becoming a physician, following multiple rejections from U.S. programs. The same applies to Canadian students, whose provincial requirements make competition for medical school admissions even higher than U.S. schools.

Many students with the potential for becoming excellent physicians feel denied a chance because of the high GPA and MCAT scores required for acceptance into U.S. medical schools. While admissions boards and panels try to take a holistic impression of applicants into account (with secondary applications, personal statement essays, and interviews), the applicant pool far exceeds the number of places available and plenty of capable students get cut in the admission process. So, they circumvent the obstacle of lower scores by completing training elsewhere.

Furthermore, nontraditional students who may have earned higher degrees before deciding to pursue medicine may not want to spend additional years reviewing material and completing prerequisite courses or the MCAT. As some foreign schools do not require these, this may be very appealing.

A few students discover during their college or high school years that they definitely want to pursue medicine and feel continuing an undergraduate degree would be a waste of time. There are pros and cons to this approach, but the decision to forego an undergraduate degree may be right for some people. Since medicine is an undergraduate course almost everywhere in the world and requires less cumulative time to earn a medical degree, they transfer or enter directly upon completion of high school. This choice can be influenced further by familial connections to another country.

Others try this route because the customary one is closed to them. For instance, a reading disability may prevent someone from achieving his or her potential on the MCAT, since the MCAT will not accommodate those with particular needs. Students in this kind of situation, given an opportunity that is not available to them in the United States, often do very well in their medical careers.

Lastly, an increasingly popular reason to train abroad is to explore a change of scenery, learn other viewpoints of the world, and experience a different culture more deeply than just a vacation there would allow. This is somewhat risky if you have not visited the location before, as first impressions can be deceiving. However, it usually leads to a very meaningful, uniquely enriching part of your life.

Note: It must be stated that the purpose of international med schools is NOT to cater to U.S. students or a U.S. system, but to provide their own countrymen with their own type of health care. The only notable exception is the Caribbean medical schools, which predominantly target the U.S. market. This sounds obvious, but is forgotten quite often as students encounter methods of administration and education different from what they're used to. Those who lose sight of this can construe their experiences very negatively and become rather embittered. So, remember to take everything in stride and have fun, no matter what frustrations you encounter along the way!

Length of training

Medical training in other countries usually follows a longer course, most often five to six years, in order to earn a degree, but the cumulative duration of education is shorter.

In the United States, medicine is a postgraduate degree completed following an undergraduate degree. Elsewhere in the world, medicine is an undergraduate degree, with students entering medical school directly from secondary school (high school). Secondary school students generally cover science and math that is more detailed than U.S. high school students (subjects like basic organic chemistry, which we don't study until college); they have completed some premed requirements while still in high school.

So, they may expect cursory knowledge of premed prerequisites before starting the course, which allows them to spend more time on fundamental medical subjects. For example, instead of cramming all of anatomy and neuroanatomy together in six months, these subjects may be spread out over two years, lessening the daily workload. However, after graduation, it often takes longer to progress through a residency in many countries, and you will find that non-U.S. IMGs apply to U.S. residency programs or fellowships with the intent of specializing faster and expediting their rise to the top of the medical practice hierarchy.

For a traditional six-year medical program, the first three years are preclinical and the last three years are clinical, so students spend one additional year in the hospital setting compared to U.S. medical students. At some schools, U.S. applicants who have completed an undergraduate degree may be placed into the second or third year of the course or be exempt from certain classes. Many schools are recognizing the merits of early exposure to a clinical environment and are advocating more than the traditional three years of clinical exposure. Also, some are starting to follow suit of U.S. schools and incorporating Problem-Based Learning (PBL) into their programs. This may be seen as an advantage, so inquire into your medical school's curriculum and ask about proposed changes to the curriculum before you apply.

Choosing a school

As discussed previously, when choosing a school, first determine its credentials. Look for long-established programs in the WHO Directory and raise a red flag to programs that tend to change allegiances frequently. If you are considering a newer school, assess its administration's openness regarding discussion of its accreditation status. Other questions about the school's financial stability, eligibility to practice in that country after graduation, and views of the school's existing and neighboring medical students can give an indication as to whether a program's quality can be assured.

Next, figure out where you want to go. Although choosing English-speaking countries is obviously more common and most convenient for the U.S. IMG, the more adventurous and those with family or friends elsewhere may choose other countries. The study of medicine is difficult enough without having to worry about translating everything. Even if you're fluent in the country's language, learning and incorporating medical terminology and colloquialisms will be an extra challenge. Be prepared to spend extra time coping with the language. Before you leave, brush up and practice conversing. If the language is new to you, take lessons or an immersion course prior to starting medical education. Language programs in certain countries (e.g., Spain) may be offered to help those who already have command of the language take the extra step in learning medical terminology. Some countries (e.g., Sweden) may require a language proficiency exam before you can study there.

Shop around and talk to students, directors, or even lecturers of a university to find out what the reputation of the school is. Look on PubMed (www.pubmed.org), a public research database, to see if the school has good research projects (which gives you an idea of its academic background), and scrutinize the school's website to find out about its curriculum. If you know any graduates from the school who are successfully practicing in the United States, ask them about their experiences. Online venues such as the Student Doctor Network forums are extremely useful in this regard, as visiting student members paint a realistic picture of life at that university and can answer any questions you may have.

Once you have secured the legitimacy of your school of interest, made your individual pros and cons list of that school and the decision to study abroad, and considered the logistics of studying there, all you have left to do is apply.

Applying to international schools

Some countries have organizations that take care of U.S. applications via centralized application services: Atlantic Bridge (www.atlanticbridge.com) for Irish universities, UCAS (www.ucas.co.uk) for British universities, and ACER (www.acer.edu.au/tests/university/gamsat/) for Australian universities (graduate entry). If your school of interest does not use an application service, contact its admissions office directly to get application materials. Also if you can, speak to students at that university and ask questions about the application process, career security, and general life as a foreigner. This can be a reassuring way to help you decide which schools you will apply for.

If you have already completed your undergrad degree, the same general admission requirements apply: GPA, letters of recommendation, personal statement, and curriculum vitae (resume). Treat the application as you would a U.S. medical school application. Because of differences in standardized tests and grading systems, your "statistics" may not be given as much weight, thus placing more importance on good letters of recommendation, curriculum vitae/resume, and essay responses.

Obviously, make your application as strong as possible. Find out if your schools of interest require the MCAT. Many programs will look at MCAT scores, so if you have taken it, send the scores along. If the school does not require the MCAT, find out what their requirements are—there may be an equivalent exam you will have to take. For those applying directly from high school, they will usually want to see SAT scores in addition to the general requirements.

As mentioned before, most overseas medical programs are undergraduate courses, and entry for native students is solely points-based (from their high school standardized tests). Since our application process and standardized tests are different, some universities may request an interview, usually either in a location in the United States or over the phone. Popular questions asked relate to why you want to leave home to attend their school, what you think you can add to their environment, and your understanding of their education process.

Make sure you complete the application early to allow for mailing time (can be several weeks even by airmail). If their medical office doesn't give you a confirmation of receipt, email or call the admissions office about two weeks after you have mailed your application materials. Unlike U.S. applications, it is not necessary to send a thank-you letter after interviews, although be courteous and gracious in personal correspondence with the appropriate admissions liaison, even if interaction has made you want to tear your hair out. Most admissions offices are receptive to questions and offer friendly correspondence.

Goals to keep in mind while studying abroad

Knowing the challenges IMGs face, you should keep some goals in mind throughout the duration of training abroad: the USMLE board exams, U.S. electives with good letters of recommendation, and involvement in meaningful extracurricular activities.

The national average score for the USMLE1 is between 215 and 220 each year. As an IMG, you will want to shoot for a score well above that to increase your chances of matching into the residency you want. IMGs are usually chosen last in the pecking order of matching for residency, regardless of U.S. citizenship, so anything you can do to enhance your application will be to your advantage.

When to take the individual steps of the USMLE exam series depends on the curriculum of your program. You should probably take Step 1 after you have completed most preclinical subjects and covered the topics that appear on the exam, especially pathology and pharmacology, and this probably corresponds with the third U.S. medical year. Clinical experience can be useful as well.

You will most likely need extra study for the USMLE (especially Step 1) in subjects that foreign schools do not hit as hard as U.S. schools, such as biochemistry and embryology. The ECFMG requires that you complete at least two years of medical school before taking USMLE1. Depending on your curriculum and your own level of preparedness, you may need to take eight to ten weeks of solid study to prepare for the exam, since you will not receive time off to study for it.

The ECFMG also recommends that you complete core clinical rotations with substantial patient interaction before taking USMLE2, including exams for clinical skills (CS) and clinical knowledge (CK). USMLE1 and USMLE2 CK exams can be taken at specified centers authorized by the ECFMG around the world, whereas Step 2 CS is only administered in Atlanta, Chicago, Los Angeles, Houston, and Philadelphia in the United States. In general, IMGs pass Step 2 CS without too much trouble, but those who run into problems may have difficulty with the English language, interpersonal skills and communication, or the activities of the patient encounter (history and physical exam).

Another extremely helpful asset to gain access to U.S. residency programs is good letters of recommendation from U.S. clinical directors. This involves completing elective rotations and clerkships in the U.S., which you will have to self-arrange unless your university has acknowledged exchanges with U.S. medical schools. Even then, availability may be limited.

You'll have to spend a lot of time online looking at medical school or student websites and contacting different programs about eligibility, as well as arranging flights and accommodation. Some programs charge overseas students (U.S. IMGs included) a fee ranging from a couple hundred to thousands of dollars, and many require students to be in their final year of medical education or prior completion of core rotations. Others will not entertain applications from international students.

Keep in mind that a few states may have additional requirements in order for your rotation to count. As already mentioned, you should look at the state medical board regulations for your particular states of interest. The American Academy of Medical Colleges (AAMC) Extramural Electives Compendium (www.aamc.org/students/medstudents/electives) may give a good guideline as to which institutions you can consider for electives, although you can contact individual hospitals as well.

You do not necessarily have to complete all your electives in the United States, but it is recommended to have at least two or three letters of recommendation from U.S. hospital department chairs, clinical directors, or prominent physicians. Some foreign schools encourage completing electives in third world countries that need assistance. Doing these can be extremely valuable teaching experiences and should be taken advantage of, especially since U.S. schools don't advertise the opportunity to do so. But, make sure you complete electives in the U.S. as well—don't neglect them.

While rotating, the opportunity may arise to personally arrange entry into a residency program outside of the Match, especially if a U.S. hospital is affiliated with the specific international or Caribbean medical school that the student attends. However, this opportunity is rare and offered only to an extremely well-performing and impressive student, and based on the individual discretion or disposition of a program chair.

A word about extracurricular activities: If you can, try to participate in research if it's of interest to you. Opportunities can be hard to find in another country where research is not as bountiful as in the United States, but you will find academics receptive to the idea if you show keen interest. It's unwise (and not much fun) to partake in activities just to try to beef up your resume, but do find meaningful organizations or hobbies to engage in. Becoming involved is a great way to meet people and really adds to your enjoyment of being in a different country.

Finally, you will need your medical school dean's letter as one of your supporting documents for application to residency programs, so be sure to coordinate with your school's medical student liaison when application time approaches. Timing can be an issue, so coordinate your medical school curriculum with USMLE testing dates and elective openings carefully. Some students choose to use an additional year post-graduation to sort out the application requirements (except electives, which must be completed pre-graduation) for residency programs.

Once you complete these requirements and are ready to apply for residency programs, you will apply through the Electronic Residency Application Service (ERAS, also used by U.S. medical school graduates), using the ECFMG as your base. If the specialty you are interested in does not participate in ERAS, check with the program directors and ask their preferred method of receiving applications. All residency program information can be found in the Fellowship Residency Electronic Interactive Database (FREIDA). There are also specific resources on the ERAS website that provide resources (like cover sheets for IMG letters of recommendation), which should be sent to the ECFMG, who will then transmit it to ERAS.

After you have completed and submitted materials for your application to ERAS, using the ECFMG to receive your dean's token (discussed in the "Residency Training" chapter), you will have to register with the National Resident Matching Program (NRMP) to "match" with a residency program. Matching is the process that compares the applicant's programs of choice with hospitals' lists of preferred applicants.

Those unsuccessful in the first round of the match (which occurs more frequently with IMGs than U.S. graduates) go through a post-match "scramble." In the scramble, residency programs that did not fill all available residency spots may choose to accept IMGs (and any other U.S. medical school graduates) who did not match outside of the match by making an independent offer at this time. This practice is currently under review by the NRMP, and so may change in the near future.

If your application passes the screening process used by residency programs, you may be invited for an interview with a program director following your applications. Make sure you are well prepared by talking with previous students who interviewed at the program regarding the kinds of questions they were asked, and by reading on current medically related events.

Your title

You will be entitled to use the initials MD upon returning to the United States, even though you will be graduating with a regional MD equivalent. This is for simplicity's sake. In the UK, medical school graduates earn an MBBS. Students may graduate with an MBBChBAO (bachelor of medicine, surgery, and obstetrics). People in Europe like letters, but they all mean the same thing. However, the letters "MD" in the UK is a higher research degree conferred upon post-graduate candidates after completion of an MBBS. It causes some confusion with U.S. doctors unfamiliar with the UK/European system. As another example, in Germany, the MD is only given to those who have completed research and thesis, etc., similar to what in the U.S. system would be an MD/PhD. But the bottom line is that upon graduating with a medical degree, you will be entitled to list yourself as an MD in the United States. Again, check with the state licensing boards about their requirements.

The IMG stigma and challenges

There is a stigma attached to the sound of "IMG" or to certain university locations (especially Caribbean schools) because of sham stories and the view that IMGs were not "good enough" to get into U.S. medical schools. Because of this, some of your colleagues or even residency admissions directors may not be receptive to IMGs and as stories go, may not even look at an application from an IMG, regardless of citizenship or scores.

Thankfully, this doesn't seem to be too common, but be aware that it does exist. At the end of the day, if you have proven yourself competent by scoring well on the USMLE and by performing well clinically, your colleagues and patients won't know and won't care where you were educated. The whole stigma thing is silly, really. Much of the same material is covered in medical schools worldwide, but using different educational structures. Some curricula are more notes-based, others require more self-direction; some are very traditional, others have started incorporating PBL. The French think their system is best, the UK students think their education is the best, and so on. In truth, a "best" probably does not exist, but there is a set level that every doctor in the world needs to reach in order to achieve competency.

The sheer number of applicants to residency programs can make the likelihood of an IMG acceptance rare in certain places. You will hear of states or residency programs that may be IMG-unfriendly, simply because demand is so high. But nothing is absolute; there is no harm in trying and putting your best efforts forward. Listening to the gossip mill and doing your own research to dig out the more receptive programs will save you time, anxiety, and money, but if you show good performance during medical school, your opportunities are plentiful.

On the flip side, if you are a U.S. IMG studying abroad, and you want to work there after graduation, those countries also take care of their own countrymen first and it might be hard to obtain a residency spot as a non-citizen, not to mention difficulties in obtaining work visas. While obtaining junior positions may not present a problem, it can be harder to progress through the ranks and advance in your career. You will find out more of the hardships and the process of working while studying there.

Canada is special

The only notable exception among international schools is Canada. Essentially, Canadian medical schools are considered equal to U.S. medical schools and you have, as a graduate, all the same rights, privileges, and residency opportunities. Both U.S. and Canadian schools are accredited by the same institutions and graduates are equally qualified and trained. Therefore, there are no limitations and Canadian graduates are in all aspects treated equally with U.S. graduates.

Caribbean medical schools

Caribbean medical schools typically only provide the basic science curriculum (first and second year) in the Caribbean on an island in a medical school setting. The third and fourth year rotations are arranged to take place in affiliated hospitals in the United States. Most of these affiliated hospitals are located on the East Coast.

As faculty members are dedicated to teaching only, these schools usually do not provide research opportunities, but students may complete research electives or participate elsewhere. Upon graduation, an MD degree is awarded.

MCAT and GPA requirements may be lower than for U.S. medical schools and some Caribbean schools do not require the MCAT at all. Applications are submitted directly to the Caribbean medical schools for consideration, and you can find applications online on their websites. At most schools, students can enroll and begin their studies three different times during the year (spring, summer, fall).

It has been noted that board pass rates are lower for Caribbean school graduates than those of U.S.-trained MD and DO graduates: USLME1 exam pass rates were 59 percent for Caribbean schools, 72 percent for osteopathic (DO) schools, and 92 percent for allopathic (MD) schools according to the NBME Annual Report for 2005.[1]

However, Caribbean graduates can be found practicing successfully all across the United States. Remember to check the state medical boards for information regarding specific Caribbean schools.

Non U.S. citizens

For non U.S. citizens looking for a place in U.S. residency programs, the appropriate visas and their requirements must be obtained, most commonly the J1 visa and the H-1B visa. These have different eligibility requirements and allowed durations of stay, and have implications for spouses or significant others who may be traveling with you. A very complete resource directed toward IMGs can be found at the VISALAW website, which is run by a large immigration law firm (www.visalaw.com/00may4/12may400.html).

Podiatry (DPM) Schools
Contributions to this section by Robert Greenhagen,
podiatry student

General information

There are currently eight colleges of podiatric medicine in the United States. Successful completion of one of these programs leads to a Doctor of Podiatric Medicine (DPM) degree. Many of these programs are affiliated and either partially or fully integrated with an MD or DO school.

The education consists of two years of basic science/general medicine courses followed by two years of clinical rotations, similar to regular medical school. These rotations are done in non-hospital-based clinics as well as major hospitals and deal with general medicine, basic podiatric medicine, and podiatric surgery. Research opportunities for medical students are available during these four years.

DPM students take the NBPME (National Board of Podiatric Medical Examiner's) boards and match for Podiatric Medicine and Surgery (PM&S) residencies. Applications for colleges of podiatric medicine are handled through the American Association of Colleges of Podiatric Medicine (AACPM, www.aacpm.org).

Podiatrists may practice in all of the U.S. states.

Podiatry schools are somewhat easier to get into than MD and DO schools due to lower average GPA and MCAT requirements, but admission is still somewhat competitive.

Residency

During the fourth year, students participate in the podiatric residency match and scramble. Applications for residency are handled through the Central Application Service for Podiatric Residencies (CASPR). Applicants interview at centralized regional interview program (CRIP) locations. These usually consist of an East, Central, and West CRIP location. While all residency programs are members of CASPR, a few programs do not attend CRIP interviews and interview separately after the CRIP dates.

Podiatric residencies are two to three years long and are termed Podiatric Medicine and Surgery 24 (PM&S-24) and Podiatric Medicine and Surgery 36 (PM&S-36) programs. DPMs rotate through various medical specialties and train in podiatric medicine, forefoot, rearfoot, and ankle surgery.

Combined degree programs

Many schools offer an optional master's degree program along with the DPM degree. Examples include Master's of Health Care Administration and Master's of Public Health (MPH) degrees. Consult specific schools for more information on opportunities.

Selecting a School

There are certainly many factors involved when trying to decide which schools to apply to.

Before selecting medical schools to apply to, you need to figure out what is important to you. Not all of the following areas or questions are relevant or important to everyone. Make a list of what matters to you, then use your list of priorities to figure out which medical schools meet your needs.

Of course, often, you cannot choose your medical school to attend. It is possible that your application is not competitive enough or you just don't get offers where you'd like to go.

In-state versus out-of-state medical schools

If you have the opportunity to go to a public medical school within your state of residence, that will be a great advantage to you. Public in-state medical schools are much cheaper (in-state tuition versus out-of-state tuition), sometimes charging you only 50 percent of what out-of-state students have to pay. Average resident tuition for public medical school was $20,370 in 2005, 46 percent less than the average nonresident tuition of $37,475 at public medical schools in 2005.[6]

Admission is usually much easier for in-state students since the state schools are given incentives or mandates from the state, and it is their mission to accept predominantly in-state students. The out-of-state applicant pool is often very large and applicants are competing for very few spots. Even many private medical schools receive some bonus or incentive from the state they are located in to accept more in-state applicants. So, the advantage may even exist at private medical schools within your state.

Other factors to consider

Here is a list of some factors that you may want to consider when making a list of potential schools:

Academics and competitiveness at schools
Is my MCAT competitive for MD, DO, Podiatry, or Caribbean medical school?
Is my GPA competitive?
Do I have sufficient extracurricular activities, research, shadowing, volunteer work, etc., for the school?
Do I meet all special course work and other requirements of the school?
Do I need to apply to more schools than the average applicant does since my MCAT and GPA are weak?
Does the school admit many out-of-state students?

Reputation and Rankings
Is the school top rated and well known/prestigious?
Does the school have top research or other awards?
Is the school known for the specialty I am interested in?
Is the school research oriented or clinically oriented and does it match my interests?

Location
Is the school where I am willing/happy to live?
Are beach, mountains, and/or entertainment close by—if important?
Is the school close to or far away from relatives or to home?
How safe is the campus, the neighborhood, and the area?

Family
Do you have parents, siblings, and/or friends around?
Is the area suitable for raising your own kids?
Does the area have good schools and is the neighborhood safe for your family?
Is reasonable and safe housing available close to the school?

Costs

Tuition costs—especially consider in-state versus out-of-state if you have that option.

Cost of living for the areas you are interested in can vary significantly and your budget is essentially the same, no matter where you go.

Commuting costs can also be significant.

Other

Are all the third- and fourth-year rotations done locally or do I have to travel all over the country?

What are the USMLE scores/pass-rate for the school?

Are there any aspects of school that are exceptional?

What do the campus and the affiliated hospitals look like? Are they in good shape or old and run down?

What were faculty, students, and other staff like on interview day?

Chapter References

1.   2005 USMLE Performance Data as published in the
        2005 NBME Annual Report,
        http://www.usmle.org/scores/2005perf.htm

2.   International Osteopathic Licensing, Educating the
        International Community, Michigan State University
        College of Osteopathic Medicine website, Dawn
        Wondero,
        http://www.com.msu.edu/communique/Spring99/
        Licensing.html

3.   Overview of Osteopathic Medicine, Osteopathic Medical
        College Information Book, 2007 Entering Class, page 4

4.   International Medical Graduates in the U.S. Workforce,
        A discussion paper, American Medical Association, page
        5,
        http://www.ama-assn.org/ama1/pub/upload/mm/18/
        workforce2006.pdf

5.   National Residency Matching Program (NRMP)
        Applicants by Type, AAMC Data Book, 2006, pages 68,
        69

6.   Median Tuition and Fees for First-Year U.S. Medical
        Students, AAMC Data Book, 2006, pages 54, 55

The Application Process

Application Process

Overview

The application process for medical school is long and intense. It really begins much earlier than when you actually fill out the application to send to the schools. It includes completion of many premed requirements, meetings with your premed advisor and premed committee, taking the MCAT, and doing well in all of your premed coursework and extracurricular activities.

Most medical schools will review applications as they are submitted on a rolling basis, extend interview invitations, and finally offer spots in their classes in the same way. This means that they fill their classes on a first-come-first-serve basis. Initially, they may have 150 spots to offer. With each passing week of conducting interviews, the admissions committee meets and extends offers and fewer and fewer spots are available. At the same time, the medical school still receives more applications, so the competition goes up and the number of available spots goes down. This means that an early application is one sure way of having the best possible chances of getting in.

Your chances of gaining admission to medical school

As you can see from the data that follows, the number of allopathic (MD) medical school applicants has decreased by about 8,000 from 45,000 applicants in 1994 to 37,000 applicants in 2005, while medical school enrollment has remained largely constant over the same time period.[1] Acceptance rates have increased from 38 to 48 percent. So, overall, almost one half of all allopathic (MD) applicants gain admission to medical school now.

The following data shows applicant and acceptance data for allopathic (MD) medical schools.[1]

Year	Applied	Accepted*	% Accepted
2005	37,364	17,978	48%
2004	35,735	17,662	49%
2003	34,791	17,542	50%
2002	33,625	17,593	52%
2001	34,860	17,454	50%
2000	37,088	17,535	47%
1999	38,443	17,421	45%
1998	40,996	17,373	42%
1997	43,016	17,312	40%
1996	46,965	17,385	37%
1995	46,586	17,356	37%
1994	45,360	17,318	38%

* Data reflects acceptances, not matriculants.

The AAMC (Association of American Medical Colleges), which is the association of allopathic (MD) medical schools, has recently (June 2006) stated that medical school enrollment should be expanded by the year 2015 by another 5,000 spots. This is an increase of about 30 percent over current levels in order to address severe shortages in the medical field over the next few decades. This should also improve chances for gaining admission to medical school.

In regards to osteopathic (DO) medical schools, the number of applicants has decreased by almost 2,000 from 10,213 applicants in 1995 to 8,255 applicants in 2005, while medical school enrollment has increased significantly by at least 1,000 (45 percent) over the same time period.[2] Acceptance rates have gone up from 22 to 40 percent.

The following data shows applicant and acceptance data for osteopathic (DO) medical schools.[2]

Year	Applied	Matriculated*	% Accepted
2005	8,255	3,308**	40%
2004	7,240	3,308**	45%
2003	6,814	3,308	48%
2002	6,324	3,079	47%
2001	6,898	3,048	44%
2000	7,708	2,927	38%
1999	8,396	2,848	34%
1998	9,554	2,745	29%
1997	10,764	2,692	25%
1996	10,781	2,535	23%
1995	10,213	2,274	22%

* Data reflects matriculants, not acceptances.
** Approximate since data was unavailable.

Note that quite a few applicants may be in both applicant pools, applying to both MD and DO schools in the same year. In 2005, there were probably fewer than the 45,619 total applicants that would be suggested by simply adding the data for both school types. Also, looking at this data by itself, it would appear that admission to DO schools is more competitive than admission to MD schools. However, as indicated by GPA and MCAT scores and a few other factors, MD schools are generally considered more competitive to get into.

No one can predict how many individuals will be interested in studying medicine and applying each year in the future, so these trends may not be the ultimate predictor of future interest in the field of medicine, especially with many potential future changes to the U.S. healthcare system.

Main events of the application process

What to Do	When to Do It	More Detail
Meet with your premed advisor to discuss your future	Freshman year (or when you decide on medicine)	The sooner the better
Take required course work	Before the MCAT (freshman, sophomore, junior years)	You need physics, chemistry, organic chemistry, and biology for the MCAT
Complete extracurricular activities (shadowing, etc.)	Before June of your junior year, when you apply	You want to be able to list these on the application, so they have to be completed by then
Take the MCAT	January through September of junior year	Take the MCAT before May 1 if at all possible
Interview with your premed committee	Before applying, junior year	If your undergrad school does that—they usually write a letter of recommendation for you
Fill out applications and write your personal statement	Right after the MCAT is out of the way	It may take you a few weeks to months to work on this, so start immediately after the MCAT is done
Return secondary applications you receive	Promptly within no more than 7 days from the day you receive them	The earlier the better; try to return these within a couple of days, if possible
Interviews	Try to accept the first possible days for interviewing	Earlier interviews are better
Acceptance	Most schools notify you within about 2 weeks, some within a few days, and some take several months after your interview to let you know if you have been accepted, rejected or wait-listed.	
Choosing your school	Allopathic (MD) schools allow you to wait until April of the year you plan to attend to decide—you hold your spot with a $100 refundable deposit, in most cases. DO schools have much stiffer deadlines a few months after extending offers and require nonrefundable deposits ranging from $500 to $1500 depending on the school. Your final decision must be made in April of the year you plan to attend.	

Early, Early, Early, EARLY, EARLY, EARLY, EARLY!!!!!

One of the most important aspects of your application relates to timing. You can talk with many applicants who applied late because they took the MCAT late (August) or they just procrastinated on their applications. You will hear loud and clear that they would recommend applying as early as possible. I strongly agree. Applying as early as possible, interviewing on the first day possible, etc., gives you a *huge* advantage.

As already mentioned, as time passes with a rolling admissions process, your chance of gaining admission decreases due to more and more spots being filled with students and more applicants still arriving to be considered. Besides this factor of increasing competition, there is also peace of mind when you have received an offer early. Let's consider each step of the application process in detail now, in light of timing.

Early MCAT (by May 1)

You should take the MCAT by May 1 so you can get your scores back around June 1, which is the first day you can submit your AMCAS medical school application. Taking the MCAT later during the summer will put you behind in the application process. Many applicants have already received interview invitations and some have already been extended offers as the admission cycle progresses. Most medical schools will not consider your application and do not offer interview invitations until your MCAT scores are received, so timing your MCAT is essential for timing your application.

Early applications

Make sure you start working on your AMCAS (MD) and/or AACOMAS (DO) applications right after the MCAT is out of the way if you didn't have time for this before you took the MCAT. It takes a few months to get the applications put together, so you should ideally start about two months before June 1 to fill out the applications or at least gather the required information and start working on your personal statement. The online applications are made available sometime around May 1 each year, although they cannot be submitted until June 1 at the earliest. It is recommended to submit your completed applications (AMCAS and AACOMAS) within the first week after you receive your MCAT scores. That would be roughly the week following June 1. It is critical to submit your applications as early as possible.

Early secondaries

Fill out all secondary applications received from the medical schools immediately and try to return them within less than seven days, ideally within two days along with the money and other information they require you to submit. Turn these around as fast as possible. Some secondaries are more involved than others and all cost money. Do not procrastinate. To obtain early interviews, turning these around quickly is a must!

Early interviews

If you have done the previous three steps very speedily (early MCAT, early application, fast turnaround of secondaries), you will have interview invitations very early and will have the opportunity to interview during the first few weeks of the interview cycle, maybe the first week or even the first day interviews begin. Try to pick the earliest day for interviewing the school offers. Ideally, you want the first day available on their schedule to interview.

Early offers

Most medical schools extend offers within two to three weeks. However, the notification time varies greatly from school to school. For example, Kirksville College of Osteopathic Medicine took three to four days in the 2005 admissions cycle. Medical College of Wisconsin took about ten days. University of Utah and University of Washington took up to four to six months (March notification).

Why the hurry?

You should know the answer to this question by now. If not, reread this section again from the beginning! Do yourself a favor and do things early. It's the one factor of your application you have complete control over—and it really pays off!

I know applicants who either took the MCAT late (in August) or took way too long submitting their applications, secondaries, etc. They were still interviewing well into March and did not hear back until the end of the entire interview season. On the other hand, some students have already received multiple offers by Oct. 15. Also, as already explained, less spots are available, as the medical schools tend to have rolling admissions. At the beginning, really all of the spots are free and the schools try to fill them more aggressively. So, people who are equally qualified have less of a chance to get in during January through April than if they had interviewed during October (or earlier if possible).

Early Decision Program (EDP)

Don't confuse the Early Decision Program (EDP) with applying early—this is a separate admissions program and not really part of the regular admission process. Not all medical schools offer the Early Decision Program.

This is how it works:

You can only apply to *one* medical school's Early Decision Program. The medical school has to make a decision by October 1 and must notify you of acceptance or rejection. If you are accepted to the school, you are obligated to attend that particular medical school and cannot participate in the regular application cycle at any other medical schools for that application cycle. So, you have to be sure the medical school you apply to with this program is really the school you want to attend since there is no changing your mind later.

There are also some huge drawbacks to the Early Decision Program, as you might have already guessed, since you can only apply to *one* medical school. If you are not accepted, you have wasted valuable time to get your application submitted to the other medical schools.

You cannot start applying to other medical schools until you have received a rejection letter from your EDP school by October 1. That is two to three months late in the application cycle! You are essentially in the same spot as if you had taken the MCAT late.

Note that if you were rejected during the Early Decision Program, you can still apply to the same medical school through the regular admissions process again and you will be considered for regular admission independently from the EDP decision. You may even get a spot in the class that way if you were rejected for EDP admission.

The Early Decision Program can be useful for very strong (exceptional) applicants or for candidates who have specifically been encouraged by the school to compete for early admissions. Generally, if you are a strong enough applicant for a spot through the Early Decision Program, you will also get a spot in the class through the regular process.

EDP drawbacks in summary

Personally, I think the Early Decision Program only limits your choices and is not very useful. Especially if you apply early (not through the Early Decision Program), you can also get offers by the middle of October. Also, the timing issue is a *huge* disadvantage, putting you way behind in the admission process if you are rejected.

Premed Advisor and Committee

Premed advisor

A competent premed advisor can make a big difference in guiding you through the admissions process successfully. Most premed students don't know anything about the admissions process or what to do to get into medical school. The premed advisor is the first stop to help you determine what courses you may have to take at your university or college to graduate with a useful degree while also fulfilling all medical school course requirements at the same time.

Basically, the advisor is there to help you gain admission to medical school. The advisor will also be familiar with local shadowing, volunteer or clinical opportunities, and may suggest faculty members who have previously worked well with premed undergraduate students on research. A premed advisor is also able to look at your specific situation and give you some direction and advice tailored to your unique circumstances.

Advisors typically have all kinds of useful information such as which medical schools give tuition breaks or scholarships to students from your state and which medical schools have admitted large numbers of students from your undergraduate institution or from your state in the past. These schools should be on the top of your list of medical schools to apply to.

Often, premed advisors or premed offices maintain email lists and distribute a lot of useful information, reminders about deadlines coming up, and meetings or forums that you can attend. At these meetings, you have a chance to meet staff from medical school admissions offices, local physicians, and current medical students who share a wealth of knowledge about medical school admission and their own experiences.

In short, premed advisors are great resources. Go see your advisor! Hopefully your school has one. If not, check to see if another school in your area has one you can make an appointment with.

Premed committee

Many undergraduate institutions have premed committees, often chaired by a premed advisor. Most medical schools require a letter of recommendation from a premed committee, or at least prefer a letter from a premed committee to other faculty letters. The premed committee may meet with you in an interview or other format to get to know you better. They then write a letter of recommendation in your behalf, which is sent to the medical schools you have applied to. This letter is sent out about the same time you are returning your secondary applications to the medical schools.

Application(s)

There are two main application services used for U.S. medical schools. The AMCAS application is used to apply to most allopathic (MD) medical schools, with a few exceptions, and the AACOMAS application is used for all osteopathic (DO) medical schools. Application to Podiatry schools is also centralized through the AACPMAS application.

All Caribbean medical schools and most international medical schools accept only individual applications, which can be found online at each school's website. You will need to visit their websites for application information.

Interestingly, most medical schools do not use the information submitted through the AMCAS or AACOMAS application to screen applicants. Instead, most of the applicants are sent secondary applications that have to be returned with another nonrefundable application fee, ranging from $30 to $100 per medical school.

How many schools should you apply to?

Some statistics show that, on average, you have to apply to fourteen schools to gain successful admission to medical school. Having said that, I know some people who only applied to one medical school and got in. I also heard about one applicant who applied to fifty medical schools and received only one offer. Also note that some applicants apply and don't receive any offers. Often, it takes one or more reapplication attempts over several years to finally gain admission to medical school.

Typically, if you are an average applicant, applying to around twelve to fifteen medical schools is probably about right. If you are a very strong applicant, applying to three to five medical schools may be sufficient. If you are a weaker than average applicant, you may want to apply to twenty schools or more.

Err on the safe side. Apply to more schools than you need rather than not enough. Sitting around for a year is no fun! You could be studying medicine! So, make sure you get in!

Allopathic (MD) and osteopathic (DO) school applications

The AMCAS application for allopathic (MD) and the AACOMAS application for osteopathic (DO) schools are quite lengthy and require some time and effort to complete. Don't think you can finish them in one day, but, you probably won't need weeks, either.

As already mentioned in the "Early, Early, Early" application section of this book, you should have your application ready for submission within a week or so after receiving your MCAT scores. If you take the MCAT later during the summer (July, August or September), you don't want to wait until you have your MCAT scores back. You need to submit your applications during the summer, before you take the MCAT. Just realize that most schools will not even look at your application further until the MCAT scores are received. When you receive your scores, they are released to the medical schools you have applied to. The schools then complete your file and make decisions about extending interview invitations. If you have already submitted your application, completing your file once the MCAT scores are received is easy and will save you a few days of processing time.

If you don't know your MCAT scores by the time you apply, you obviously cannot easily determine how competitive your overall application will be fore sure. This makes it harder to decide which medical schools to apply to.

Both applications (AMCAS and AACOMAS) ask you for the following information:

1. Personal, contact and biographical information
2. Education background including high school and all colleges/universities, degrees, etc.
3. All college courses ever completed by type, course number, name, and grade earned
4. Any special tests completed with scores (MCAT, SAT, ACT, and others if applicable)
5. Experiences, including work and extracurricular activities
6. Personal statement/comment
7. List of schools you wish to apply to

Note also that the MCAT scores are automatically released to AMCAS (for MD schools), but not to AACOMAS (for DO schools). You have to actually release your MCAT scores to AACOMAS on the MCAT Testing History System (https://services.aamc.org/mcatthx/) if you are applying to osteopathic (DO) schools. You will need to have all of your transcripts from any college or university ever attended sent directly to AMCAS and AACOMAS for verification of your course work.

If you fill out the AMCAS application (MD) first, then the AACOMAS application (DO) is easier to fill out since the latter requires shorter answers and explanations on everything, including the personal statement. So, start with the AMCAS application, print it out, then fill in the AACOMAS application if you plan to apply to both MD and DO schools.

One last bit of advice about the applications: Check everything for spelling, grammatical, and other errors and mistakes, especially the personal statement, which is part of the application.

Here are the links to the AMCAS application and the AACOMAS application:
    AMCAS: www.aamc.org/students/amcas/start.htm
    AACOMAS: https://aacomas.aacom.org/

Allopathic (MD) schools not participating with AMCAS

There are MD schools that do not participate with AMCAS. These schools include all the public Texas medical schools and a couple more, for a total of eight medical schools. The Texas medical schools use their own centralized application, the Texas Medical and Dental School Application Service (TMDSAS, www.utsystem.edu/tmdsas). The other schools require direct submission of an application to the individual school.

The following allopathic (MD) medical schools are not participating with AMCAS (in 2007):
    1.   University of Missouri—Kansas City School of

Medicine
2.   University of North Dakota School of Medicine and
      Health Sciences
3.   Texas A & M University System Health Science Center
      College of Medicine
4.   Texas Tech University Health Sciences Center School of
      Medicine
5.   University of Texas Medical Branch at Galveston
6.   University of Texas Medical School at Houston
7.   University of Texas Medical School at San Antonio
8.   University of Texas Southwestern Medical Center at
      Dallas Southwestern Medical School

Cost of applications

Everything costs money. This is no different when you apply to
medical school. AMCAS and AACOMAS both charge money per
medical school you wish to have your application forwarded to.
There is a base fee for the first school and then you are charged an
additional amount for each additional school.

For AMCAS, the application fee in 2007 for the first school is
$160 and each additional school costs $30. For example, applying
to fourteen allopathic (MD) schools would cost $550.
Fees for osteopathic schools are very similar, with the first school
fee of $155, the two-school fee of $190, and any additional school
cost of $30. Applying to fourteen osteopathic (DO) schools would
cost $555.

Both application services have fee assistance programs that you
may be able to qualify for. Here are links to the AMCAS fee
assistance program and the AACOMAS Fee Waiver:
      www.aamc.org/students/applying/fap/
      www.aacom.org/home-applicants/fee-waiver.html

The fee waivers may be worth a try, but you have to show that you
meet some very specific conditions to qualify, and qualifying for
these fee waivers is hard.

Also, remember that it takes up to $100 per secondary application and $300 to $500 per interview you attend due to flights, food, and hotel costs. In the end, your total application costs can easily reach $5,000 by the time you add in all the costs associated with applying to medical school and navigating the admission process. But remember, "Don't trip over pennies on your way to dollars."

The Personal Statement or Application Essay

The personal statement or essay is probably the most dreaded and feared part of the actual medical school application.

YOUR statement

The first thing to know is that this is *your* personal statement. It is yours. No one else can write it for you. Reading other people's statements in preparation to write your own may be helpful in some cases, but not always. No single person will be in exactly your circumstances or have exactly the same background and extracurricular and other experiences you have.

Through the essay, the admissions committee wants to see who you are. They only have your sterile application in front of them, listing all of your accomplishments, your course work, and other information. The personal statement allows them to see you as a person, not just in terms of numbers and lists of accomplishments. The statement is also used by the people who interview you. Interviewers usually review your file and application essay before the interview. I was asked about my personal statement in every interview I had, and most likely, you will be too.

Other people's statements

Reading other people's statements may make you feel inferior since you have not even started to think of yours. You will be astonished by how well other people are able to write, how neat their stories are, how entertaining their essay is, and how well it flows. What you don't see is that they went through the same turmoil you are going through now, that they may have spent several months writing, rewriting, and refining every sentence and every word to make it flow and sound that good. They may even have involved an English professor or other people to help them finalize their statements. So, don't panic or think you could never come up with something that good. By the time you are done, people will be in awe about your statement when they first start out writing theirs.

Before I started writing my statement, I bought two books that contained forty actual essays of successful applicants. With each additional essay I read, I got more frustrated and convinced that I could never write anything like that. I also was drawn into how they wrote and thought and saw certain phrases or wording that I wanted to use because they sounded good. However, reading other applicant's essays may lead to problems—you may end up using their language and expressions rather than your own.

I had to unload all of these essays from my brain and start over to actually write *my own* statement. Once I did that, things began to work and the statement started to come together. I wrote my own personal statement and did not use any fancy phrases or language from other essays. It was truly my own statement.

Some basic guidelines

1. Show your motivations and why you are interested in medicine.
2. Show your qualities, strengths, and accomplishments by illustration/story rather than factual statements.
3. Spelling, grammar, and neatness count (do not rely on your spellchecker—ask others to read your statement).
4. Do not overdo selling yourself. ("I'm Superman; I will defeat all evil, stamp out disease, and save the planet.")

The medical school is really interested in hearing about you and your motivations in becoming a physician. The trick in telling them about yourself is to tell stories or write about what you have done to show how you interact, what type of person you are, and what feelings and motivations you have.

So, rather than saying, "I am compassionate, hard-working, love to help people, and have all the qualities to become a great physician," which may all be correct, factual statements about you, you need to spend some time showing this through activities you have done and through stories. Support your hypothesis with data—ever heard this before? That means you may have to describe how you felt when you saw the results of your tutoring efforts of high school students rather than factually explaining your tutoring—they know what tutoring is and can see that that you have done this on the application anyway. You may want to focus on how you felt when the little boy was treated by the physician you shadowed or what moved you when you volunteered at the soup kitchen or what lesson you learned from an experience. It is very hard to express this in your essay, but this will make your essay come alive to the reader and show your personality, character, and attributes favorably instead of just listing them.

In short, the admissions people want to hear about you and your story as well as your motivations for medicine. Write about the lessons you have learned, your feelings, and motivations. What are the things that convinced you to pursue medicine? If you have dreamed of becoming a physician all your life, write about that. But you had better have some evidence to support that claim in the form of stories and experiences that have validated that choice. Maybe you have had some serious event in your life that caused you to pursue medicine. Write about it.

Your statement does not have to be completely about premedical pursuits, etc. If you love sports or any other activity that totally defines you and has taught you great lessons or shows your positive qualities and attributes, you can use that as your story. The personal statement is intended to *tell your story*, overall, whatever that story is. Just make sure that what you write about still meets the general idea and you answer the question "Why medicine?" Show how your qualities will make you a great physician.

You don't absolutely have to answer the "Why medicine?" question if you don't want to, even though it is recommended, as long as you can show your qualities and demonstrate that you will be a great physician based on the story you tell. Telling the story does not mean making up anything. Be truthful, don't lie about anything, and be careful with exaggerations.

You can capitalize on your unique situation. Are you a nontraditional student? Write about it. Write about why you changed your mind and what led you to medicine.

Your personal statement should also be used to explain any poor performance or major gaps in your education or work experience. If you have deficits or major questionable items on application, the personal statement is the place to address some of these.

How to come up with your qualities

So, you think you are plain boring and have nothing to share? Ask yourself and others (others often know you better than you do) about your qualities and make a list of them. Are you energetic, driven, focused, organized, a leader, a team player, or compassionate? Come up with a list and pick the top three to five of them that really define you the most. Try to bring these qualities out as you write the statement. When your statement is done, ask yourself "Are each one of these reflected in this statement?" If not, try to rewrite some parts to incorporate them.

Here are some basic traits to jumpstart your thinking (in no particular order):

1. You care about others.
2. You are compassionate.
3. You are driven.
4. You are energetic.
5. You are motivated.
6. You have a strong work ethic.
7. You have goals.
8. You are responsible.
9. You are friendly and easy to get along with.
10. You get along well with others.
11. You are easy going and good to work with.
12. You are a team player.
13. You are a leader.
14. You motivate others.
15. You get stuff done.
16. You enjoy helping.

How to come up with your motivation for medicine

What made you decide to pursue medicine?
What events (shadowing, volunteering, or other events) appealed to you or opened your eyes or led you down this path to medicine?
Imagine you had to convince your spouse or a close friend who is skeptical about your decision that medicine was your thing, what would you tell him or her? How would you back up your claim?
Do you love the sciences, the cutting edge of biology, curing diseases, dealing with people, helping others, intellectual stimulation, challenges?

If you are having a hard time with this, you probably haven't spent enough time with extracurricular activities that involve you in patient care, actively or as an observer.

Don't overdo it

You want to sell yourself, but without bragging or giving the impression you are the best thing that ever happened to planet Earth. People reading your statements can immediately sense if you are insincere or bluffing. They have read thousands of statements throughout the years and are pros, so take them seriously. Don't lie, don't exaggerate too much, and don't brag. Stress your strong points.

A note about the AMCAS and AACOMAS statements

The AMCAS statement (for MD schools) is limited to 5,300 characters (about one page), including spaces. Use Word to give you word and character counts and if you are over this limit, try eliminating words or phrases that are nonessential to your story. You may have to rewrite a few sentences to save characters.

The AACOMAS statement (for DO schools) is limited to 3,000 characters, including spaces. You can trim down your AMCAS statement if you are applying to both types of schools or write a separate one from scratch.

Secondary Application

Overview

Medical schools send out secondary applications once they receive your AMCAS or AACOMAS application information. Getting a secondary application does not necessarily mean that you have passed any screening processes at the school. Most schools do not screen your application until they have received your secondary application. However, a few medical schools do screen first and then send out secondary applications.

At times, you wonder if medical schools just mail you a secondary application without prior screening, so that they can collect the additional fee you have to submit along with the application. In most cases, the secondary application fee is somewhere between $40 and $100, depending on the school. What makes you wonder even more about the need for a secondary application is the fact that many medical schools don't even ask you for any new significant information. Some just ask you to verify the information you submitted through AMCAS or AACOMAS or ask something new (but insignificant).

Some secondaries actually ask you for new information, to answer some more questions, including why you are interested in attending the specific medical school or specific questions like "Why medicine?" You may have to write a small essay and answer some other related questions.

Timing

Return all secondary applications you receive promptly within no more than one week from the day you receive them. Fast turnaround is essential and shows you are committed and interested in the school. Ideally, secondaries should be turned around within two days.

The earlier you return the secondary application to a medical school, the earlier the school will schedule an interview, and the earlier you will be able to receive an offer.

Interview

Overview

You have made it past some severe screening and have been invited to an interview. By this time, your application has already been sifted and sorted a couple of times. Usually, medical schools weed out many applications and only invite about 20 percent of all applicants for an interview.

If you made it this far, the medical school typically considers you able to handle the rigors of medical school academically and your credentials look promising. Now, you just have to show them what type of person you are up close. Mainly, they are trying to see if you will fit in at their school and if you will fit into medicine as a person.

In particular, the interviewer is going to evaluate your character, personality, communication skills, how easy it is to get along with you; how confident, honest, and sincere you are; and if you are truly interested in medicine.

Read what successful applicants have to say about the interview in the "Medical Student Answers" section of this book.

Some general pointers:

1. Dress professionally and conservatively. Complete suit and tie for men. Shave! A dress or formal business attire for women. You should look your best.
2. Be on time!
3. Give yourself plenty of time to get to the interview in the morning. Even traffic accidents and detours can happen to you (or your cab driver). I had planned to be at an interview thirty minutes early and arrived only two minutes early due to an unexpected accident on the freeway that blocked traffic. Schedule extra time to be

there early. It is better to sit around and wait for the interview day to start than to be late!

4.   Make your flight and hotel reservations early for best prices and availability. Before you book your travel, ask the medical school for hotels close by. Most of the hotels nearby have arrangements to give you a huge (sometimes 60 percent off) discount if you are flying in for an interview at the medical school. Also, arrange transportation services (taxi or shuttle) the night before (ask the school or hotel for more info).

5.   For preparation, review some of the information about the medical school you are about to interview with.
You may be asked why you are interested in attending that particular school. These reasons can also include the fact that you like the area or town the medical school is in or the lakes and mountains (water sports, skiing, etc.) that are close by. So, your reasoning does not have to be limited to what the school itself has to offer.

6.   Send a thank-you letter after the interview.

Interview day

If you have to travel far, get into town the night before. That way you can relax and be ready for your interview day, which usually starts at 8 a.m. or so and may last until 3 to 5 p.m.

Interview day usually includes one to three interviews, conducted one on one, panel style, or with a group of fellow applicants being interviewed by the same panel at the same time. Most interviews are one on one or small panels.

Most of the time, interviews are conducted by basic science and/ or clinical faculty members. Additional interviews may also be held with third- or fourth-year medical students.

Other highlights of the interview day are typically a tour of the medical school and facilities, including cadaver labs and classrooms (where you will live for the next few years), lunch and/or meetings with current medical students, a financial aid presentation, and other miscellaneous presentations.

You should be able to get a good feel for the medical school, the faculty, the students, facilities, etc., while you are there. That is part of the reason you are there—to help you decide if you would like to spend the next four years there (or not).

Timing

Medical schools typically contact you by mail or email to invite you to an interview. Most likely, they will offer you several days to choose from, sometimes spread out over several months. If possible, try to take the first interview day offered to you. Get right back with the medical school to schedule your interview so that your interview slot is reserved right away.

Interviewing on the first day possible is advantageous to you since the medical school has not yet filled most of the spots available in the class. Also, the earlier you attend the interview, the earlier you will be able to receive an offer.

Some common interview questions

It is usually helpful to reflect on and work out some answers to common questions you may be asked in the interview. You don't want to memorize answers (or at least not make it look like you did), but if you have never thought about some topics, it is very hard to come up with a good answer on the spot.

If you are given a question you don't know the answer to, you can always state that you had never thought about that before or that you don't know the answer to the question. Honesty is best. Interviewers can see through insincere responses.

Some common questions you should probably answer for yourself (or rehearse with a friend) before you go to any interview are:

1. Why medicine?
2. Why do you want to be a doctor?
3. Where do you see yourself in ten years?
4. What are your strengths and weaknesses?
5. What do you do for relaxation?
6. How do you deal with pressure and stress?
7. What are your greatest qualities? (Or your worst?)
8. If you could cure a disease, which would it be and why?
9. What is the greatest challenge facing medicine today? How would you fix it?
10. Tell me about yourself.
11. You wrote in your personal statement that… What did you learn from that?
12. Your application shows… What did you learn from that?
13. What will you do if you are not accepted? …and again next year?
14. This physician says… about you in this letter. What did you do to convince him of that?
15. Tell me about your research project.
16. Tell me about your… activity.
17. What do you like to do?
18. Ask me a question now.
19. What do you see as your greatest challenge?
20. Why would you be a good physician?
21. What characteristics does a good doctor have?
22. What three things would you change about yourself?
23. Discuss your volunteer work, clinical experiences, shadowing.
24. Tell me about a life-changing experience you have had. What did you learn from it?
25. What is your favorite book or movie?
26. What are your thoughts about nationalized/socialized medicine?
27. What issues face our health care system today or in the future?
28. What is your specialty interest?
29. Why is there such a discrepancy between your MCAT score and your GPA?
30. What do you like most about medicine and being a physician?

31. How will your weaknesses affect you as a medical student and as a physician?
32. What would your best friend say about you?

Some ethical question examples are listed in the next few paragraphs.

Some topics you should be familiar with

All of these topics often come up in interviews, so you should be familiar with these, at least:

1. Antibiotic resistance
2. Insurance and the uninsured
3. Health care costs
4. Abortion
5. Euthanasia
6. Drug costs
7. National health care/socialized medicine
8. Stem cell research
9. Life support for persons in persistent vegetative state (example: Terri Schiavo)

Ethical questions

First, let's clarify what ethical questions are for: Interviewers want to see how you think, if you can navigate difficult scenarios. The answer you give supporting one position or another is not as important as your reasoning. In fact, often, reasoning through both choices openly with them and stating that this is hard to resolve is the best way to go. It shows that you understand the dilemma and that you can navigate through it on both sides. What they care about is your reasoning.

Let's discuss some examples (the potential answers shown here are not the correct answers, because there are no correct answers— they are only potential answers to illustrate how these types of questions are handled). You may be able to come up with better answers yourself. Use these as some thought starters.

Question

Your patient's HIV test is positive. He does not want his family to know. His wife calls later that day to ask about the test results. Would you tell her? What if she is in danger of contracting the disease herself?

Answering this question

Good ways to handle this is through discussing the patient's wishes and his privacy rights (which reign supreme legally) and showing your reasoning why the patient's rights are very important here. Then, you may state "However…there are other implications on the other side of this as well…" and elaborate on the problems of responsibility in preventing problems for the wife. The physician also has a duty to warn others. Show your thinking.

Question

Would you perform an abortion if a patient came to you requesting one?

Answering this question

This really is not a question about abortion, per se. It is about how you would handle the patient in this case. Do you respect the patient's wishes? An answer like "Absolutely not." is probably not going to go over well. However, if you are opposed to abortion personally, an answer along the lines of "I would not perform an abortion. I would discuss alternatives and let the patient think about them for a few weeks. If she still desires an abortion, I would tell her that I don't do those myself and provide a referral for her." As a physician, you don't get to decide for other people what they should do. You are a consultant. That is the point here. How do you resolve your personal convictions with patients' wishes if they are not the same?

Some other thoughts

Be aware of legal implications. Euthanasia (assisted suicide) is illegal in most places, for example. So, elaborating on how you would assist a patient would be a bad idea even if you support the idea in general. You may want to state "I don't know about the legal side of this issue, but assuming it would be legal, I would..." Then present your position. This shows you are thinking and would certainly obey the law.

If ethical questions totally freak you out, you can also buy or check out a book on the subject and do some reading about the issues you will encounter in interviews and in your future training and practice. A good book on the topic is *Resolving Ethical Dilemmas: A Guide for Clinicians* by Bernard Lo. It is some rather deep reading on almost all ethical issues you could possibly encounter and what some of the "right" answers and legal aspects are. Also, you can find books on the same topic at your local bookstore, online, or at the library.

You may also want to check out the "Interview Feedback" section available on the Student Doctor Network website, which includes actual questions applicants have been asked at specific schools in the past.

Acceptance, Rejection, and the Wait List

The three ultimate outcomes of your application to medial school are acceptance, rejection, or a spot on the wait list.

Normally, medical schools have to make more offers than they have spots available in their class to fill each class. This works in your favor. If a school has 100 spots to fill for that year, they may have to extend 150, 200, or 300 offers to get 100 students to actually attend their school. If the medical school is very prestigious, then they typically have to extend fewer offers to fill the class. If they are the backup school for many applicants who would rather go elsewhere, then they have to extend more offers.

Acceptance

Celebrate your acceptance letters! Congratulations! You made it! All the hard work in preparation has paid off!

Of course, you want to get acceptance letters from medical schools—at least from one medical school. Acceptance letters are mailed within about two to four weeks from your interview date by most medical schools. A few schools notify students within a few days and some even take several months to notify applicants of their decisions. Other medical schools notify most of their applicant pool at once—on a given day, rather than on a rolling basis.

You are typically given ten to fourteen days from the day you receive the acceptance letter from a medical school in the mail to make a deposit and indicate that you are interested in attending there. Once the deposit is made and you respond to the school, the medial school will hold a spot for you in the incoming class.

Make sure you pay your deposit and have the school hold the spot for you! This does not mean that you actually have to attend this particular school in the end. Once you have made deposits at several schools (with several offers), you can still decide where you really want to study medicine, after considering all of your options. By making the deposit, you don't promise or commit to attend that particular school.

You typically have until about April 15 to make your *final* decision of where to attend. You cannot hold spots at different medical schools past this date, so you have to decide if you are still holding spots at different medical schools at that time.

For most allopathic (MD) schools, the deposits are usually only $100, but there are exceptions with higher deposit amounts. The deposits are typically refundable or will be applied toward your tuition if you attend there eventually. However, for most osteopathic (DO) schools, the deposits are between $500 and $1,500 and are most often nonrefundable.

Rejection

Most applicants get some rejection letters. It is certainly hard when the first letter you receive back is a rejection. Don't give up. Some rejections are normal. Often, it depends on the interviewer you had that day and whether or not you connected with that person. It may have nothing to do with your application or your personality.

If you did not receive any acceptance letters at all (and you applied to a dozen or more schools), you will need to reevaluate your options. Don't despair. This does not mean that you are not meant to be a physician. I know several individuals who applied at least two years in a row before being accepted. For some, it even takes three tries.

You will need to analyze your overall application and see which areas can be improved within another year, before applying again. Read the "Reapplying" section of this book for more info and strategies to increase your chances.

Wait list

Medical schools maintain lists of students who are qualified for admissions, but just missed making the first cut to fill the class. These students are placed on the wait list, which is typically numbered, so each student is assigned a specific numbered spot on the list.

Most medical schools will reveal how many students, who were initially placed on the wait list, were offered spots in previous years. This way you can get an idea if you really have a chance to get an offer by the time classes begin. There is some fluctuation every year. Also, a medical school may not let you know the exact number you are on the list or how many students on the wait list were eventually offered spots in the class in previous years.

As an example, if the school typically takes ten applicants from their wait list every year, and you are number nine on the list this year, you may have a chance. But, I know of some students who were in a similar spot and that particular year the school only took 50 percent of the number they accepted off their wait list in previous years; so, it's no guarantee. It all depends on how many other applicants decline offers at that medical school late in the game. For sure, if you are in the top three or four on the wait list, you will most likely have very good chances.

Being on a wait list can be good and bad. Obviously, if you don't have any other offers, a wait list spot is better than nothing. Also, you may have other offers, but your first-choice school, where you would rather study medicine, has placed you on the wait list. In this case, you can wait until you have to decide (usually around April 15, when you have to tell all your schools if you are going to attend—you cannot hold spots at different schools after that point) to see if your wait list spot turns into a real spot in the class.

All you have to do when April 15 comes around is make a decision among the offers you have already received. Any medical school that has offered you a spot in the class demands an answer of yes or no. Hopefully, you have at least one offer, which you can accept at that point. This does not apply to wait lists—you can remain on different wait lists until class begins, even if you have accepted a spot at a different medical school already.

Even once you have told another medical school that you will be attending there, you can still change your mind, up to the day you actually begin class and pay your tuition. It is possible, in theory, to receive a phone call from a medical school notifying you that your wait list spot has turned into a real spot until the day class starts.

In fact, there are people who had already moved to attend one medical school and received such a call from their first-choice school where they had been wait-listed. There are those who pack up again and move, just about a week before classes actually start to attend their first-choice school.

Reapplying

Overview

Many applicants do not succeed the first year they apply. In fact, a large percentage of students in each class are successful reapplicants. Generally, admissions offices look at reapplication favorably. It strengthens the applicant's position and shows the commitment and interest to become a physician.

There are three main reasons why you may have to reapply:

1. You were not prepared sufficiently or your overall application was not strong enough.
2. You applied to too few schools—maybe only the one or two medical schools in your state.
3. You applied only to top schools or the wrong set of schools.

If your application needs improvement

There are some very important considerations before reapplying. If you have done nothing to improve your overall application since the previous year, reapplying to the same schools will most likely do nothing for you. You have to show improvements in your application by increasing your MCAT score, doing more research, shadowing, etc. You don't have to show improvement in each area, but overall your application should become stronger.

Spend some additional time in a medically related job or volunteer opportunity and do some serious research, for example. If your MCAT was particularly weak, that may warrant some new preparation and retaking the MCAT.

If you applied to too few schools or the wrong schools

Some applicants only apply to one or two schools. That is a mistake. Although a few applicants still get into medical school by applying to only one or two schools, most applicants are putting themselves at a serious disadvantage if they do this. An average applicant should be applying to at least a dozen schools.

Just as it is essential to apply to enough medical schools, it is also important to apply to the right medical schools. If your MCAT, GPA, and other parts of your application (extracurricular activities, research, etc.) are extremely good, applying mostly to top medical schools will probably be fine. However, most applicants, whether very competitive or not, should have a good mix of schools they are applying to, including some of the less competitive schools.

If your MCAT is a little lower, don't expect to easily get into the top medical schools in the country—although you still might be able to. Apply and reapply accordingly. You can still include some top medical schools in the mix—and may well have a chance—but be sure to include mostly medical schools that take more average applicants and not just the most elite applicants.

Also, consider applying to more osteopathic (DO) schools if you haven't already. These typically have lower MCAT and GPA requirements, among other things. A good alternative can also be podiatry schools if you're interested in that. Caribbean schools and other international schools are also an alternative to U.S. medical schools, but be sure to read more about Caribbean and international medical schools and some of the cautions before considering this option.

Chapter References

1. U.S. Medical School Applicants, Matriculants, Enrollment, and Graduates, AAMC Data Book 2006, pages 8–10

2. 2004 Annual Report on Osteopathic Medical Education, AACOM, pages 17, 20, http://www.aacom.org/data/annualreport/index.html

Money and Finances

Money and Finances
Contributions to this section by Mark Piedra, MD

Overview

You may have already heard this quote, but here it is anyway:

Live like a doctor now, live like a student later.
Live like a student now, live like a doctor later.

You don't want to overspend while in medical school. Try to stay on a limited budget while in school. Obviously, the less money you borrow while in medical school, the less you have to pay in interest and the less your payments are going to be when you are done. Don't max out your student loans just because you can. Use the loans if you have to, but not to buy toys.

Interest never sleeps. It accumulates 24 hours per day, 365 days a year. Interest always works against you.

Medical school is very expensive, with many students accumulating between $100,000 and $250,000 in debt by graduation. In 2005, the average indebtedness for graduates who attended public MD medical schools was $110,000 and for those who attended private MD medical schools was $138,093.[1]

Although a few students or their parents may have the financial resources to pay for medical school, most students do not. Rather, they rely heavily on loans and occasionally scholarships to fund their medical education. Note that all types of financial aid, loans, scholarships, etc., are handled through the financial aid office of the medical school you attend.

First, it is important to know that you can usually qualify for financial aid fairly easily to pay for medical school. Your parents' finances are not considered, which is usually good. This ensures that you can get financial aid even if your parents are doing fairly well financially, but not well enough to pay you $50,000 per year to cover your medical school expenses.

Most of the aid comes in the form of student loans, which are deferred while you are in medical school. These loans can also easily be deferred until the end of residency training once you graduate from medical school.

The financial aid office at the medical school has a lot of say about the financial package you receive while attending medical school. To understand how the finances work, we need to review what is meant by the student budget or "cost of attendance."

Cost of attendance or student budget

Cost of attendance is *not* the amount of money you think you need or the amount you actually need to attend medical school. It is the amount of money the financial aid office at the medical school thinks (or rather calculates, estimates, and averages) you need to survive and make it through medical school each year.

Cost of attendance is a dollar amount that the medical school's financial aid office comes up with, based on federal guidelines, which are rather strict. It includes all costs such as tuition, fees, books, commuting expenses, and living expenses that the average normal single student would have to pay during one school year. As already mentioned, the medical school has to follow government guidelines to set up the budget and does not have much ability to change the budget (so they claim).

This magical dollar amount called cost of attendance is the same for each student, regardless if he or she is married or has children, lives alone, or with roommates. The medical school only considers the expenses of the student by him- or herself. Family members such as spouse and children are not considered and do not increase the amount of money allotted to the student for living expenses.

The cost of attendance is usually broken down into the student budget, which shows each item (tuition, books, rent, utilities, commute, clothing allowance, etc.) separately. Financial aid, in the form of loans and scholarships, will only cover the cost of attendance. Financial aid is not available for any higher amount than the cost of attendance or total student budget. Government loans, scholarship money, and alternative loans can be used to cover the cost of attendance.

Your change check

For example, if your financial aid office says that your total cost of attendance is $50,000 per year, including all living expenses, tuition, etc., and you happen to qualify (because you are so good looking or whatever) for some fancy scholarship worth $80,000 per year, your financial aid office will limit your financial aid package to $50,000, since that is your cost of attendance. The other $30,000 is not available to you at all. You would receive a check of whatever money is left of the $50,000 (not the $80,000) after subtracting tuition, fees, etc., for the year for you to live on.

As illustrated by the example, taking the total amount specified by the cost of attendance and subtracting out the tuition, fees, books, supplies, and mandatory insurance leaves you with the amount that will be paid out to you each year to cover living expenses. The school usually mails a change check to you every semester. It is your responsibility to budget that money to last the entire semester to pay your bills.

The summer break is not included in the budget, either. So, you only receive money for nine of the twelve months of the year, since that is the only time you are in school (for the first two years). During years three and four, your budget is calculated using all twelve months since you don't get summers off anymore.

That means that the financial aid office only considers you to be a student for nine of the twelve months of a year (during the first two years) and only budgets enough financial aid for the nine months during which you are actually a student. If you don't have a job over the summer, you will have to stretch the limited change check to also pay your bills over the summer.

Note that generally the annual change check is just under $11,000 (or $5,500 per semester) at most medical schools. That is not a lot to live on, especially if you have kids or other unique circumstances. It comes to about $900 per month if budgeted over twelve months.

More cost of attendance info

In most cases, the schools calculate your budget with the assumption that you will have roommates to share rent expenses, so the budgeted rent expense in your student budget is very low and not enough to really afford your own place.

Again, to make this point very clear, even if you hypothetically qualified for say $200,000 in loans, scholarships, etc., per year, the school will only allow you to fund (from all these sources combined) the total budget amount specified—NO MORE!

Having said that, a few exceptions allow you to increase your cost of attendance. Child care expenses fall in this category. If you have child care expenses because you are attending school, you can add this expense to your student budget and get a larger change check to cover these expenses. But this does not give you more money to live on each month. Also, this is a loan that you will have to pay back.

If you need to purchase a computer or laptop for school, this also counts as an allowable expense to increase the budget. You purchase the computer or laptop and then turn in the receipt to be reimbursed. Reimbursement only works if you still have some unused financial aid available to cover the additional student budget expense. Most of the time, this is not an issue since you can typically qualify for additional private loans if you need them.

You have to provide documentation in the form of bills, receipts, and signed statements from other people involved (e.g., daycare providers) to be reimbursed for child care expenses. A receipt is sufficient for reimbursement of a computer purchase.

You can also qualify for some one-time money if something unexpected happens; say, your car is stolen, you have to have a brain transplant, or some other major one-time expense comes up that would sink your boat. These circumstances can be considered for additional aid. However, this is limited and only approved on a case-by-case basis. Note that you have to be able to qualify for this money in loans or scholarships first. If you are at a very expensive school and max out your loan amounts, there may be no additional money available for this or you have to access private loans.

You cannot increase your change check by qualifying for extra aid or alternative loans. The different loan programs and scholarships only determine where that money comes from, not how much in total you get. All government loan programs have caps or maximum amounts you can borrow and some medical schools are more expensive than what you can borrow through government loans.

That is what alternative loans, available through the financial aid office, are for—to bridge the gap if your cost of attendance exceeds the amount the government is willing to loan to you each year.

Be sure to read the details about the different loan types and scholarships available for pros and cons about each.

Buying a car or home

Many applicants will ask if financial aid can be used to purchase a car. While a car or a car payment is not a line item in the student budget, once a financial aid disbursement is made to the student, the student can use the money as they see fit. The transportation line item in the student budget is meant only for commuting expenses (for example, gasoline, maintenance, or mass transit expenses) and not for a car itself. When determining your financial plan for medical school, be sure transportation costs beyond what the school will offer are considered. For some students, a car is just a luxury during the first two years of medical school, but may be required for the clinical years.

Some students will consider buying a home or condominium while in medical school. This can be a huge advantage in terms of building equity and having an investment that may increase in value (although increases in real estate prices are never guaranteed) rather than paying rent. But it is important to realize that one of the major benefits of owning a home over renting is a tax benefit, which may not help a medical student. The IRS allows homeowners to deduct mortgage interest payments (often the majority of a mortgage payment in the early period of repayment) from their income on their tax return. Because most medical students do not work or pay little income tax, they cannot assume this benefit.

In addition, remember that your time commitment during your clinical years and in residency may not allow you enough free time to take care of regular household maintenance, such as mowing the lawn, shoveling snow from the driveway, making minor repairs, and home improvements. A condominium or townhouse that requires far less upkeep than a house may be a better alternative for a medical student.

Process of getting your aid

The process of securing medical school financial aid begins in January before your matriculation (graduation from your undergraduate institution). After completing your IRS tax return, you will complete the Free Application for Federal Student Aid (FAFSA, www.fafsa.ed.gov). Sometime between March and the start of school, the medical school financial aid office will send you your financial aid package. This package will detail the school's calculated cost of attendance, your expected contribution to this cost, and amounts of aid in the form of scholarships and loans. You then decide which aid you will accept or decline.

For most students, the next step is to complete a Master Promissory Note, which is your loan agreement for federal loans. At this time, most students will choose a lender (often from a list provided by the school, although the school may be the lender). The money that you accept is paid in two disbursements directly to the school. The first disbursement occurs at the start of school. The school will take tuition and fees from the disbursement and give you the remaining funds in the form of a check or direct deposit to your bank account. This usually occurs during the first couple of weeks of school. The second disbursement is typically in the following January.

It is important to note that financial aid will never cover certain items, such as car payments or consumer/credit card debt.

The school's financial aid office will take the cost of attendance and subtract from it your expected family contribution to determine the amount of need-based aid for which you will be eligible. The expected family contribution is determined using the Free Application for Federal Student Aid (FAFSA). This is the same FAFSA completed to apply for financial aid during your undergraduate education.

The FAFSA is completed each school year, and the new application is available in January. You should complete your FAFSA as soon as you can each calendar year. You will be required to have completed your tax return before completing the FAFSA, so it is to your advantage to do that as early as possible. Don't wait until April 15! The federal deadline for completing the FAFSA is not until the end of the upcoming school year, but each medical school will set their own deadline for when they will require you to complete the FAFSA to make you eligible for institutional aid.

During your medical school application year, you should complete the FAFSA as early as possible, even if you have yet to be accepted.

On the FAFSA form, include schools to which you will likely be accepted. You can always add more schools later.

Financial aid eligibility

Most schools will determine your eligibility for financial aid in two ways: the federal and institutional methodology. The federal methodology assumes that all medical students, regardless of their tax status, are financially independent. This means that your parent's income and financial status is not included in determining your federal expected family contribution. Included in calculating your expected family contribution are:

1. Gross adjusted income as reported on last year's tax return
2. Total value in bank accounts and investments
3. Age
4. Marital status

The expected family contribution does not take into account retirement accounts or equity in a primary residence you might own. Your age and marital status are used to determine the amount of your savings and investments, which will be protected. For the most part, the higher your federal expected family contribution is, the less eligible you will be for need-based aid.

The institutional methodology for determining need-based aid will take into account the expected family contribution from your FAFSA but might also consider parental information including income and investments. Some schools do not ask for your parent's financial information, and all schools will allow you to opt out of this if you wish. Typically, it will never hurt you to provide your parental information. The rationale behind using parental information is to help the school gauge which students are truly in financial need or come from a financially disadvantaged background. They will use your financial information and your parents' to help determine your eligibility for institution-specific need-based aid, such as the Perkins loans and scholarships.

If you are in the position of being estranged from your parents, or are an older student who has been financially independent for several years, you should contact the medical school financial aid office to see if you can still be considered for institutional need-based aid without providing parental information. Some schools will provide exceptions for these students. If you are happy with the standard Stafford loans, then you can choose not to provide the parental information. The parental information, whether supplied or not, should not affect your eligibility to qualify for the full loan amounts each year.

Foreign students can find it difficult to obtain financial aid to attend medical school in the United States. To be eligible for federal student loans (including Stafford and Perkins loans), you must be one of the following:

1. U.S. citizen
2. U.S. national including natives of American Samoa and Swain's Island
3. U.S. permanent resident with an I-151, I-551, or I-551C (alien registration card)
4. A foreign citizen with an I-94 card stamped with one of the following:
    a. Refugee
    b. Asylum granted
    c. Cuban-Haitian entrant status pending
    d. Conditional entrant stamped prior to April 1, 1980

Students with an I-171, I-464, F-1, F-2, J-1, or J-2 visa are not eligible for federal student aid. Private loans are available for students under these circumstances, but these require a cosigner who has a U.S. credit history.

Medical students with spouses and/or children are in an especially difficult financial situation. A variety of problems can arise. If a spouse works and the student files a joint tax return, much of the spousal income will be included in the expected family contribution and taken into consideration when determining eligibility for need-based aid. Therefore, the student may become ineligible for aid and offered next to nothing in his or her financial aid package. In this case, the married student should ask the financial aid office for unsubsidized Stafford loans up to $38,500 or the COA, whichever is higher. Your expected family contribution should not be a factor for the unsubsidized Stafford loans since all medical students should be eligible for the maximum, regardless of need.

The older medical student will have some unique financial concerns, especially if he or she is entering school with a previous high-paying job. The FAFSA does not take into consideration the fact that a student will no longer be earning money while in medical school and will take the income reported on the student's tax return as income for the upcoming year, even though the student will likely not be earning that income when school begins. The expected family contribution will be very high for students who are entering school after leaving a high-paying job.

Any student in this situation should contact the financial aid office soon after completing the FAFSA to explain this situation so that the office can adjust the expected family contribution accordingly. In some cases, the student may not be eligible for need-based aid, such as subsidized and Perkins loans in the first year of medical school. Also, any savings accounts or investments (excluding retirement accounts and equity in a primary residence) will be included in the expected family contribution. A student with a high level of savings who does not wish this money to be included in the expected family contribution can protect this by using it to pay off a mortgage on their primary residence or putting the maximum amount allowed in a retirement account before they complete the FAFSA.

Loans and Scholarships
Contributions to this section by Mark Piedra, MD

Overview

A combination of different loan types and potential scholarships makes up your total financial aid package, which will match your total cost of attendance. There are different types of loans. Most people take out loans through the U.S. federal government loan program and supplement these with institutional aid as well as alternative private loans if total cost of attendance exceeds the amount provided through the federal program.

Quite a few students choose to participate in a military scholarship or the National Health Service Corps scholarship, which both pay for all costs in the student budget and sometimes a little more. This allows students to complete medical school debt free but graduates have to pay back the particular service by committing to work in the program for less pay for usually four years.

Subsidized and unsubsidized loans (Stafford loans)

Both subsidized and unsubsidized loans are federal loans.

For subsidized loans, the U.S. government pays the interest for you while you are in medical school and during other deferral periods, so these loans are the best deal you can get. However, only a portion of the loan package is comprised of these types of loans and you cannot get more.

The other portion of the loan package is made up of unsubsidized loans on which interest and interest on interest accumulates from day one when the loan amount is paid out to you. A good portion of your loan money is of this type and you really have no choice in this.

Both of these loans are deferred until after graduation and the interest rate is capped—it can never exceed some 8.5 percent or so during the life of the loan. Note that you can make interest-only payments on the unsubsidized loans while in medical school to prevent accumulation of interest, but you don't have to, and most people don't. These loans also qualify for further deferral during residency, so that no payments need to be made during residency training, either.

Pretty much everyone qualifies for these loans, although there are income and asset limits that can reduce eligibility, and everyone is treated equally for qualifying. These are part of the package of financing your cost of attendance and not extra money beyond that.

The yearly limit for these loans is $8,500 in subsidized and $30,000 in unsubsidized aid. So, if your student budget exceeds $38,500 per year, these extra costs have to be covered by other sources of financial aid. In addition to the yearly limits of $38,500, there is also a lifetime limit of $189,125, which cannot be exceeded as a grand total for your student career.
Stafford loans offer various repayment terms ranging from ten to thirty years.

Institutional loans and scholarships

Institutional aid usually has the best terms, but is also typically in very short supply. Interest is either very low or not charged at all. Federal Perkins loans fall in this category as well because the medical school can give these out at its own discretion and the school acts as the lender. The school gives these preferentially to students with greatest financial need.

Often these institutional loans and scholarships are based on financial need, academic merit, or something similar. Some medical schools have small scholarships available that also fit in this institutional aid category. Of course, with scholarships, there is no payback, because they are not loans.

The amounts awarded in this category are usually small in comparison to the whole cost of attendance, ranging from $1,000 to $5,000 or so per year, but they have the best conditions with low interest, etc. So, this is a great source, but only makes a small contribution to your overall aid package. Again, these are part of the package of financing your cost of attendance and not extra money beyond that.

There are many dubious scholarship-finding enterprises that will charge you money to search for scholarships or file for federal aid and other such things. Most of these are scams, designed to take your money without delivering anything of value to you. All financial aid info and help is available for free through the government, the financial aid office, and banks. So, do not buy into a scam!

The Primary Care Loan (http://bhpr.hrsa.gov/DSA/pcl.htm) is a federal loan offered by some medical schools for students who are certain they will enter a primary care field after medical school. The interest rate is fixed (5 percent) and interest does not begin to accrue until one year after you graduate (similar to the subsidized Stafford loans). The amount you can borrow is determined by the medical school offering the loan. To use this loan, you must choose to enter into a primary care field. These are limited to family medicine, internal medicine, pediatrics, preventive medicine, or osteopathic general practice. When choosing to take this loan, you agree that you will practice in that primary care field until the loan is repaid (ten-year repayment period). If you choose not to enter a primary care field, your interest rate is increased to 18 percent.

Alternative (private) loans

A note up front: Private loans are dependent on your credit rating. If you have poor or no previous credit history, you may need a cosigner to qualify for these loans. The problem is that the student budget at most medical schools exceeds the Stafford loans available per year ($38,500 per year), so many medical students have to depend on this loan type to cover their budget and many medical schools require a credit report be sent to them before any offers are finalized.

These are available through the financial aid office as well. The financial aid office applies this money to the tuition and fees owed before giving you a change check. Banks extend these loans and charge the going variable interest rate starting on day one when the loan amount is paid to you.

Interest rates fluctuate just like a variable car or home loan and there is no interest cap. These loans are only used to fill gaps if the other loans, subsidized and unsubsidized, and scholarship money did not cover the entire cost of attendance as this is the type of loan that typically caries the worst conditions.

If you are lucky enough that your in-state tuition falls below the money available each year in subsidized and unsubsidized loans, you may not need these loans at all. In most cases, the federal and institutional aid alone may not be enough to cover your cost of attendance and alternative loans are the only way to get additional money to cover these expenses.

Part-time and full-time scholarships offered by medical schools

Some medical schools offer full- or part-time scholarships based on MCAT, GPA, and other merits. As an example, Mayo Medical School offers a part-time scholarship to *all* students accepted there. For the 2005 year, Des Moines University considered all medical students for part-time or full-time scholarships if they had an MCAT greater than 30 and a GPA greater than 3.5.

These are just two examples. Check with individual medical schools to see what they offer.

Working while in medical school

It is almost impossible to work while attending medical school. The course work is too intense to maintain any kind of employment, with maybe two exceptions.

The first exception is if you can get a job that has been tailored to medical students. Some schools look for students to cover the help desk in the library for a few hours a week (prime study time in the library) or to help make sure all the lecturers have access to microphones, markers, etc., during lectures. These jobs are typically very limited and take either no time or very little time. Don't expect any regular type of employment. You don't have time for it.

The second exception may be if you are on a five-year extended curriculum instead of the regular four-year program. Usually, either first or second year is stretched over two years and you technically have more spare time since you are only taking half the load for that time.

During your clinical years (third year and fourth year), you will be unable to hold any kind of job due to irregular hours spent on rotations.

Military scholarships

The Health Professions Scholarship Program, or HPSP for short, is available through the military. You choose to enter the Army, Navy, or Air Force. All of these branches have to offer pretty much the exact same incentives and benefits, with minor difference, so the program is almost identical no matter which branch you choose.

Military scholarships pay for your tuition, fees, books, and anything else that is directly related to medical school. They also pay you a monthly stipend while in medical school. The stipend can be around $1,400 or so per month (in 2005).

In return for getting your four-year medical education paid for, the military expects four years of active duty medical service after residency and four more years of reserve duty. It's a year-for-year payback. If you only use the HPSP program for three years, you only owe three years of military service. The minimum payback is three years, regardless of how many years you use the program.

Also, if your medical school allows it, you are expected to serve four forty-five-day active duty tours during medical school. These are similar to shadowing and medical school rotations, which allow you to get involved in military medicine.

This is what typically happens for the HPSP program:

1. You graduate from undergrad with a four-year degree.
2. You apply for the HPSP scholarship program through your military branch of choice (Army, Navy, Air Force).
3. They review and approve your application.
4. You attend the medical school of your choice that you selected just like you would without the militaryscholar ship. During your medical school experience, you are not in uniform, but are a student like everyone else. You receive a monthly stipend and all school expenses paid for. You spend the first summer at a military hospital for shadowing or at Officer Indoctrination Training (learning how to be an officer).
5. You have to go through Officer Indoctrination Training for forty-five days. Many people try to get this done the summer before medical school and that is an advantage since you gain some additional officer benefits and pay from that.
6. When you graduate from medical school, you apply for residency through the military match, which is different from the civilian residency match. In some cases, you can go through the civilian match and complete a civilian residency but for the most part, you are expected (with little choice) to enter a military residency. From day one of residency, you are an officer and paid as such with vacation, benefits, etc. Pay (officer's pay) is slightly better than resident pay in civilian residencies. Military residencies are completed in and around

military hospitals, prominently where big bases are—
Bethesda, Maryland, being the largest, for example.

7.   After residency, you pay back your four years of service obligation. Pay is considerably less than for civilian doctors, but still fairly decent.

8.   After four years of active duty service in the military, you can stay by choice in the military or leave and work as a civilian physician like any other private physician. You are still considered reserve for four years and can be called back up for active duty whenever needed. You need to check what implications that may have to see if this route is a good one for you.

Supposedly, medical students and residents are not deployed while in training, but fully trained physicians may be deployed during the payback period. However, I have also heard that some residents, but relatively very few, were deployed to some of the more recent wars after completing their first year of residency training.

The recruiters say that most medical students can pretty much choose their specialties just like in the civilian world, with most of the competitive specialties being the same as in the civilian world, but students have to go through the military match to get into their residencies.

The military, however, has been known to overrule people's career choices on occasion and make them choose specialties the military needs at the time. So, if your residency choice matches their need, and they have enough openings for that particular specialty training at the time, you can pursue that training.

If they do not have openings in your specialty of interest that particular year, whether you don't match, the specialty is not offered at all that year, or they need more specialists in a particular field, you may end up having to choose a different specialty instead. Not all specialties are offered every year, especially the less common ones.

In other words, depending on the military branch's need at the time, they may make you choose a specialty you did not want to enter. You may have to pursue specialty training in which you are not interested to start out your medical career. Then, after some time, you can apply to your choice residency again to retrain. This is especially possible if you plan to stay in the military for a little while. If you train as a general medical officer or flight surgeon and serve in that capacity, your chances for choosing and getting into the specialty of your choice increase significantly.

During your service payback time, you are typically stationed at a base hospital within the United States. However, you may also be sent abroad for up to three months at time, up to four times during your commitment without your spouse or children, if you have them. Being stationed overseas more permanently is unusual unless requested. Generally, you don't have much say about where you are stationed, although you can make requests, which may or may not be considered, based on the needs of the military.

Note that the military can decide to force you to stay in the military if needed, as in the case of war or crisis. That means that the military can essentially force individuals, not just physicians, to stay in the military beyond their contract time, so you would be unable to leave the military, even if you have fulfilled your payback.

Besides the HPSP program and the Uniformed Services University of the Health Sciences, there are additional programs available through the military after completion of medical school or residency. Some of these include loan repayment options, but all carry a military service commitment as a physician.

Three final thoughts on the military scholarships

Read your contract, including all fine print. Do not just trust the recruiter. They often forget to mention some of the finer points, or may not think they are important. Payback commitments for active and reserve duty vary somewhat. Be sure you know what you are getting into and that you know what you will be signing!

Be sure that you enjoy being in the military. Financially, with the military, it is true that you are not piling up debt while in medical school, but that does not necessarily mean that you will be better off in the end. Comparing students who used the military programs with those who used loans, there is no significant difference after five to ten years in practice when factoring in physician pay in the military and in private practice. In fact, for most non–primary care specialties, it is not advantageous to use the military option (due to higher compensation in private practice) looking at it from a financial perspective only.

Once you have signed up for this program, it is almost impossible to withdraw from it. There are also very heavy penalties financially, often requiring payback of 300 percent of the amounts paid by the service for your education. Be sure to speak with several current participants in these programs before deciding on one of them.

Uniformed Services University of the Health Sciences

The Uniformed Services University of the Health Sciences is a medical school owned and operated by the military. It is similar to HPSP in some aspects, yet different. You apply to the Uniformed Services University of the Health Sciences (USUHS) directly through AMCAS as you would to any other medical school. If you are accepted, when you begin medical school you are immediately commissioned as an officer in one of the three military branches with the corresponding officer pay throughout medical school and rank advancements begin immediately.

School is free. On this path, you can only enter military residencies (practically no civilian paths are possible unless a particular specialty training is not offered through the military at all) and you owe a total of seven years of service payback after residency.

Medical students at this medical school are in uniform during medical school, and are part of the active duty military, although they pretty much concentrate on nothing else but medicine while in training. They do not deploy medical students while in training. Some physicians stay in the military until retirement; others just fulfill their minimum payback time.

National Health Service Corps

As with the military scholarships, the National Health Service Corps (NHSC) scholarship pays for all school-related expenses and a monthly stipend while you are in medical school. To be considered, you must commit to practicing in a primary care specialty when you begin medical school.

When done with medical school, you complete your primary care residency. After that, you have to fulfill your four-year service requirement. This is done by practicing medicine for four years in an underprivileged area with a shortage of physicians in your specialty.

You are asked to open a practice or find employment in one of those areas. In many cases, that is where physicians remain for the rest of their careers once settled. Since all of those specialties are in short supply almost anywhere, you can find opportunities in nearly any city and town in the United States that is considered underserved.

You can check the current listings at http://nhsc.bhpr.hrsa.gov/jobs/search_form.cfm to get an idea and do some digging. You'll be surprised that most likely your own backyard is considered underserved or at least some areas close to home. Most often, underserved areas are in areas that are more rural or within inner cities.

As with the military programs, once you have signed up for this program, it is almost impossible to withdraw from it. There are also very heavy penalties financially; again, often requiring payback of 300 percent of the amounts paid by the service for your education. Be sure to speak with several current participants in these programs before deciding on one of them.

The other alternative loan

You can always qualify for loans on your own, outside of the boundaries and rules of the financial aid office. However, you will generally need to show an income (or spouse's or co-borrower's income) and have a good credit history. Also, the terms are usually not as good and you accumulate interest at a higher rate. It is more like a personal loan. Do not confuse these with the alternative private loans available through the financial aid office mentioned previously.

Most financial aid offices will not be able to give you much information on these loans since they usually only work within the framework of the cost of attendance and never outside of this box.

These alternative loan programs mentioned in this section do not require school certification. This is the key. If any loan requires school certification, it is administered through the financial aid office and the rules of the cost of attendance apply. Therefore, the loan would be part of the financial aid package, not to exceed cost of attendance.

For example, Bank One offers a loan program that does not require school certification (more banks offer this type of loan if you look around). It is an alternative loan program for graduate/professional education that is targeted at the medical school and other professional school students.

Another nice feature of this particular loan offered by Bank One is that the loan repayment is deferred during medical school and can be deferred up to eight years maximum, which essentially includes residency. Most other alternative loan programs do not have deferment options, but go into repayment the day you sign the loan, just like a car loan, house loan, or other personal loan.

You can find the loan application and information at educationone. com. Choose the Graduate/Professional Education loan. This loan type requires good credit, an income, and/or a cosigner and is not needed by most medical students. Most medical students should be fine with the amount of money available through the financial aid office; so, stick with that.

Making It Financially

Since all medical schools only consider the medical student, without spouse and children, for financial aid purposes and calculating the cost of attendance, it is not surprising that they only provide about $11,000 or less per year for students to live on. That is less than $1,000 per month to pay for it all—rent, utilities, food, transportation, recreation (what recreation?), clothing, etc. It is a pretty tight budget.

You may have to share an apartment and try to save wherever you can. One of the most quoted phrases that you will hear over and over "Live like a doctor now, live like a student later." That means essentially that you need to live within your budget. Live like a student now, poor and humbly, and you will reap the rewards of the doctor life later. If you have a spouse and children, it will be nearly impossible to live on this limited budget and your spouse will most likely have to work to bring in extra money.

You will be unable to work during medical school. There is not enough time in a day to get all the material studied, let alone work. Another important aspect to consider, especially if you have a family, is what other government assistance programs are available.

Government assistance programs include food stamps, Medicaid, subsidized housing, and help with child care, utilities, and cash assistance. Many students and their families utilize one or more of these programs while going through school. Qualification for these programs is based on income. With the absence of income or potentially low income through contribution by a spouse, most medical students and family qualify for these programs. Check with local agencies to find out what you have to do to get on these programs if you need them. Food stamps and Medicaid are typically the easiest programs to qualify for and are especially useful for families with little or big children. Childcare assistance may be another useful program.

Keep in mind that you will be paying back into the system with large tax contributions when you are a physician.

Chapter References

1.   Educational Indebtedness of U.S. Medical School
        Graduates, AAMC Data Book 2006, page 58

The Medical School
Experience

A Taste of Medical School—What You Do
Contributions to this section by Audrey Stanton, DO, MPH

Overview

Medical school is an extremely intense experience. Course work consists of about 24 credits of upper-division science courses per semester with labs. Most medical students would tell you that it is doable; it just requires a lot of hard work.

There are two general approaches to teaching medicine today in medical school:

1. Traditional curriculum
2. Integrated/Problem-Based Learning (PBL) curriculum

In the traditional curriculum, the first two years of medical school are classroom based and dedicated to studying the basic sciences to give you a basis for clinical medicine (don't be misled by basic; it does not mean easy). This is followed by two more years in clinical rotations, for a total of four years spent in medical school. See the sample schedule posted later in this chapter to get an idea of what the curriculum looks like.

Students complete courses in a semester format, usually several courses at the same time. Anatomy is studied, then physiology, then pharmacology, etc., each as a distinct course, although not just one course per semester as simplified in this example, from beginning to end. Patient contact is primarily reserved for the last two years, although some patient interaction usually occurs on a limited basis. This approach generally provides a good foundation and immersion in the basic sciences.

In the Integrated/PBL curriculum, the courses are more integrated, as the name implies. All courses are taught at the same time on the same topic. For example, the heart may be the topic and students learn all the anatomy, physiology, pharmacology, etc., related to the heart. So, the material is learned more by topic/system rather than by course. Early patient contact and clinical integration is more emphasized as well in this model. This approach provides earlier patient interactions, but may not provide as much depth in the basic sciences, as some contend.

Problem-Based Learning (PBL) curriculum involves self-directed learning using patient cases to learn the same information that is covered in a traditional curriculum in an integrated manner. In PBL programs, students meet in groups and work through a patient case, directed by a faculty facilitator. The amount of direct instruction is minimal in a full-PBL program, so students take responsibility for their own learning and for presenting material to the small group.

First and second year

The following schedule is for the Medical College of Wisconsin. Most medical schools will have a very similar schedule, although they may integrate or place some courses in different semesters, drag some courses out over several semesters, or combine them into one semester. However, all medical students are required to pass the board exams (USMLE or COMLEX) and, therefore, need to cover essentially the same material and topics. The following is an example of the traditional curriculum discussed previously.

First semester
Clinical Human Anatomy/Gross Anatomy
Biochemistry
Human Development
Clinical Continuum (medical interviewing, etc.)

Second semester
Physiology
Cell and Tissue Biology (histology)
Neurosciences
Clinical Continuum

Third semester
Microbiology
Pathology
Foundations of Clinical Psychiatry
Clinical Continuum (physical exam, etc.)

Fourth semester
Pathology
Foundations of Clinical Psychiatry
Pharmacology
Clinical Continuum

As already mentioned, all medical schools have a similar curriculum, although there is some variation. The goal is to prepare students for the USMLE1 (or COMLEX1 for DO students). This exam and later licensing exams are required for graduation, obtaining a residency, and practicing medicine.

The USMLE1 or COMLEX1 board exam is particularly important since it is used by residency directors to assess your abilities when you apply to residency programs, similar to the MCAT for premeds.

Third and fourth year

In third year, you begin with rotations. Rotations are the clinical part of medical school with most time spent in a hospital or other clinic setting, depending on the rotation. The following are typical rotations during third year (list is from Medical College of Wisconsin):

Third-year rotations
Family Medicine - 1 month
Pediatrics - 2 months
Ob/Gyn - 1.5 months
Psychiatry and Neurology - 1.5 months
Internal Medicine - 2 months

Clinical Procedures (Anesthesiology, Trauma Surgery, Emergency Medicine, Radiology) - 1 month
Surgery - 2 months
Elective Rotation or Vacation - 1 month

Third year usually contains mostly core rotations intended to give you a good foundation in all major fields and are required by all medical schools and needed for you to pass the USMLE2 (or COMLEX2). During the fourth year, and occasionally during the third year, you can choose more rotation electives. Quite frequently, however, the fourth year also includes some required core rotations.

Fourth-year rotations
Subspecialty in Internal Medicine, Pediatrics or Family Medicine - 1 month
Subspecialty in Surgery - 1 month
Ambulatory Medicine in a Subspecialty (Cardiology, etc.) - 1 month
Integrative Clinical Selective - 1 month
Elective Rotations - 5 months
Vacation - 2 months

Electives give you opportunities to experience other specialties or augment knowledge in areas that relate to future residency training. For example, a family medicine resident may want to spend some time rotating in dermatology, oncology, or other areas that may benefit and be useful to family medicine rather than doing another family medicine rotation.

The fourth year is usually more flexible, with more time do elective rotations. Typically, during this time, you can also go abroad or to other areas of the country for rotations, participate in medical missions in third world countries, schedule extra research, and *vacation!*

In terms of the calendar

First year
Class from August to May
Summer is off—many students participate in research or become clinically involved over the summer via externships

Second year
Class from August to May
Six weeks off after class—you take the USMLE1 (or COMLEX1) during this time before third-year rotations begin

Third and fourth years
Rotations from July (beginning of third year) until May (end of fourth year)
You can schedule eight to twelve weeks of vacation during this two-year time period

Many people assume that they will have plenty of time rotating through many different specialties before they have to make their residency and specialty choices. However, residency choice and applying to residency programs happens early during the fourth year, before completing many rotations.

So, most medical students may only have their core rotations and maybe one or two other elective rotations completed before having to decide on a specialty.

The Medical School Experience
Contributions to this section by Audrey Stanton, DO, MPH

Overview

If you look over the class schedule, you may not get the impression that medical school is that difficult. After all, you probably have taken four courses per semester at your undergrad institution before. What is different in medical school is the amount of material covered in each course. Despite the fact that you only take four courses or so at a time, these courses still combine to over 24 credits per semester. Medical school is difficult due to the large amount of material presented and tested in each course.

First and second year

Make no mistake about it, medical school is intense and time consuming.

For many students, the hardest first-year course appears to be biochemistry. It is a very intense experience and a course some students have to repeat during the first summer to make up for a poor grade. Especially for students without any or little biology background, this seems to be a tough course.

Gross anatomy or clinical anatomy is the other heavy-duty course during the first semester. This course usually gets all the attention—most people have heard about the cadaver dissections. Other courses, especially physiology, pathology, and pharmacology are also very intense. If you ask students which course is the hardest, you may get varied responses, but typically biochemistry and pathology top the list.

It takes long hours studying and memorizing to do well in each course.

By the time you are in second year, the excitement of being in medical school has worn off to some degree and the intensity and difficulty seem to increase slightly. By this time, most students say they are getting tired of studying, are getting burned out, and are ready to move on to clinical rotations. Third- and fourth-year clinical rotations are much closer to practicing medicine than the basic science course work completed during the first two years.

Learning and study habits

Learning and study habits vary by student; some students read the textbooks, others attend lectures, and yet others study notes. Interestingly, most students report that they do not have time to do all three.

However, some study habits can also vary by course. Some courses have very comprehensive class notes and all exam materials are drawn from them. Studying the notes is, therefore, the most effective way to study. Other times, exam material is drawn more from textbooks, so reading the textbook is most beneficial.

It appears that you figure out which method of absorbing the material works best for you, and then you spend your time putting that method to use. It's best to start the first semester doing whatever (memorization) method worked best for you in the past, but be ready to make changes quickly if things don't work out. For example, if you always memorized notes by rereading them over and over, stick with that method. If things worked best by rewriting your own notes and memorizing them, keep doing that.

Realize that the key is a lot of repetition. Most likely, you will have to spend many hours studying, for two reasons:

1. The amount of material covered in one month in medical school was covered in one or two semesters in undergrad.
2. The level of detail you are expected to know is unbelievable-way beyond what you had to know for undergrad.

So, if you were the type of person who could score "A's" in undergrad by studying the day before the exam, don't try this in medical school, even if it worked for you in undergrad. Essentially, forget about the hours you studied in undergrad. When talking about study method, consider what way you best memorize, not how many hours you could get away with (not) studying.

There are exceptions on both sides of the spectrum when it comes to study habits and time spent studying. However, many students report something close to the following schedule during their first two years of medical school:

Monday through Friday
8:00 am to 5:00 pm — Attend lecture and lab and/or spend time studying
5:00 pm to 8:00 pm — Eat dinner, relaxation, family or free time
8:00 pm to 11:00 pm — Study time (may vary)

Saturday and Sunday
Study varies on the weekend. Some students take one of the two days off; others take both days off. Yet, others spend one or two half-days on weekends studying. Before exams, most people study through the weekend.

Before major exams
The week before exams, most students also report an increase in time spent studying. So, the schedule outlined previously is more typical for non-exam-preparation weeks. During exam preparation (for a week or two leading up to exams), many students appear to be busy studying from early morning until late at night every day.

Note that some students study much more—basically every waking moment—and others do not study as much. Generally, students seem to take time for some limited hobbies, family, or going out on the weekend. But, much less time is available for these types of activities while in medical school.

Did you ever hear: "You cannot cram in medical school"? Well, apparently some medical students don't know that, because there are a few students who cram a week or two before exams and still do okay. Some of them may not be in the top of the class, but they are doing well, nonetheless. It all depends on what type of person you are.

However, cramming does not tend to work very well in medical school. For most students, it takes a lot of time on an ongoing basis to keep up with the material. Even most people who were successful crammers in undergrad have to change their study habits. Only few people (perhaps the very brightest) can get away with cramming or little studying during medical school. So, don't plan on being able to cram for a day or so before exams, even if you did so in undergrad.

In most cases, chances are that when you go into exams, you will still not actually know the material as well as you would like to, despite many hours of studying.

A note about grading and ranking students

Note that regardless of grading and ranking (as described in the following sections), the drawbacks and advantages are not that significant. You will do fine at any medical school with any grading and ranking system and be able to get into any residency, regardless of the systems used at that particular medical school.

Pass/Fail

Many medical schools use a pass/fail system and do not award other grades than these. This supposedly cuts down the competition among students and makes the school experience less stressful. On the other hand, this also makes it harder for residency directors to sift through the applications, which means that you will not be able to stand out on your grades. So, your grades will not be able to help you in your quest for getting into residency, which is generally considered a drawback, and more of the decision is based on board scores.

Honors/High Pass/Pass/Low Pass/Fail

As you might have imagined, this system is very near the A/B/C/D/F system, just with different names and used by many medical schools as well. The pros and cons are obvious from the prior discussion of the pass/fail system. Supposedly, there is more competition among students and the experience is more stressful. At the same time, it is easy to show residency directors that you are a top student (or not) in your class with your transcript and GPA. High pass and especially honors grades help you look good to residency directors, so this grading system is generally considered more helpful than the pass/fail in regards to finding a residency spot.

Grades and Residency

Some people claim that the grades of your preclinical medical school years (the first two years) don't matter much when it comes to your residency application. It is true that your third-year rotation grades are much more important. Typically, your third-year grades count twice as much as your preclinical grades. So, they are less important, but not unimportant, either.

Class rankings

Most medical schools will rank all students in a class academically from first to last. So, it is easy to find out if you are in the top 20 percent or bottom 20 percent of the class since you will be given an exact number rank. If there are 150 students in the class, you will look favorable if you're toward the top and less favorable if toward the bottom. This ranking is also sent to residency directors when you apply for residency spots. It can help or hurt you.

Some medical schools have decided not to rank the students in their classes for the same reasons mentioned above for the pass/fail system, mainly to limit competition among students. Not being ranked can also be a drawback, since it is harder to stand out, similar to the pass/fail system.

Success in the pre-clinical years

When you first get to medical school, the best thing to do is talk to as many students who are a year ahead of you as you can. Find out about each class and what to study. You'll find that for some courses, the notes are complete and reading the textbooks is a waste of time and money. Some professors only test what they teach in lectures, others expect you to know everything in a textbook chapter, whether mentioned in class or not.

Students who went down this path before you at your school are an invaluable source of information in this regard. Often, they also have old exams you can look over to get a feel for what will be expected of you or as a study aid.

Don't think you can outsmart everyone else. After telling some brand new first-year students how to study for each course during the first year, some of them gave answers similar to these "Study method varies by person. I have done well in undergrad and know what I'm doing and what's important. I don't need your help. I'm a book studier, so that's what I'll keep doing." Well, they didn't do well and were much more interested in listening to advice after the first exams. Unfortunately, the first exam had gone poorly and disqualified them from reaching honors grades in that course for the rest of the semester, regardless of the performance on the rest of the exams.

Make sure you talk to more than one student. You don't know if you are talking to the student who finished first or last in the class you are asking about or how this particular student feels about the importance of grades, etc. If you are all about trying to achieve honors and are interested in a very competitive specialty, you really wouldn't want to take advice from the guy whose motto is *Pass = MD* and who could care less about grades. On the flip side, when someone tells you that you have to spend 150 hours per week studying, I'd say you'd need to talk to someone else. Talk to at least five to ten people and ask them how they did in the course you are inquiring about.

Textbooks, attendance, and exams

While every class seems to have a long list of required textbooks, there is absolutely no way that you'll have enough time to actually read them. It is best to talk to second-year students to see which books they found to be most useful and which ones they never needed. At the beginning of the semester, limit the books that you buy to a bare minimum; much of the time you can start the first semester with an anatomy atlas alone.

Many schools have copies of the required texts on reserve in the library. These can be checked out for short periods of time as needed. As the semester progresses, you will get a better feel for which books you actually need to purchase. This can save you a significant amount of money. Another way to save money is to avoid buying books from the campus bookstore. These stores are convenient, but have significant markups. Many websites sell new and used textbooks, so if you can wait for them to be shipped, you can get some good deals.

You may also find it helpful to complete board review books pertaining to the subjects as they are being taught. This may help you organize and think about the important concepts. For instance, as you are completing pharmacology, a pharmacology board review book will provide questions for you to think about the main concepts. This strategy will help you prepare for the medical boards (USMLE or COMLEX).

Attendance policies vary from school to school and may include mandatory attendance at lectures and/or labs. Some schools have mandatory attendance, but don't really enforce the policy. Others require strict sign-ins for some or all classes or labs. It is good to investigate school policies while you are still in the application process. When you attend interviews, ask current students about how the school addresses class attendance.

Exams may be spread out throughout a semester, often with significant clusters of exams around midterms and finals. Block schedules have shorter courses and fewer classes at a time followed by a more compressed testing period, usually a week of exams finishing out the block, with a block ending every four weeks.

While it may sound easy to largely have multiple-choice tests in medical school, it is critical to note that medical school professors are masters at designing challenging multiple-choice questions. The types of questions you will see will blow your mind. You have not experienced multiple-choice testing until you have seen medical school tests.

Third and fourth year (clinical years)

Once the USMLE1 (or COMLEX1) is out of the way and third-year rotations begin, life apparently improves significantly for most medical students. This is usually a very exciting time and an overdue transition out of the classroom and into clinical medicine.

During third and fourth year, lots of time is spent learning basic clinical skills and gaining general clinical knowledge and experience in preparation for residency.

During rotations, many of the less pleasant chores fall on the medical student since they are the junior members of the medical team and stuff rolls downhill. The residents don't want to do many of these chores and had to do plenty of them already during medical school. So, medical students get to do them. "Oh, that looks like a good job for a medical student."

As part of the medical team, you are also given responsibility for patients (with the help, guidance, and supervision of residents and attendings). Responsibilities include patient histories, reporting on the patients on rounds with the team and learning about their health problems, treatments, etc., in the process (and being able to answer questions about them).

Most rotations are followed by some sort of test (shelf exam), which becomes part of a grade earned on each rotation besides subjective written evaluations from the attending physicians and/or residents during the rotation.

Some rotations are more intense than others. Generally, the third year is one during which you will not see your spouse or other friends and family much. Particularly ob/gyn, surgery, and internal medicine can be very intense with long hours from early morning (sometimes 5:00 a.m.) until very late at night with little sleep in between. A few rotations require very long hours and many rotations require taking call.

A few rotations have been described as easier than others, including those that are not involved in inpatient services. Examples may be psychiatry, outpatient pediatrics, family medicine, and various others (typically outpatient), which may have hours from 8:00 a.m. to 5:00 p.m. or so.

Fourth year is "easier" with fewer hours spent in the hospital, but it really depends again on the types of rotations you choose for your electives. If you pack your schedule full of exciting surgical rotations or other inpatient oriented rotations, expect to have long hours. You have some ability to choose your schedule by selecting your elective rotations and thereby can influence the intensity of fourth year somewhat.

At the end of the four years, or at the beginning of your residency, you take the USMLE2 (board exam) for MDs or COMLEX2 for DOs.

The USMLE1 (or COMLEX1) score, reflecting mastery of the basic sciences learned in the first two years of medical school, is used heavily in the residency selection process by residency directors. The USMLE2 (or COMLEX2) is required, but the score is much less important, since most residency decisions are not influenced by them, although a few very competitive residencies or fellowships may use this score as well.

Success in the clinical years (rotations)
Written by Ai Mukai, MD

Most rotations will have a standardized shelf exam at the end. Grading is usually based on a subjective evaluation by attending physicians and/or residents and the objective shelf exam. Most schools will require you to get honors in both components to earn honors for the rotation.

Various strategies have been suggested for students who have the option of scheduling their third-year rotations. Most say to try to schedule the field they may want to go into around the middle of the year. That way, you will have some experience (learn how to do basic history and physical fairly efficiently, get used to talking to patients, learn the computer system, etc.) and you will have time to change your mind and schedule your fourth-year electives.

In addition, if you are interested in internal medicine, first rotating in pediatrics and family medicine (especially if it has an inpatient component) will help prepare you for internal medicine, so you can try to schedule them earlier. If you are interested in pediatrics, internal medicine and family medicine can help you. If you want to do surgery, ob/gyn can give you some basic OR skills (knots, sutures, sterile field, etc.) and ER (if it's an option) may allow you to see traumas. If you are interested in ob/gyn, surgery (for previously described reasons) and family medicine can help prepare you. For psychiatry, neurology and family medicine may be helpful. For neurology, psychiatry and medicine will be helpful.

If you are pretty sure you know what field you want to go into, you can also try asking the rotation director/secretary to schedule you to rotate with one of the big shots (i.e., department chairs, residency program directors, etc.). This will allow you to secure a good letter of recommendation early.

Basic things you should know how to do by third year: components of a good history and physical exam (H&P). (Hopefully, you learned how to do this during your second year.) You can build on your skills as the year goes on. Various specialties will have aspects they will want you to focus on when writing your H&P, SOAP notes, etc. You will gain some familiarity with minor procedures/ physical examination skills (i.e., rectal exams, pelvic exams, blood draws, IVs, etc.). Basic physiology and pharmacology are important. Also, you have to understand the hierarchy of a team— attending physician, senior resident, intern/junior resident, then medical student (yes, that's you).

Good things to have in your pocket include: pen light, stethoscope (around your neck, on your waist with a clip for those of you with neck pain, or in your pocket), reflex hammer, Maxwell Cards (contain most important clinical formulas, normal values, etc.) or equivalent, Pharmacopea (abbreviated drug information booklet) or equivalent (can be in your PDA), Sanford antimicrobial guide, lots of pens, calipers (if reading EKGs), alcohol swabs, and portable snacks (granola bars, etc.). There are little pocket cards you may find useful with templates for H&Ps, physical exams, etc.

There are good pocket-sized review books for most rotations. The best thing to do is stick with a series. Find a style you like and stick with that. Some of the more popular titles include: PreTest, Recall, Blueprints, Step-Up, First Aid, and Appleton & Lange. *Pocket Medicine* also seems to be a popular book for internal medicine rotations, as well as the MKSAP series for internal medicine. The Boards and Wards series is good for Step 1 and 2. Many students may find it useful to get a pocket reference guide and a question book. If you can find other students with different schedules, you can share your books. For internal medicine, you may need an EKG book. Many students have reported that pimping questions in surgery come straight out of Surgery Recall. You may consider purchasing the Swanson textbook for family medicine because many residents use it to study for Step 3. (A favorite for Step 3 is *Crush Step 3*) The key is to find a maximum of three books per rotation and find the style of book that seems to be the best fit for you.

The Politics

There usually seems to be students who excel during their first and second year who don't do as well during their clinical years and vice versa. And, of course, there are those people we love to hate who seem to be good at everything. First- and second-year grades are usually more objective. They're based on tests and recall of information. Third and fourth year (most fourth-year evaluations are purely subjective) are based on both evaluations and tests. The tests are similar to other tests you have encountered and will encounter in medicine—standardized multiple-choice questions. The evaluations are where most students start realizing the politics of medicine. There will be students who resort to major kissing up, telling attendings in every rotation that they are interested in that field. Others will refuse to kiss up and try to push through purely with their intellect.

Both those types will fail. Most attendings can smell a fake and rigidity will get you nowhere. You want to go for a happy medium. You are not expected to know what you want to do with the rest of your life early your third year. You can evade the dreaded "so, what are you interested in going into?" question early your third year with "I don't know yet, but I like the fact that... (insert field of the rotation and what you like about it). You should be able to name at least one thing you like about a field. If you know what you want to do and you are doing a rotation in that field, feel free to share that. If you don't want to lie (even white lies), you can be honest and say you are interested in another field—but it may be helpful to state a reason why the field you are doing the rotation in is relevant to the field you are interested in. (For example, neonatal rotation is very interesting to someone interested in ob/gyn.)

The Golden Rules of rotations
1.   Don't ever try to make anyone else look bad, whether it be a fellow student, resident, or attending, especially in front of the patients and/or attendings. That will come back to haunt you. Don't take over other students' patients unless asked to do so by a resident or attending.

2. Try not to contradict anyone above you in public (especially in front of patients but also in front of anyone else). It is okay to ask why they chose to do what they did later, in private.

3. Don't use too much sex appeal to be liked. A little flirting is natural; soliciting and being seductive is not.

4. Show up early, leave late if there are things to do. Never look bored. Never leave before your work is done. Even if you absolutely hate the rotation, the attending, or the resident, tell yourself that this is a temporary situation and "this too shall pass." You can do anything for a few weeks. If there's nothing to do and you're just standing around, ask, "Is there anything else I can do to help?" This will often lead to an early dismissal (permission to go home).

5. Volunteer for extra work, presentations, etc., but always strike a balance between rule number one and this rule.

6. Don't ask questions just to ask questions. Don't ask questions just to show off what you know and don't ask stupid questions. If you have a gut feeling that you should probably already know what you are about to ask, you may be exposed by some attendings: "Why don't you know that? You should have read about that already." That would be bad. Learn what's appropriate to ask and what's not. In other words, don't showcase that you weren't prepared even with the basics for the rotation.

7. Be nice to everyone including nurses, patient care aides, secretaries, etc. You never know who people know—secretaries and nurses may be married to department chairs, etc. Nurses can be your worst enemy or your best friend. You choose which one.

8. When in doubt, err on the side of being conservative—whether it is about clothing or shoes. You never know who is watching.

9. Show interest. Most evaluators look for signs of genuine interest, self-motivation, and ability to retain/learn. Most negative evaluations seem to commonly mention disinterest, inability to work with others, laziness,

cockiness, inability to communicate effectively, and other behavioral problems. Being quiet may be misconstrued as disinterest. Request mid-point evaluations to identify these potential negatives and correct them before they become a permanent part of your record! (Most dean's letters will contain excerpts or copies of your third-year evaluations.) If you get a negative evaluation, challenge it as quickly as possible and see if there is any way to get it changed.

Electives

Late third year or early fourth year, you will have the opportunity to do "away" rotations in the field you think you may be interested in. The application process for these rotations can be quite frustrating. The best place to start is on the Internet. Try to find the residency Internet page and look for links for applications to do away electives. If there is no such link, try the main academic institution page (usually the student affairs page). Finally, if you have no luck at all finding information, try emailing the contact person for the residency. You can consider emailing the program director but you will most likely be referred to the secretary.

Some spots fill up fast, especially if the program/field is competitive or small. You may be required to get a form from your medical school vouching for malpractice coverage. You may also need to get a physical exam form from your student health office. Many programs seem to wait until the last possible moment to notify the students of their approval/disapproval for the rotation. This leaves some students with nowhere to go with only a few weeks to spare. You might want to consider applying to more than one rotation or asking the contact person how likely it is for you to *not* get the rotation; having your dean or advisor make a phone call may also help.

Board Exams
Contributions to this section by Audrey Stanton, DO, MPH

Overview

In the United States, all physicians are required to have passed the board exams for licensure and being able to practice medicine.

For allopathic (MD) students, the board exam series is the USMLE1, USMLE2, and USMLE3. For osteopathic (DO) students, the board exam series is the COMLEX1, COMLEX2, and COMLEX3. For Podiatry students, the board exam series is the NBPME1, NBPME2, and NBPME3. All other international medical school graduates (IMGs) are required to pass the USMLE series in order to qualify for U.S. residency training and licensing.

The USMLE Step 1 (USMLE1)

This exam is the first of the series and is typically taken after the preclinical basic science years (first two years) of medical school. Passing this exam is required by most medical school for progression into the clinical years of medical school (third and fourth years).

The USMLE1 scores are also heavily used by residency programs in making decisions about which residency applicants to accept for training. So, this exam is the most important one of the entire series. It is given much weight (similar to the MCAT for premeds) when applying for residency training.

The exam is computerized and takes one day (eight hours) to complete. It includes seven sixty-minute test blocks each containing about fifty multiple-choice questions, for a total of about 350 questions. Each question is to be answered with one best answer out of up to eleven answer choices.

The key in the exam is integration of information from various courses presented in the first two years of medical school. It includes table, chart, and data interpretation, and interpretation of radiological and other images or pictures of different specimens. The exam tests the student's ability to apply basic science knowledge to clinical situations.

The topics covered include anatomy, biochemistry, microbiology, physiology, pathology, pharmacology, and behavioral sciences. About 70 percent of the exam questions cover pathology and pharmacology alone, so these two topics are of particular importance in preparation and review for the exam.

According to the USMLE website, the official purpose of Step 1 of the exam is to assess "whether medical school students or graduates understand and can apply important concepts of the sciences basic to the practice of medicine."

The exam is scored on a scale from 0 to 300 points, 300 being the theoretical best score, but really impossible to achieve. Even a score of 280 is unheard of and never achieved. The average is normally around 215 to 220. Some of the more competitive specialties may have averages of 230 to 235 for applicants who were accepted into their programs.

The minimum passing score for the USMLE1 is 185 out of 300, which requires answering about 60 to 70 percent of the questions correctly.

Osteopathic (DO) students may also take the USMLE1 examination, which will help them to enter allopathic (MD) residency training.

To find out more, you can visit the official website at usmle.org.

The USMLE Step 2 (USMLE2)

This exam is the second of the series and is typically taken after third or fourth year, the clinical years, of medical school. Passing this exam is required by most medical school for graduation and for beginning residency training.

The USMLE2 scores are not used by residency directors in evaluating residency applicants since most applicants will not have taken it by the time they apply and interview for residency. However, there are a few instances in which it is very advantageous to take the USMLE2 earlier and make sure the residency programs receive the USMLE2 score before the interview. It is up to the applicant to release the score to the residency programs.

If your USMLE1 (Step 1) score was not very good, it can make a significant difference to take the USMLE2 (Step 2) early. If the Step 2 scores are much higher, it can make up for the poor performance on the Step 1 exam and allow residency directors to see this improvement. This is a huge benefit and can make the difference in getting the residency spot!

On the other hand, if your Step 1 score was very good and your residency application is otherwise strong, knowing your Step 2 score can only hurt you. If it is a good score, it does not improve your residency application any more—it is already strong. If your Step 2 score has dropped from your Step 1 score, this is only going to weaken your application.

So, if your Step 1 score was low, take Step 2 early. You can then decide whether or not to release the score to the residency programs you are applying to. If it is low, don't release it. If it is high, release it. The same is true if your Step 1 and overall residency application are already strong. If you still decide to take Step 2 early, you are not obligated to release the score until after your interviews.

Residency directors may ask you about your Step 2 score anyway. So, if your Step 1 and overall residency application are already strong, there is no reason to rush Step 2 (or check your score) and risk being asked about it.

As you can see, the Step 2 score is a strategic tool in your hands. Use it wisely.

The exam is computerized and takes one day (nine hours) to complete. It includes eight sixty-minute test blocks each containing about fifty multiple-choice questions, for a total of about four hundred questions.

This includes questions about the core rotations offered during the clinical years of medical school, such as internal medicine, family medicine, surgery, ob/gyn, pediatrics, psychiatry, public health, and preventive medicine. Most of the questions are clinical scenarios in which you are expected to make a diagnosis or a prognosis or determine appropriate steps in medical care, similar to what is encountered in real practice.

According the USMLE website, the official purpose of the Step 2 exam is to assess "whether medical school students or graduates can apply medical knowledge, skills, and understanding of clinical science essential for provision of patient care under supervision."

The exam is scored on a scale from 0 to 300 points, 300 being the theoretical best score, but really impossible to achieve. The minimum passing score for the USMLE2 is 182 out of 300, which requires answering about 60 to 70 percent of the questions correctly.

This exam also includes a clinical exam/physical exam component that evaluates the student's ability to perform a physical exam and evaluate the medical problem presented by standardized patients. This component of the testing consists of eleven to twelve patient encounters over eight hours. The patient encounters are similar to situations experienced with real patients. Students elicit a medical complaint and history, perform a physical examination (with the exception that certain parts of the examination must not be done: rectal, pelvic, genitourinary, female breast, or corneal reflex examination), answer any questions the patient may have, and inform the patient of the diagnosis and plan. Immediately after each patient encounter, the examinees will have ten minutes to complete a patient note. The patient note is similar to a real medical record that includes complaint and history, examination findings, assessment, and plan. The encounters consist of common medical problems seen in the clinic, doctor's office, emergency department, or hospital setting. Synthetic models, mannequins, or simulators may also be used to test physical examination techniques relating to specific medical problems.

The USMLE Step 3 (USMLE3)

This exam is the last of the series and is typically taken after graduating from medical school, often during the first year of residency training. Passing this step is required for full licensure as a physician. Interns and residents cannot moonlight until they have passed the exam and physicians cannot practice independently without passing all three USMLE steps. This last step of the series has to be completed within seven years from the time Step 1 was passed.

The exam is computerized and takes two days (eight hours each) to complete. It includes one and a half days for answering about 480 multiple-choice questions. The other half-day is taken up with nine computer-based case simulations. The multiple-choice questions are single best answer, and may be stand alone or grouped together in sets of two or three items along with a clinical vignette. The computer-based case simulations test the examinee's ability to manage patients via free-text entry of clinical orders. Buttons and check boxes are used for advancing the clock, changing the patient's location (e.g., emergency room, inpatient, or discharge to outpatient), reviewing previously displayed information, and obtaining updates on the patient. Each case simulation ends when a final end point is reached: patient's condition improves, patient fails to get better due to incorrect management, or the patient dies.

This exam is intended to test your ability to take care of patients as a generalist physician without supervision and mimics scenarios seen in practice.

According the USMLE website, the official purpose of the Step 3 exam is to assess "whether medical school graduates can apply medical knowledge and understanding of biomedical and clinical science essential for the unsupervised practice of medicine."

The exam is scored on a scale from 0 to 300 points, as the other two exams. The minimum passing score for the USMLE3 is 182 out of 300, which requires answering about 60 to 70 percent of the questions correctly.

The COMLEX series (osteopathic)

This exam series essentially mirrors that of the USMLE, with some minor differences, and it is limited to osteopathic (DO) medical students. It also includes a section on OMM (osteopathic manipulative medicine), which is unique to the COMLEX. COMLEX1 tends to be slightly more clinically oriented than USMLE1, but COMLEX2 and 3 are very similar to USMLE2 and 3. In all other aspects, exam timing and importance is similar to that of the USMLE.

All three COMLEX exams are scored on a scale from 200 to 800. The mean for Parts 1 and 2 is 500 and the minimum passing score is 400. COMLEX Part 3 has a mean of 500 and a minimum passing score of 350.

If osteopathic graduates are planning on obtaining MD residencies (two-thirds of DOs do), it is also a good idea to take the USMLE1 and/or USMLE2 board exams along with the COMLEX exams since some MD residencies absolutely require the USMLE score. Even if a residency program does not require the USMLE score, it is usually best to have taken the USMLE anyway because MD residency directors are more familiar with the USMLE scoring system.

To find out more, you can visit the official website at nbome.org.

The NBPME series (podiatry)
Contributions to this section by Robert Greenhagen, podiatry student

The National Board of Podiatric Medical Examiners (NBPME) is the board series for podiatric medical students. Similar to USMLE and COMLEX, it is a three-part series, NBPME Part 1, 2, and 3.

Part 1 is generally taken after the second year of podiatric medical school. Similar to the USLME, it tests the candidate's understanding of the basic science areas including general anatomy, biochemistry, physiology, microbiology, immunology, pathology, and pharmacology. Part 1 also includes a unique area, lower extremity anatomy. The test is 150 written, multiple-choice questions and is scored in a range of 55 to beyond 75. A score of 75 and above is required to receive a passing score. The test is reported as pass/fail with 75 to 80 percent of the candidates achieving a passing score.

Part 2 is generally taken near the completion of the fourth and final year of school. It tests the candidate's knowledge of the clinical science areas including general medicine, dermatology, radiology, orthopedics, biomechanics, surgery, anesthesia, hospital protocol, community health, and jurisprudence. The test is 150 written, multiple-choice questions and is scored in a range of 55 to beyond 75. A score of 75 and above is required to receive a passing score. The test is reported as pass/fail with 80 to 85 percent of the candidates achieving a passing score.

Part 3 (PMLexis) is designed to determine whether a candidate's knowledge and clinical skills are adequate to safely practice on his or her own. It tests the candidate's ability to evaluate, diagnose, and treat patients. Part 3 is used by state licensing boards for licensure for independent and unsupervised general practice. Candidates must hold a DPM degree, have passed NBPME Parts 1 and 2, and have applied for a license in one or more of the participating states to take Part 3. The test is completed on a computer terminal and is scored in a range of 55 to beyond 75. A score of 75 and above is required to receive a passing score, though each state licensing board has the final say in establishing a passing score. The test is report as a pass/fail with 85 percent of the candidates achieving a passing score.

To find out more, you can visit the official website at nbpme.org.

Residency Training

Residency Training
Contributions to this section by Natalie J. Belle, MD

Getting into residency and the residency match

You get into residency by applying for residency spots during fourth year of medical school and interviewing for those residency spots. Many factors are important in being able to get into your residency of choice:

1. Board scores (very important, especially if applying to a competitive specialty or program)
2. Grades and honors
3. Recommendation letters from the dean and faculty members in the specialty of interest
4. Research (required for some residencies)—ideally within the field
5. The decision-makers know you personally (doing an effective rotation there can be key)
6. A good interview

After interviewing all candidates, the residency programs make a rank list with the most desirable applicant they want in their program on top and the least desirable at the bottom. Students do the same, making a rank list with their first-choice program in the first spot, listing five to ten programs (more if the specialty is very competitive or the applicant is less competitive) from most desirable to least desirable.

On Match Day (middle of March) each year, a computer matches applicants with positions ("The Match" or more officially called the National Residency Match Program (NRMP)) and you find out where you will spend the next few years for training. Most people match in their first choice or at least in the first two or three.

The match is a computerized application process that allows applying to multiple programs using the same application. Fourth-year students and graduates of U.S. medical schools are given tokens for participation in this program by the deans of their medical schools. After registering with the NRMP, U.S. graduates and fourth-year students are eligible to complete an ERAS (Electronic Residency Application Service) application that includes dean's letters, a personal statement, letters of recommendation, medical school transcripts, and USMLE scores. The completed application may be sent to hundreds of programs through this centralized application service. There is a fee schedule based on the number of programs applied to for this service.

The completed applications are downloaded by residency programs reviewing the application materials and choose applicants for an interview. The more competitive the specialty, the more interviews are needed to ensure being matched by the match computer. Following selection for interview, applicants schedule interviews and travel to programs to be interviewed by teaching faculty and program directors. This process is similar to an employment interview and similar to the interview process that the applicant underwent for admission to medical school. Interviews may range from questions about an applicant's desire to enter a specific program to questions that indicate an applicant's knowledge base in the specialty. The interview is traditionally an opportunity for the applicant to meet some of the residents currently in the program and gather information about the program.

The rule of thumb is not to rank a program that one would not want to spend their years of residency because an applicant can potentially match at any program on their rank list provided they were invited for an interview by the program.

MD and DO residencies

There are roughly 16,000 graduates from U.S. allopathic (MD) medical schools[1] and about 3,000 graduates from U.S. osteopathic (DO) medical schools[2] each year, all of which participate in different residency match programs to get into residency. In addition to these 20,000 U.S. graduates, approximately another

12,000 international medical graduates (IMGs) also participate in the residency match programs each year.

The NRMP, primarily catering to the MD graduates but also accessible to DO graduates and IMGs as independent applicants, offers by far the most residency positions—about 21,000 per year. The osteopathic match offers another 1,000 residency spots to DO graduates, although this is insufficient to offer all DO graduates residency positions (more about this later).

So, after a little math, it is apparent right away that there are fewer positions available (roughly about 22,000 spots including MD and DO residencies) than applicants for residency (32,000 total applicants including U.S. graduates and IMGs). If only considering U.S. medical school graduates, including both MD and DO, there is actually a surplus of residency positions since there are only approximately 20,000 total graduates and 22,000 residency spots available each year.

When looking at the 32,000 or so applicants for residency, many graduates do not match at all—particularly IMGs. In the 2005 NRMP match, 94 percent of MDs matched, 69 percent of DOs matched, and 55 percent of IMGs matched. It is also interesting to mention that about 10 percent of the residency positions of the NRMP match were not filled that year.[1] Also, many osteopathic physicians match through the DO match rather than the NRMP (MD) at higher percentages.

Note that many applicants and some residency programs never go through the match. Applicants can arrange their own residencies without going through the match and some residency programs just don't use the NRMP. Also, there are a few specialty matches for the very competitive residency programs, such as plastic surgery, urology, ophthalmology, neurosurgery, neurology, and a few others, which add more residency spots to the total number of spots available each year. These don't participate in the NRMP, but use the San Francisco Match Service (www.sfmatch.org), which is separate from the NRMP match and is completed earlier than the NRMP. Essentially, if you don't make it into one of the San Francisco match specialties, you still have time to go through the regular NRMP match for the same year.

Residency overview

Residency is considered a continuation of medical education and had been cast in a gray area between education and employment. Residents or physicians-in-training are paid a stipend that starts around $40,000 and increases slightly over the period of their training, prompting the Bureau of Labor Statistics to place medical/surgical among the ten most underpaid professions in the country based on the number of hours worked and the take-home wage.

After successfully matching in a residency position, the next steps depend on the type of residency position that you have matched into. If you have matched into a categorical position, this means that barring poor performance on your part or loss of accreditation by the program, you are expected to complete the residency training in that location. If you have matched into a preliminary position, it is expected that you will complete your residency in another department or location (prearranged) for a designated preliminary resident or to be arranged for a non-designated preliminary resident. Generally, preliminary positions are offered in internal medicine and general surgery only for medical graduates who will be going on to complete residencies in orthopedic surgery, neurosurgery, anesthesia, dermatology, ophthalmology, otolaryngology (ENT), radiology, pathology, and some psychiatry programs. Other options for these residents are to do a transitional year before beginning their residency at the PGY-2 (Post Graduate Year 2) level.

After completing your PGY-1 or internship year, many residents will start their specialty training in their chosen field by rotating through the various services of their chosen field. For example, medical residents will have rotations in cardiology, nephrology, pulmonology, outpatient, and critical care medicine. Surgical residents will rotate through pediatric surgery, vascular surgery, critical care, hepatobiliary surgery, transplant surgery, and other surgical specialties. The level of responsibility of the resident is dependent on the year of training with PGY-1s generally handling the ward duties; PGY-2s and 3s handling critical care and more complex cases.

In addition to patient care, residents who are more senior are responsible for teaching the junior residents. The senior residents teach most procedures and patient care skills to the residents who are less senior. While the attending physician is in charge of education on their service, the senior resident is generally in charge of making sure that patient care is carried out on the service. The attending physician and senior resident will generally share the responsibility of running the service and the education of the residents.

In the special cases of the surgical specialties, residents who are more senior tend to do most of the surgical cases while the junior residents are responsible for getting the ward duties completed before they can get into the operating room. Surgeons have the added responsibilities of having to learn multiple operative procedures in addition the medical care of their patients, which adds years to their post-graduate training.

In most surgical or surgical subspecialties, the resident learns surgical procedures by operating with an attending surgeon. A minimum number of operative procedures must be logged in addition to the number of years of surgical residency before a residency graduate may be eligible to sit for specialty board certification.

In every residency program, a yearly in-training examination is taken by all residents to assess their progress in mastery of the basic and clinical science of their residency. Most residency programs use these scores for remediation in the case of a poor performance or to assess the effectiveness of their training. Performance on these exams is generally a good indicator of the ability of the resident to pass specialty boards at the end of their training. At the completion of residency, most physicians elect to go into practice either at the academic level or privately. Some elect to enter fellowship for further training in a subspecialty.

Training

Most residency training is anywhere from three to seven years in length, often followed by a fellowship for additional subspecialty training. For example: Internal medicine residency (3 years) followed by a cardiology fellowship (3 years) or anesthesia (4 years) followed by a pain management fellowship (1 year) or plastic surgery (5 years) followed by a hand surgery fellowship (1 year). The minimum is three years (internal medicine, family medicine, pediatrics) and the maximum is around seven years (neurosurgery and others with fellowship). Most surgery specialties are about five years without additional subspecialization such as thoracic surgery.

Physicians are paid a salary during residency. The salary ranges from about $35,000 to $45,000 per year (2007 numbers), depending on specialty, location, and years of experience (years in residency). If you are on a military scholarship, and therefore in a military residency, your salary and benefit package can get close to $60,000 per year for residency, depending on various factors.

Residencies and specialties vary greatly in their intensity and time commitment. Some residencies are forty-five hours per week (dermatology, oncology, etc.) with little or no call. Others are brutal, like most surgical, internal medicine, or other inpatient residencies with eighty hours or more a week.

At the end of residency, you take the last board exams (Step 3) for board certification in your specialty.

Also, during residency training, the more senior residents are involved in teaching the more junior ones and often some medical students as well. You often hear "see one, do one, teach one" when referring to residency training. So, residency training, most often, includes learning and teaching those who follow behind to some extent.

Schedule

Due to ACGME requirements for residency program accreditation, residency programs are officially limited to work their residents no more than eighty hours per week, but quite a few programs still ignore that limit and residents in these programs often exceed eighty hours per week. A few years back, there were no limits and residents routinely worked 100 to 120 hours a week.

The first year of residency (often still called the internship year) is crazy. Don't plan to see your family. Almost regardless of specialty, you have a heavy call schedule with every fourth night you stay at the hospital—for up to thirty hours at a time. You are still at the bottom of the hill and it all rolls downhill.

Usually things improve somewhat after the first year of residency and it gets better. Some people say that it is during the first year of residency where you learn 90 percent or more of all you'll ever need to know and it is a very intense experience. It is also after the first year or residency that you can get licensed in most U.S. states, and, depending on specialty, you can start moonlighting (working outside of residency) to earn some extra money on the side. Of course, this is not true for all specialties. Moonlighting is not possible after completing just the first year of most surgical residencies, for obvious reasons.

Again, the eighty-hour limit, imposed a few years ago, is not necessarily followed by all residency programs yet. Also, programs can file for an exemption to increase hours from the eighty-hour workweek, which some programs have done. It pays to check out the hours residents put in at a residency program you are interested in. Things are likely to improve with time and perhaps hours will be reduced to some number under eighty, eventually.

DO residency considerations

Most of the available residency positions in the United States are ACGME-approved for MDs, while only very few residency positions are funded and approved by the AOA (American Osteopathic Association) for DOs alone.

There are about 3,000 DO graduates per year, compared to only about 1,000 AOA (DO) available residency positions. This creates a problem for DO graduates and most of them will have to enter MD residency programs for training each year. Military residencies are also approved for DOs by the AOA, so this presents another alternative to stay with AOA residency programs.

So, what's the fuss about AOA-approved residencies and why would a DO graduate really care? Well, the ACGME (for MDs) and the AOA (for DOs) handle physician licensing in each state and the AOA does not like DO physicians to train outside of its approved programs. The AOA may prevent you from getting a medical license in some states if you have completed a non-AOA-approved internship (first year) program.

To prevent this from happening, DOs can enter AOA-only accredited internships, AOA-ACGME programs with dual accreditation or military residency programs, which are typically accredited by both. Also, the AOA can approve additional residency programs that are currently not AOA-accredited on a case-by-case basis.

Also note that it is very difficult for DOs to compete in some of the more competitive specialties for some of the same reasons IMGs are "discriminated" against. Particularly some of the surgery subspecialties, such as otolaryngology (ENT), urology, pediatric surgery, neurosurgery, and a few others are almost off-limits for DOs.

Military residency

All graduates of the Uniformed Services University of the Health Sciences (USUHS) medical school have to go through the military match. Also, generally speaking, all graduates of any other medical school who participated in the military HPSP scholarship are required to go through the military match.

In the case of HPSP, the military is more lenient in allowing graduates to complete civilian residencies in some cases and then returning to the military to serve the payback period afterward. Also, for a few limited specialties, the military does not offer any residency positions at all. Neurosurgery is an example. In this case, only civilian residencies are an option and the military allows individuals to pursue civilian residency training in this case.

The results of the military match are announced in December instead of March. If you are interested in a particular specialty, you can rank both military residencies and civilian residencies at the same time. However, if you match in the military residency, you are required to accept that residency position and to withdraw from the civilian match.

Note that the actual time spent in the military residency does *not* count as your service payback time. So, here are a few quick examples.

If you were on the HPSP program for four years during medical school, you owe the military a four-year active duty commitment and a four-year reserve duty commitment after residency. However, if your residency training takes longer than five years, you will owe one additional year of active duty service and one additional year of reserve duty service for each year over the five-year limit.

So, let's assume your residency and fellowship training take six years to complete, combined. You would owe the military five years of active duty payback and five years of reserve duty payback instead of four years each in this case. If your residency training only takes three years to complete, you still owe four years each in payback.

If you have attended the UHSU, the minimum payback is seven years. Any additional time is added to this as well.

As already mentioned in previous discussions, military residencies are most often accredited by both ACGME (for MDs) and AOA (for DOs), although there are some disparities in the competitive surgical specialties, which are almost off-limits to DOs, as also discussed previously.

Other info

The FREIDA website (www.ama-assn.org/ama/pub/category/2997. html) is the official site for most residency and fellowship program information. You can find all types of great info, including average weekly work hours, resident salaries, etc.

Fellowship training

Most fellowships require that the physician has completed a residency program. Depending on the residency program, various fellowships are available such as nephrology, cardiology, pulmonology/critical care, or for internal medicine graduates or vascular, cardiothoracic, trauma/critical care, and plastics/hand for surgical graduates. In addition, graduates from pediatrics may elect to subspecialize in areas such as pediatric cardiology, pediatric nephrology, pediatric pulmonology, neonatology, or pediatric critical care. Other residency graduates will have other subspecialties that are open to them so see the listings at the end of this chapter.

Fellowships require applications that are similar to residency application and match into a program. It is generally a good idea to start looking for a fellowship program two years before you anticipate finishing your residency. The application and match procedures take place the year before completing your residency.

For residency graduates interested in fellowships, your in-training examination scores, evaluations by your teaching faculty, and your research achievements during residency are key to securing these positions. Fellowships may be one, two, or three years in length depending on the fellowship location. Fellowships are generally located in academic teaching centers and tertiary care centers where the patient volume will allow concentration in a medical or surgical subspecialty.

Fellows may have the rank of junior attending physician or they may be ranked above the senior resident on a particular service. Fellowship pay may be slightly better than residency pay but far less than an attending physician's salary unless you have a junior-attending appointment. Fellows are expected to take call and handle all patients in their subspecialty. They are expected to perform the required number of procedures in order to sit for their subspecialty board examinations, which may be oral and written.

Specialty Selection

Overview

How do you know what specialty is right for you? Most medical students decide during their third and fourth year clinical rotations which specialty training to pursue. Students have to start applying to residency programs early fourth year and go on interviews during fourth year. The residency match occurs in the middle of March.

Many students already have ideas early during medical school about which specialty they may want to enter eventually. However, it has been found that about 70 to 80 percent of medical students change their minds while in medical school.

Check out the list of specialties in this book.

Selection factors

When considering which specialty is the right one, there are many important factors to consider:

1. Does the specialty interest you?
2. Could you do this for a living, rather than just shadowing or spending a couple weeks on a rotation?
3. Is the lifestyle what you want for yourself?
4. Are you fine with the hours worked by physicians in this specialty?
5. Are you fine with the compensation offered in this specialty?
6. Are you fine with the length of training for this specialty?
7. Are you fine with the intensity of residency training for this specialty?
8. Are you interested in academic medicine?
9. Is this specialty going to change significantly within the near future?
10. Are you competitive for the specialty?

Probably the most important factor on this list is specialty interest. Make sure you are truly interested in the specialty. Don't choose a specialty just because it pays well or is the most prestigious. Physicians who are miserable in their specialties most often made decisions due to those two factors, rather than focusing on what they would have most enjoyed to practice.

Your medical career will most likely last a long time and you do not want to be stuck in a specialty you hate. At the same time, realize that you can still change specialties even if you have already begun or completed residency once. So, it is never too late, but it is painful to start over again.

Also, spending some time shadowing or rotating in a specialty may give you a false impression, depending on where and who you rotate with. Often, your experience can be much better or worse than what you would see if you were in practice yourself and may influence your decision in the wrong direction. Keep that in mind.

Lifestyle, compensation, and hours

Lifestyle, compensation, and hours are probably the most important factors for most people besides the factor of liking the specialty itself. It is generally known that surgeons have longer workdays and more call than most other specialties. Also, dermatology, ophthalmology, and a few other specialties are known as the cush specialties, with little call, very good compensation, and relatively normal workweeks.

You have to decide which of these factors are most important to you. The surgical specialties are typically the most intense where sixty to eighty hours per week is not uncommon—the most call, but with the highest compensation and the most prestige. Many specialties with great work hours and little call are also often the ones that are less well compensated and least prestigious.

Realize that medicine, in general, is an intense profession. Most physicians in specialties that are considered to have better workweeks quite often still work fifty hours or more a week. Most employers require the physician to work forty hours per week doing direct patient care. Any extra paperwork, charting, etc., is considered extra work, so realistically, most physicians don't ever work just forty hours per week, although you can find some exceptions. As one physician put it, "Forty hours in medicine is part time."

Certain specialties are extremely competitive and hard to get into because they offer a favorable compromise between compensation (still fairly high), time spent each week (relatively low), and call schedule (not very intense). These include dermatology, ophthalmology, radiology, radiation oncology, anesthesiology, emergency medicine, pathology, and some others for various reasons. These specialties and a few others offer a relatively decent lifestyle.

A rule of thumb for compensation is that the more procedures the physician does, the more he or she is paid. So, a specialty that just sees patients in the office (internal medicine, family medicine, pediatrics), prescribes medications, and is involved in thinking, etc., is not as well compensated as one that actually does probing, scoping, cutting, suturing, etc.

Averaging all specialties and all practice types, the average employed (not in private practice) physician earns approximately $210,000 per year in the United States. Surgical subspecialties and some other (highly procedural) specialties like cardiology can reach $400,000 or more per year, whereas most office based medical specialties such as family medicine, internal medicine, and pediatrics are closer to $150,000. Many different salary surveys can be found that all slightly vary on these numbers, so these numbers may fluctuate somewhat. You can find salary surveys with salaries listed at:

> http://www.allied-physicians.com/salary_surveys/physician-salaries.htm

> http://www.cejkasearch.com/compensation/amga_physician_compensation_survey.htm

Also, there can be great variation in pay depending on whether or not physicians work for themselves in private practice; are employed by a physician group, hospital, or other organization; or work in academic or military medicine.

You have to decide how much time you want to spend at work each week versus spending time with your family or doing other things and balance this with your interests and compensation. Naturally, there is also great variation within each specialty. For example, a pediatrician who works very long hours every week has the potential to earn more than another pediatrician who works shorter hours.

Length and intensity of training

As is true for practicing medicine, the surgical specialties are also the ones that typically have the most intense and the longest residency training. Generally, surgical residents tend to have the longest workweek and the most call. Cardiology and some other specialties also have long hours and lots of call. Dermatology and a few others, again, have much less call and a much less-intense schedule. General surgery is notorious for having one of the worst and most intense residencies, but some of the other surgical subspecialties are not quite as intense.

Note that long hours and call schedules are not restricted to surgical specialties, however. Pediatrics, for example, and many other specialties, which do not have extremely long hours once in practice, can have long hours and lots of call during residency.

Academic medicine versus private practice

In 2005, of the 15,736 MD medical school graduates, 32.8 percent (or 5,161) entered academic medicine (4,752 entering clinical academic medicine and 409 entering basic science academic medicine), 35.2 percent (or 5,539) entered private practice, and 8.1 percent (or 1,274) took salaried clinical positions (976 hospital employed, 62 HMO employed, and 236 state or federal employment).[3]

Academic medicine involves teaching medical students and residents, and doing research. Typically, compensation of academic physicians is only about 50 to 60 percent of the compensation paid to physicians in private practice.

Many physicians particularly like or dislike academic medicine for some of the same reasons. Private practice compensation is substantially higher, but there are also differences in the work itself. Obviously, research and teaching involvement are not usually part of a private practice career.

Also, the types of patient cases seen on regular basis may vary quite a bit. Being in a major academic center can provide a different set of patients. Often, academic physicians can subspecialize more in a specific area of interest within their specialty and become a "super expert" if they wish to do so. Academic surgeons may also see more variety and cases that are more difficult in their academic practice and stay current on all the surgical skills needed to perform many different surgeries. Once in private practice, several of these surgeries may be so rarely encountered that they no longer feel adequately practiced in the surgery and refer all of these cases to a larger academic center from then on.

Similarly, in internal medicine, the academic practice can be almost or entirely inpatient, whereas most private practice settings are mostly outpatient settings. Also, in the academic world, physicians tend to see many more interesting and complicated cases on a regular basis (because they have been referred to the academic center), which are rarely seen in private practice.

How competitive are you?

Certainly, your board scores, grades, and a few more factors determine if you will be competitive for a specialty. Some specialties are very competitive because there are very few residency training positions available and because the specialties provide a nice lifestyle, good hours, good pay, and little call, as previously discussed.

Comparing some of the extremes by numbers only, there are about 140 entry-level residency spots for neurosurgery and 180 for plastic surgery compared to 6,600 in internal medicine.

The average USMLE1 score is 215 to 220 each year. The average for accepted residency applicants in the very competitive specialties can be around 230. Since this is an average, there are also people who get in with average board scores.

You should not give up on your dreams or ideas of becoming a particular specialist just because you feel that you are not going to be competitive enough. Most students can get into the field they are interested in, but just like getting into medical school, they may have to make up for a lower board score and lower GPA with other activities to be competitive. Also, they probably will have to apply to many more residency programs to get interview invitations.

Aptitude test and evaluation

During the third and fourth year, most medical schools put together presentations and workshops to help students with the specialty decision-making process. As part of these workshops, students work through various assessment tools, which may help them focus on a list of potential specialties that may match their interests or personalities.

If you are interested in seeing which types of residencies you may want to consider or which ones may be a good fit for you now, you can visit med-ed.virginia.edu/specialties/ and complete the aptitude test.

Note that you should repeat this type of test again later in the process if you are just beginning with medical school or premed. The test results will most likely change with time and as some of your priorities change.

This aptitude test is actually used by some of the workshops during third and fourth year. You will answer 130 questions and the program generates a list of specialties for you from best to worst fit. The test only takes about fifteen to twenty minutes to complete.

Medical Specialties

This list may not include every specialty available. These specialties are shown with their respective subspecialties indented. Entering subspecialty training requires completion of the main specialty first.

Note: Some specialties can be reached by pursuing different paths. Also, some specialties may use a preliminary year (surgery most often) that may or may not be completed at the same site as the actual specialty residency training that follows. Otolaryngology (ENT), for example, has some residency programs which require completion of one or two preliminary years of general surgery before entering four years of ENT residency training. Alternatively, other ENT residency programs offer integrated programs lasting five years. For this reason, some specialties may be listed independently while others may be listed under the preliminary discipline.

Aerospace Medicine (4 years)
Anesthesiology (4 years)
    Adult Critical Care — via Anesthesia (5 years total)
    Pain Medicine (5 years total)
    Pediatric Anesthesiology (5 years total)
Dermatology (4 years)
    Clinical and Laboratory Dermatological Immunology (5 years total)
    Dermatopathology (5 years total)
Emergency Medicine (4 years)
    Hyperbaric Medicine (5 years total)
    Medical Toxicology (6 years total)
    Pediatric Emergency Medicine — via Emergency Medicine (6 years total)
    Sports Medicine (5 years total)
Family Medicine (3 years)
    Geriatric Medicine — via Family Medicine (4 years total)
    Osteopathic Manipulative Medicine (OMM) (5 years total)
    Sports Medicine (4 years total)
Family Medicine and Emergency Medicine combined (5 years)
Family Medicine and Osteopathic Manipulative Medicine combined (3

years)
Family Medicine and Psychiatry combined (5 years)
General Surgery (5 years)
   Adult Critical Care—via Surgery (6 years total)
   Cardiothoracic Surgery (8 years total)
   Colon And Rectal Surgery (6 years total)
   Hand Surgery—via General Surgery (6 years total)
   Neurological Surgery (6 years total)
   Otolaryngology (ENT) (5 years total)
      Facial Plastic and Reconstructive Surgery (7 years total)
      Head and Neck Cancer Surgery (7 years total)
      Otology—Neurotology (7 years total)
      Pediatric Otolaryngology (7 years total)
      Plastic Surgery—via Otolaryngology (7 years total)
   Pediatric Surgery (7 years total)
   Plastic Surgery—via General Surgery (6 years total)
   Trauma Surgery (7 years total)
   Urology (5 years total)
      Pediatric Urology (6 years total)
   Vascular Surgery (7 years total)
Internal Medicine (3 years)
   Adult Critical Care—via Internal Medicine (5 years total)
   Allergy and Immunology (5 years total)
      Clinical and Laboratory Immunology (6 years total)
   Cardiology (6 years total)
      Cardiac Electrophysiology (6 years total)
      Interventional (invasive) Cardiology (7 years total)
      Nuclear Cardiology (7 years total)
   Endocrinology (5 years total)
   Gastroenterology (6 years total)
   Geriatric Medicine—via Internal Medicine (4 years total)
   Hematology—via Internal Medicine (5 years total)
   Hematology and Oncology combined (6 years total)
   Infectious Disease (5 years total)
   Nephrology (5 years total)
   Oncology (5 years total)
   Pulmonology (5 years total)
   Rheumatology (5 years total)
   Sports Medicine (4 years total)
Internal Medicine and Dermatology combined (5 years)
Internal Medicine and Emergency Medicine and Critical Care
combined (6 years)

Internal Medicine and Emergency Medicine combined (5 years)
Internal Medicine and Family Medicine combined (4 years)
Internal Medicine and Medical Genetics combined (5 years)
Internal Medicine and Neurology combined (5 years)
Internal Medicine and Nuclear Medicine combined (4 years)
Internal Medicine and Pediatrics combined (4 years)
Internal Medicine and Physical Medicine and Rehabilitation combined
(5 years)
Internal Medicine and Preventive Medicine combined (4 years)
Internal Medicine and Psychiatry combined (5 years)
Medical Genetics (4 years)
Neurology (4 years)
    Clinical Neurophysiology (5 years total)
    Pain Medicine (5 years total)
Neurology and Diagnostic Radiology and Neuroradiology combined (7
years)
Neurology and Physical Medicine and Rehabilitation combined (5
years)
Neurology and Psychiatry combined (5 years)
Nuclear Medicine (3 years)
Obstetrics and Gynecology (OBGYN) (4 years)
    Gynecological Oncology (7 years total)
    Maternal-Fetal Medicine (7 years total)
    Reproductive Endocrinology (Fertility) (7 years total)
    Urogynecology/Reconstructive Pelvic Surgery (7 years total)
Occupational Medicine (4 years)
Ophthalmology (4 years)
Orthopedic Surgery (5 years)
    Adult Reconstructive Orthopedics (6 years total)
    Foot and Ankle Orthopedics (6 years total)
    Hand Surgery—via Orthopedic Surgery (6 years total)
    Musculoskeletal Oncology (6 years total)
    Orthopedic Sports Medicine (6 years total)
    Orthopedic Surgery of the Spine (6 years total)
    Orthopedic Trauma (6 years total)
    Pediatric Orthopedic Surgery (6 years total)
    Plastic Surgery—via Orthopedic Surgery (7 years total)
Pathology (4 years)
    Blood Banking and Transfusion Medicine (4 years total)
    Chemical Pathology (4 years total)
    Cytopathology (4 years total)
    Forensic Pathology (4 years total)

Hematology—via Pathology (4 years total)
Medical Microbiology (4 years total)
Neuropathology (5 years total)
Pediatric Pathology (4 years total)
Selective Pathology (4 years total)
Pediatrics (3 years)
    Adolescent Medicine (6 years total)
    Allergy and Immunology (5 years total)
       Clinical and Laboratory Immunology (6 years total)
    Child Neurology (5 years total)
    Developmental-Behavioral Pediatrics (6 years total)
    Medical Toxicology (5 years total)
    Neonatal and Perinatal Medicine (6 years total)
    Pediatric Cardiology (6 years total)
       Cardiac Electrophysiology (6 years total)
       Interventional (invasive) Cardiology (7 years total)
       Nuclear Cardiology (7 years total)
    Pediatric Critical Care (6 years total)
    Pediatric Emergency Medicine—via Pediatrics (6 years total)
    Pediatric Endocrinology (6 years total)
    Pediatric Gastroenterology (6 years total)
    Pediatric Hematology and Oncology (6 years total)
    Pediatric Infectious Disease (6 years total)
    Pediatric Nephrology (6 years total)
    Pediatric Pulmonology (6 years total)
    Pediatric Rheumatology (6 years total)
    Pediatric Sports Medicine (4 years total)
Pediatrics and Dermatology combined (5 years)
Pediatrics and Emergency Medicine combined (5 years)
Pediatrics and Medical Genetics Combined (5 years)
Pediatrics and Physical Medicine and Rehabilitation combined (5 years)
Pediatrics and Psychiatry combined (5 years)
Physical Medicine and Rehabilitation (4 years)
    Neuromuscular Medicine and OMM (6 years total)
    Pain Medicine (5 years total)
    Pediatric Rehabilitation Medicine (4 years total)
    Spinal Cord Injury Medicine (5 years total)
Plastic Surgery (6 years)
    Craniofacial Surgery (6 years total)
    Hand Surgery—via Plastic Surgery (6 years total)
Preventive Medicine (3 years)

Medical Toxicology (5 years total)
Psychiatry (4 years)
   Addiction Psychiatry (5 years total)
   Child and Adolescent Psychiatry (5 years total)
   Forensic Psychiatry (5 years total)
   Geriatric Psychiatry (5 years total)
   Pain Medicine (5 years total)
Public Health (4 years)
Radiation Oncology (5 years)
Radiology (diagnostic) (5 ycars)
   Abdominal Radiology (5 years total)
   Cardiothoracic Radiology (5 years total)
   Endovascular Surgical Neuroradiology (5 years total)
   Interventional (Vascular) Radiology (5 years total)
   Musculoskeletal Radiology (5 years total)
   Neuroradiology (5 years total)
   Nuclear Radiology (5 years total)
   Pediatric Radiology (5 years total)

Transitional Year (1 year)

Chapter References

1.   National Residency Matching Program (NRMP)
        Applicant by Type, Data Book 2006, pages 68, 69

2.   2004 Annual Report on Osteopathic Medical
        Education, AACOM page 22
        http://www.aacom.org/data/annualreport/index.html

3.   U.S. Medical School Graduates by Race and
        Ethnicity, AAMC Data Book 2006, page 27 and
        First Choice of Career Activity by Percent for
        Graduating U.S. Medical Students, AAMC Data
        Book 2006, page 35

The Nontraditional Applicant

The Nontraditional Applicant and Medical Student

Contributions to this section by Audrey Stanton, DO, MPH

Overview

Nontraditional applicants and medical students face some additional challenges during the application process and the medical school experience itself. Nontraditional applicants may already have families of their own or may be returning students who have been out of school for quite some time. Many have pursued an entirely different career previously. There are some advantages and disadvantages to being a nontraditional applicant and medical student.

Financial burdens

There are several aspects to the financial burden:

1. Giving up a well-paid job, retirement, and other benefits
2. Starting over with a student life and budget
3. Paying your bills (especially if you have a family) on a tight budget

It is a very difficult decision to give up a well-paid job, retirement, and health and other benefits and return to school for many years to become a physician. In the end, once a physician, things are not too bad, but what happens in the many years before that? It may take ten to fifteen years of your life, depending on where you are in the education process, before you will be earning your own physician's pay—that is a long time!

Giving up your current job is not only a difficult decision, but it also results in having to cut back to the student lifestyle due to a significant drop in income. Many times, it is possible to maintain a job part time while taking premed courses, but this is not always the case.

Also, at the latest during medical school itself, there is no more opportunity to maintain a job—part time or full time. Medical school is very time consuming, leaving minimal time for anything else, including employment. For many nontraditional students, this is even compounded. There is hardly any time available; yet, there is an increased need to spend time with a spouse and/or children.

If your spouse works, the financial burden may be lessened somewhat and you can focus on your studies during premed and medical school. Note that it is financially difficult to go through medical school supporting your entire family financially without an income. Financial aid provides for minimal living expenses based on single students without children. Some schools' financial aid packages can be adjusted for family expenses, but there are limits to what you can borrow.

In order to continue to pay your bills, there are several options:

1. Your spouse works and supports your family while you go to school.
2. You have sufficient savings and/or cashed out retirement or assets to last for the duration of school.
3. You have other extended family or friends who will help you out financially while you are in school.
4. You take out additional private loans with a cosigner to cover your living expenses.

Many nontraditional students go from full-time employment to medical school. The fact that you had previous income may limit your ability to get subsidized loans from the federal government when applying for financial aid, but shouldn't affect your ability to get loans overall. Even if you don't qualify for the subsidized portion of the loans your first year, after you have a tax year without working, you may then qualify depending on your spouse's income level.

Family and time constraints

As already mentioned, medical school leaves you little free time. This creates some challenges for medical students with families. Although much time is required to study and attend class, there still is time available to spend with family. It is most important to make a schedule (and abide by it) for class and study time and family time. There usually are a few hours available every day and some time on weekends that is actual free time but right before exams, this time becomes very limited and studying becomes very intense. Sometimes study demands mean that you don't see your family much right before exams.

You may have to sacrifice some of your own personal time and your own personal hobbies to spend more time with your family. Since time is very limited in medical school, it is really up to you on how you spend it. Also, a lot of it depends on what grades you are willing to accept. It takes much more time to get honors grades than it takes to pass, but there are also other considerations about grades in the "Medical School Experience" section of this book.

Make no mistake about it, medical school is hard and time intense. It requires that you and your family make sacrifices, especially your spouse. After many long hours spent at the library in preparation for exams, you will know what this feels like and there will be times when the strength of your relationship with your spouse and children will be tested. So, do not underestimate the intensity of this experience. It gets very hard at times, but it is temporary and things improve to acceptable levels again.

In comparison to the average working person, you are spending more time away from home, that's for sure. But depending on your study habits and ambitions, it varies from person to person. For most students, a sixty-hour week is probably about normal for most weeks, but it may approach eighty to one hundred hours per week easily when preparing for exams, and the prolonged hours can last for a week or two at a time.

Returning to school after a long time

Another challenge for many nontraditional students is the fact that they have not been in school for a long time. Most likely, any previous educational pursuit has been a while and it may even be challenging to return to take the required premed courses and the MCAT. A good way to get started back into premed may be a post-baccalaureate premed program if you have already completed a baccalaureate degree previously.

These programs specialize in preparing students for the MCAT while fulfilling the required premed course work. There are other options, such as returning to any college or university to take the remaining courses or starting over and graduating with a baccalaureate degree.

Keep in mind that tutoring programs are available for your premed pursuits and while in medical school. It may take you some time to get back into studying and learning how to study, but it is possible. Make sure you get the help you need. It is available.

If you did not complete a degree the first time you went to college, some of your course work may have expired after a certain number of years and is no longer recognized for credit or transfer to another college or university. In some instances, this can also happen if you did complete your degree. For example, having completed physics, general chemistry, organic chemistry, and general biology courses twenty years ago may not be enough to fulfill those prerequisites for medical school today, even if you graduated with a biology degree then.

Specifically related to MCAT preparation, many nontraditional students who have been out of school for a while find MCAT prep courses (such as those offered by Kaplan) to be a good systematic review and preparation for the MCAT. However, keep in mind that if you have been out of school for many years, the MCAT prep course will not be sufficient to teach you what you need to know. These courses are only review courses for students who have just recently completed all of the required premed courses and are not intended to teach you new concepts you have never heard before (or concepts you studied a decade ago and hardly remember).

Another issue for returning premeds is related to recommendation letters if they have been out of school for a long time. Most professors will not remember you and will be unable to write effective letters for you.

It is important to focus on getting good *new* recommendation letters from the professors when you take any courses in preparation for medical school. If you are only taking the very basics to qualify for medical school admissions (general chemistry, physics, organic chemistry, general biology), then you will have to focus on getting good letters from at least two of those professors. Also, most of the medical schools require a premed committee letter to be sent, so be sure to find out about any available premed advisors and committees at your institution so you can get this letter. As is true for any recommendation letter, provide the letter writer with a current resume to make it easier for the letter writer to mention your other accomplishments and circumstances in the letter. This is probably even more important if you are a nontraditional applicant.

Medical school application

Medical schools have been looking favorably at applicants who have prior life experience as nontraditional students have. Nontraditional students have a unique view and many experiences with society, people, and work. Most of them have made significant sacrifices and put a lot of energy into pursuing medicine. It is very apparent that they are serious about pursuing medicine.

Many applicants who do not have this perspective may have decided one day that medicine sounds like a cool field to be in, so they signed up for it. Their commitment may not be as strong as that of a nontraditional applicant who has made all sorts of sacrifices to be there. In general, being a nontraditional applicant can be very positive, in most cases.

It is important to promote your experiences in your application and interviews and explain how your background makes you a great applicant. Think of how these and your unique life have shaped you, and use them to make yourself stand out. If you started out in college with a less-than-stellar GPA, point out grade improvements over time. If there was an extenuating circumstance behind some of the grades, it might be helpful to mention it but beware of coming across as whiny or looking as if you are making excuses for yourself.

Family support

There is also a positive side to having a spouse and family while going through premed and medical school. A spouse and children can bring some balance and force relaxation time into your life. Your spouse and children can also support you. One person once told me, "I couldn't have gone through medical school without my family. I don't know how people do it without family." You can share your troubles and cares with your spouse, and have instant cheerleaders who care about you.

There is no way to truly prepare for all of the trials and adjustments that go along with medical school, but there are things that can be done to help. It is a good idea to talk with current medical students and their families to see what problems they had to address and what worked for them.

Medical spouses and medical students have given a variety of suggestions on SDN:

> "My partner is an M4 (fourth year medical student). We've talked about this issue quite a bit and the things she appreciated the most in the last three years were... First, I do the majority of the housework, bill paying, shopping, cooking, etc., which means when she does have a little

free time, we can do something fun together instead of chores. During a couple of the less intense rotations (e.g., family practice, peds), she pitched in as much as she could. Second, I have my own group of friends, so I'm not always waiting around for her to finish studying so we can do something. That takes a lot of pressure off of her, and she doesn't feel guilty about neglecting me. I choose to do more active things with my friends (sports, street fairs, etc.) and save mellow activities, like going to the movies, with my partner. Of course, I think it's important to talk this out too, so your partner realizes you still WANT to spend time with him or her, but that you are just trying to give him or her the time needed for the demands of medical school."

—blueskytraveler (SDN forum member)

"What I hear the most that the student would like is more patience/understanding. The cycle can be bad for relationships that aren't strong. The medical student studies, so he or she can't spend time with significant other so the significant other is short-tempered when they do have time together, which leads the medical student to study and be gone more."

—Wifty (SDN forum member)

"Understand when he or she doesn't have time for cleaning, etc. It's good to have your own life, but don't forget to plan stuff with just him or her. Just be there."

— Gwyn779 (SDN forum member)

"While I completely understand a desire to avoid all of the 'gross medical stuff' and, actually, all scientific-related junk altogether (I'm the liberal-arts major in the relationship!), it has helped that my husband DOES share what he does with me. I still remember how ecstatic he was the first time he came home from anatomy lab. It sounded (and SMELLED) disgusting, but looking at the enthusiasm in his eyes helped me to know that we had made the right decision, that our sacrifices were worth it. As he studied for various tests/the

USMLE, etc., I helped him study with flashcards. Now that he is on rotations, we discuss some of his more interesting/ troubling cases. You get the idea. Essentially, while it may bore me silly sometimes (and often grosses me out), it makes me feel like a true part of this process."

—k's mom (SDN forum member)

A common theme is that both the student and the family be willing to give and take and to communicate their needs and frustrations. The family has no way to really understand what the student is going through, and the student doesn't have a full understanding of the frustrations felt by family members.

Having a parent in medical school can be a difficult situation for a child, especially during the clinical years when the student has no control over their schedule. It is not unusual for a child to try to make the parent feel guilty for their time away from home. Whenever possible, include your children in the process—and get creative. Elementary aged and older kids can quiz you from flashcards and study guides, or they can simply do their homework with you while you're studying.

You can practice your clinical skills, such as taking blood pressures and using your otoscope and ophthalmoscope, on them. Some schools seek children to be model patients for clinical skills labs, which can be a fun process for various ages. They can also be involved by helping to bring you picnic lunches and dinners if you're stuck at school studying all weekend. These kinds of activities not only give you more time with your children, but they also let the kids feel involved in the process.

Useful Medical School Statistics

U.S. (MD) schools with the highest number of out-of-state applicants (2005)

Applicants	Interviewed		Accepted		Medical School	City, State
10058	0	0.00%	174	1.70%	George Washington University S	Washington, DC
8853	942	10.60%	132	1.50%	Boston University School of Me	Boston, MA
8380	1183	14.10%	168	2.00%	Drexel University College of M	Philadelphia, PA
7915	1298	16.40%	187	2.40%	Georgetown University School o	Washington, DC
7634	624	8.20%	107	1.40%	Tufts University School of Med	Boston, MA
7267	746	10.30%	130	1.80%	New York Medical College	Valhalla, NY
6670	506	7.60%	150	2.20%	Jefferson Medical College of T	Philadelphia, PA
6602	753	11.40%	113	1.70%	Tulane University School of Me	New Orleans, LA
6575	549	8.30%	94	1.40%	New York University School of	New York, NY
6460	725	11.20%	83	1.30%	Temple University School of Me	Philadelphia, PA
6445	348	5.40%	75	1.20%	Loyola University Chicago Stri	Maywood, IL
5963	669	11.20%	126	2.10%	Northwestern University, The F	Chicago, IL
5868	511	8.70%	66	1.10%	University of Chicago Division	Chicago, IL
5523	533	9.70%	109	2.00%	Johns Hopkins University Schoo	Baltimore, MD
5515	0	0.00%	147	2.70%	Chicago Medical School at Rosa	North Chicago, IL
5363	386	7.20%	64	1.20%	Wake Forest University School	Winston-Salem, NC
5342	652	12.20%	141	2.60%	Harvard Medical School	Boston, MA
5321	528	9.90%	72	1.40%	Albany Medical College	Albany, NY
5252	843	16.10%	105	2.00%	Saint Louis University School	St. Louis, MO
5099	520	10.20%	108	2.10%	Medical College of Wisconsin	Milwaukee, WI
5080	515	10.10%	59	1.20%	University of Vermont College	Burlington, VT
5046	484	9.60%	66	1.30%	Mount Sinai School of Medicine	New York, NY
4921	653	13.30%	110	2.20%	University of Pennsylvania Sch	Philadelphia, PA
4898	940	19.20%	100	2.00%	Albert Einstein College of Med	Bronx, NY
4877	613	12.60%	78	1.60%	Emory University School of Med	Atlanta, GA
4786	1001	20.90%	119	2.50%	Columbia University College of	New York, NY
4741	711	15.00%	85	1.80%	Duke University School of Medi	Durham, NC
4698	447	9.50%	108	2.30%	Creighton University School of	Omaha, NE
4662	662	14.20%	78	1.70%	Pennsylvania State University	Hershey, PA
4465	710	15.90%	125	2.80%	University of Pittsburgh Schoo	Pittsburgh, PA
4437	590	13.30%	75	1.70%	Dartmouth Medical School	Hanover, NH
4259	728	17.10%	91	2.10%	Yale University School of Medi	New Haven, CT
4247	278	6.50%	64	1.50%	Brown Medical School	Providence, RI
4213	610	14.50%	123	2.90%	Case Western Reserve Universit	Cleveland, OH
4110	298	7.30%	115	2.80%	Howard University College of M	Washington, DC

4078	606	14.90%	67	1.60%	Joan & Sanford I. Weill Medica	New York, NY
4019	333	8.30%	81	2.00%	Virginia Commonwealth Universi	Richmond, VA
4017	1013	25.20%	91	2.30%	Vanderbilt University School o	Nashville, TN
3992	595	14.90%	99	2.50%	University of Michigan Medical	Ann Arbor, MI
3842	1144	29.80%	117	3.00%	Washington University in St. L	St. Louis, MO
3579	297	8.30%	54	1.50%	Stanford University School of	Stanford, CA
3253	256	7.90%	86	2.60%	University of Illinois College	Chicago, IL
3201	345	10.80%	44	1.40%	Oregon Health & Science Univer	Portland, OR
3120	407	13.00%	91	2.90%	Ohio State University College	Columbus, OH
3097	474	15.30%	63	2.00%	University of Rochester School	Rochester, NY
2996	0	0.00%	28	0.90%	UMDNJNew Jersey Medical Sc	Newark, NJ
2980	250	8.40%	27	0.90%	University of Maryland School	Baltimore, MD
2966	0	0.00%	68	2.30%	Meharry Medical College	Nashville, TN
2927	65	2.20%	22	0.80%	Rush Medical College of Rush U	Chicago, IL
2903	274	9.40%	49	1.70%	University of Virginia School	Charlottesville, VA
2877	240	8.30%	42	1.50%	Baylor College of Medicine	Houston, TX
2669	326	12.20%	37	1.40%	Eastern Virginia Medical Schoo	Norfolk, VA
2567	217	8.50%	27	1.10%	David Geffen School of Medicin	Los Angeles, CA
2560	0	0.00%	28	1.10%	University of California, San	San Francisco, CA
2550	250	9.80%	32	1.30%	Mayo Medical School	Rochester, MN
2480	279	11.30%	40	1.60%	University of Cincinnati Colle	Cincinnati, OH
2447	100	4.10%	32	1.30%	University of Miami Leonard M.	Miami, FL
2298	108	4.70%	20	0.90%	University of North Carolina a	Chapel Hill, NC
2292	100	4.40%	16	0.70%	University of Washington Schoo	Seattle, WA
2252	200	8.90%	20	0.90%	University of Connecticut Scho	Farmington, CT
2245	158	7.00%	47	2.10%	Keck School of Medicine of the	Los Angeles, CA
2173	233	10.70%	56	2.60%	University of Minnesota Medica	Minneapolis, MN
2165	377	17.40%	45	2.10%	University of Iowa Roy J. and	Iowa City, IA
2140	160	7.50%	25	1.20%	Michigan State University Coll	East Lansing, MI
1973	126	6.40%	29	1.50%	University of Wisconsin Medica	Madison, WI
1916	243	12.70%	35	1.80%	University of Colorado Health	Denver, CO
1872	178	9.50%	52	2.80%	Medical University of Ohio at	Toledo, OH
1841	178	9.70%	29	1.60%	Wayne State University School	Detroit, MI
1816	133	7.30%	27	1.50%	UMDNJ-Robert Wood Johnson	Piscataway, NJ
1794	107	6.00%	10	0.60%	University of California, San	La Jolla, CA
1774	148	8.30%	22	1.20%	Morehouse School of Medicine	Atlanta, GA
1742	80	4.60%	10	0.60%	Wright State University School	Dayton, OH
1686	195	11.60%	89	5.30%	Loma Linda University School o	Loma Linda, CA
1589	469	29.50%	164		Uniformed Services U of the He	Bethesda, MD

1483	217	14.60%	24	1.60%	State University of New York D	Brooklyn, NY
1335	268	20.10%	33	2.50%	State University of New York U	Syracuse, NY
1308	89	6.80%	29	2.20%	University of Louisville Schoo	Louisville, KY
1272	125	9.80%	16	1.30%	University of Alabama School o	Birmingham, AL
1157	116	10.00%	9	0.80%	University of Hawaii John A. B	Honolulu, HI
1144	136	11.90%	33	2.90%	University of Kansas School of	Kansas City, KS
1120	164	14.60%	41	3.70%	West Virginia University Schoo	Morgantown, WV
1116	88	7.90%	23	2.10%	University at Buffalo State Un	Buffalo, NY
1009	28	2.80%	8	0.80%	Medical University of South Ca	Charleston, SC
979	60	6.10%	9	0.90%	University of South Carolina S	Columbia, SC
839	57	6.80%	9	1.10%	Stony Brook University Health	Stony Brook, NY
831	30	3.60%	5	0.60%	University of Florida College	Gainesville, FL
793	95	12.00%	18	2.30%	University of Nebraska College	Omaha, NE
779	16	2.10%	4	0.50%	University of California, Davi	Sacramento, CA
774	36	4.70%	5	0.60%	University of New Mexico Schoo	Albuquerque, NM
749	10	1.30%	2	0.30%	Medical College of Georgia Sch	Augusta, GA
717	121	16.90%	39	5.40%	University of Texas Southweste	Dallas, TX
716	44	6.10%	11	1.50%	East Tennessee State Universit	Johnson City, TN
715	36	5.00%	10	1.40%	University of Nevada School of	Reno, NV
647	161	24.90%	28	4.30%	University of Utah School of M	Salt Lake City, UT
620	31	5.00%	17	2.70%	University of Oklahoma College	Oklahoma City, OK
620	74	11.90%	29	4.70%	University of Kentucky College	Lexington, KY
618	38	6.10%	11	1.80%	Joan C. Edwards School of Medi	Huntington, WV
573	26	4.50%	2	0.30%	University of South Dakota Sch	Sioux Falls, SD
558	76	13.60%	13	2.30%	University of MissouriColumbi	Columbia, MO
550	3	0.50%	2	0.40%	University of California, Irvi	Irvine, CA
539	0	0.00%	7	1.30%	University of Texas Medical Sc	Houston, TX
522	7	1.30%	5	1.00%	Northeastern Ohio Universities	Rootstown, OH
515	12	2.30%	7	1.40%	University of South Florida Co	Tampa, FL
500	151	30.20%	9	1.80%	University of Texas Medical Sc	San Antonio, TX
487	51	10.50%	9	1.80%	University of Tennessee Health	Memphis, TN
449	0	0.00%	9	2.00%	University of South Alabama Co	Mobile, AL
435	84	19.30%	12	2.80%	University of Texas Medical Br	Galveston, TX
427	69	16.20%	9	2.10%	University of Arkansas for Med	Little Rock, AR
368	40	10.90%	9	2.40%	Texas A & M University System	College Station, TX
327	28	8.60%	10	3.10%	Texas Tech University Health S	Lubbock, TX
262	96	36.60%	32		University of Missouri-Kansas	Kansas City, MO
245	2	0.80%	1	0.40%	Louisiana State University Sch	Shreveport, LA
206	14	6.80%	1	0.50%	University of Arizona College	Tucson, AZ

204	16	7.80%	5	2.50%	Louisiana State University Sch	New Orleans, LA
151	0	0.00%	0	0.00%	Florida State U College of Med	Tallahassee, FL
123	60	48.80%	17		University of North Dakota Sch	Grand Forks, ND
122	16	13.10%	2	1.60%	University of Massachusetts Me	Worcester, MA
118	0	0.00%	0	0.00%	Brody School of Medicine at Ea	Greenville, NC
40	3	7.50%	0	0.00%	Southern Illinois University S	Springfield, IL
6	0	0.00%	0	0.00%	Mercer University School of Me	Macon, GA

U.S. (MD) schools with the highest out-of-state acceptance rates (2005)

Applicants	Accepted		Medical School	City, State
123	17	13.80%	University of North Dakota Sch	Grand Forks, ND
262	32	12.20%	University of Missouri-Kansas	Kansas City, MO
1589	164	10.30%	Uniformed Services U of the He	Bethesda, MD
717	39	5.40%	University of Texas Southweste	Dallas, TX
1686	89	5.30%	Loma Linda University School o	Loma Linda, CA
620	29	4.70%	University of Kentucky College	Lexington, KY
647	28	4.30%	University of Utah School of M	Salt Lake City, UT
1120	41	3.70%	West Virginia University Schoo	Morgantown, WV
327	10	3.10%	Texas Tech University Health S	Lubbock, TX
3842	117	3.00%	Washington University in St. L	St. Louis, MO
4213	123	2.90%	Case Western Reserve Universit	Cleveland, OH
3120	91	2.90%	Ohio State University College	Columbus, OH
1144	33	2.90%	University of Kansas School of	Kansas City, KS
4465	125	2.80%	University of Pittsburgh Schoo	Pittsburgh, PA
4110	115	2.80%	Howard University College of M	Washington, DC
1872	52	2.80%	Medical University of Ohio at	Toledo, OH
435	12	2.80%	University of Texas Medical Br	Galveston, TX
620	17	2.70%	University of Oklahoma College	Oklahoma City, OK
5515	147	2.70%	Chicago Medical School at Rosa	North Chicago, IL
3253	86	2.60%	University of Illinois College	Chicago, IL
5342	141	2.60%	Harvard Medical School	Boston, MA
2173	56	2.60%	University of Minnesota Medica	Minneapolis, MN
4786	119	2.50%	Columbia University College of	New York, NY
3992	99	2.50%	University of Michigan Medical	Ann Arbor, MI
1335	33	2.50%	State University of New York U	Syracuse, NY
204	5	2.50%	Louisiana State University Sch	New Orleans, LA
368	9	2.40%	Texas A & M University System	College Station, TX
7915	187	2.40%	Georgetown University School o	Washington, DC
558	13	2.30%	University of Missouri-Columbi	Columbia, MO
4698	108	2.30%	Creighton University School of	Omaha, NE
2966	68	2.30%	Meharry Medical College	Nashville, TN
793	18	2.30%	University of Nebraska College	Omaha, NE
4017	91	2.30%	Vanderbilt University School o	Nashville, TN
6670	150	2.20%	Jefferson Medical College of T	Philadelphia, PA
4921	110	2.20%	University of Pennsylvania Sch	Philadelphia, PA
1308	29	2.20%	University of Louisville Schoo	Louisville, KY

4259	91	**2.10%**	Yale University School of Medi	New Haven, CT
5099	108	**2.10%**	Medical College of Wisconsin	Milwaukee, WI
5963	126	**2.10%**	Northwestern University, The F	Chicago, IL
427	9	**2.10%**	University of Arkansas for Med	Little Rock, AR
2245	47	**2.10%**	Keck School of Medicine of the	Los Angeles, CA
2165	45	**2.10%**	University of Iowa Roy J. and	Iowa City, IA
1116	23	**2.10%**	University at Buffalo State Un	Buffalo, NY
4898	100	**2.00%**	Albert Einstein College of Med	Bronx, NY
3097	63	**2.00%**	University of Rochester School	Rochester, NY
4019	81	**2.00%**	Virginia Commonwealth Universi	Richmond, VA
8380	168	**2.00%**	Drexel University College of M	Philadelphia, PA
449	9	**2.00%**	University of South Alabama Co	Mobile, AL
5252	105	**2.00%**	Saint Louis University School	St. Louis, MO
5523	109	**2.00%**	Johns Hopkins University Schoo	Baltimore, MD
487	9	**1.80%**	University of Tennessee Health	Memphis, TN
1916	35	**1.80%**	University of Colorado Health	Denver, CO
500	9	**1.80%**	University of Texas Medical Sc	San Antonio, TX
4741	85	**1.80%**	Duke University School of Medi	Durham, NC
7267	130	**1.80%**	New York Medical College	Valhalla, NY
618	11	**1.80%**	Joan C. Edwards School of Medi	Huntington, WV
10058	174	**1.70%**	George Washington University S	Washington, DC
6602	113	**1.70%**	Tulane University School of Me	New Orleans, LA
4437	75	**1.70%**	Dartmouth Medical School	Hanover, NH
2903	49	**1.70%**	University of Virginia School	Charlottesville, VA
4662	78	**1.70%**	Pennsylvania State University	Hershey, PA
4078	67	**1.60%**	Joan & Sanford I. Weill Medica	New York, NY
122	2	**1.60%**	University of Massachusetts Me	Worcester, MA
1483	24	**1.60%**	State University of New York D	Brooklyn, NY
2480	40	**1.60%**	University of Cincinnati Colle	Cincinnati, OH
4877	78	**1.60%**	Emory University School of Med	Atlanta, GA
1841	29	**1.60%**	Wayne State University School	Detroit, MI
716	11	**1.50%**	East Tennessee State Universit	Johnson City, TN
3579	54	**1.50%**	Stanford University School of	Stanford, CA
4247	64	**1.50%**	Brown Medical School	Providence, RI
8853	132	**1.50%**	Boston University School of Me	Boston, MA
1816	27	**1.50%**	UMDNJ-Robert Wood Johnson	Piscataway, NJ
1973	29	**1.50%**	University of Wisconsin Medica	Madison, WI
2877	42	**1.50%**	Baylor College of Medicine	Houston, TX
6575	94	**1.40%**	New York University School of	New York, NY

7634	107	**1.40%**	Tufts University School of Med	Boston, MA
715	10	**1.40%**	University of Nevada School of	Reno, NV
2669	37	**1.40%**	Eastern Virginia Medical Schoo	Norfolk, VA
3201	44	**1.40%**	Oregon Health & Science Univer	Portland, OR
515	7	**1.40%**	University of South Florida Co	Tampa, FL
5321	72	**1.40%**	Albany Medical College	Albany, NY
5046	66	**1.30%**	Mount Sinai School of Medicine	New York, NY
2447	32	**1.30%**	University of Miami Leonard M.	Miami, FL
539	7	**1.30%**	University of Texas Medical Sc	Houston, TX
6460	83	**1.30%**	Temple University School of Me	Philadelphia, PA
1272	16	**1.30%**	University of Alabama School o	Birmingham, AL
2550	32	**1.30%**	Mayo Medical School	Rochester, MN
1774	22	**1.20%**	Morehouse School of Medicine	Atlanta, GA
5363	64	**1.20%**	Wake Forest University School	Winston-Salem, NC
2140	25	**1.20%**	Michigan State University Coll	East Lansing, MI
6445	75	**1.20%**	Loyola University Chicago Stri	Maywood, IL
5080	59	**1.20%**	University of Vermont College	Burlington, VT
5868	66	**1.10%**	University of Chicago Division	Chicago, IL
2560	28	**1.10%**	University of California, San	San Francisco, CA
839	9	**1.10%**	Stony Brook University Health	Stony Brook, NY
2567	27	**1.10%**	David Geffen School of Medicin	Los Angeles, CA
522	5	**1.00%**	Northeastern Ohio Universities	Rootstown, OH
2996	28	**0.90%**	UMDNJ New Jersey Medical Scho	Newark, NJ
979	9	**0.90%**	University of South Carolina S	Columbia, SC
2980	27	**0.90%**	University of Maryland School	Baltimore, MD
2252	20	**0.90%**	University of Connecticut Scho	Farmington, CT
2298	20	**0.90%**	University of North Carolina a	Chapel Hill, NC
1009	8	**0.80%**	Medical University of South Ca	Charleston, SC
1157	9	**0.80%**	University of Hawaii John A. B	Honolulu, HI
2927	22	**0.80%**	Rush Medical College of Rush U	Chicago, IL
2292	16	**0.70%**	University of Washington Schoo	Seattle, WA
774	5	**0.60%**	University of New Mexico Schoo	Albuquerque, NM
831	5	**0.60%**	University of Florida College	Gainesville, FL
1742	10	**0.60%**	Wright State University School	Dayton, OH
1794	10	**0.60%**	University of California, San	La Jolla, CA
779	4	**0.50%**	University of California, Davi	Sacramento, CA
206	1	**0.50%**	University of Arizona College	Tucson, AZ
245	1	**0.40%**	Louisiana State University Sch	Shreveport, LA
550	2	**0.40%**	University of California, Irvi	Irvine, CA

| 573 | 2 | **0.30%** | University of South Dakota Sch | Sioux Falls, SD |
| 749 | 2 | **0.30%** | Medical College of Georgia Sch | Augusta, GA |

U.S. (MD) schools with the highest acceptance of out-of-state interviewees (2005)

Interviewed	Admitted		Medical School	City, State
7	5	71.40%	Northeastern Ohio Universities	Rootstown, OH
3	2	66.70%	University of California, Irvi	Irvine, CA
12	7	58.30%	University of South Florida Co	Tampa, FL
31	17	54.80%	University of Oklahoma College	Oklahoma City, OK
2	1	50.00%	Louisiana State University Sch	Shreveport, LA
195	89	45.60%	Loma Linda University School o	Loma Linda, CA
74	29	39.20%	University of Kentucky College	Lexington, KY
298	115	38.60%	Howard University College of M	Washington, DC
28	10	35.70%	Texas Tech University Health S	Lubbock, TX
469	164	35.00%	Uniformed Services U of the He	Bethesda, MD
65	22	33.80%	Rush Medical College of Rush U	Chicago, IL
256	86	33.60%	University of Illinois College	Chicago, IL
96	32	33.30%	University of Missouri-Kansas	Kansas City, MO
89	29	32.60%	University of Louisville Schoo	Louisville, KY
121	39	32.20%	University of Texas Southweste	Dallas, TX
100	32	32.00%	University of Miami Leonard M.	Miami, FL
16	5	31.30%	Louisiana State University Sch	New Orleans, LA
158	47	29.70%	Keck School of Medicine of the	Los Angeles, CA
506	150	29.60%	Jefferson Medical College of T	Philadelphia, PA
178	52	29.20%	Medical University of Ohio at	Toledo, OH
38	11	28.90%	Joan C. Edwards School of Medi	Huntington, WV
28	8	28.60%	Medical University of South Ca	Charleston, SC
60	17	28.30%	University of North Dakota Sch	Grand Forks, ND
36	10	27.80%	University of Nevada School of	Reno, NV
88	23	26.10%	University at Buffalo State Un	Buffalo, NY
44	11	25.00%	East Tennessee State Universit	Johnson City, TN
16	4	25.00%	University of California, Davi	Sacramento, CA
164	41	25.00%	West Virginia University Schoo	Morgantown, WV
333	81	24.30%	Virginia Commonwealth Universi	Richmond, VA
136	33	24.30%	University of Kansas School of	Kansas City, KS
447	108	24.20%	Creighton University School of	Omaha, NE
233	56	24.00%	University of Minnesota Medica	Minneapolis, MN
278	64	23.00%	Brown Medical School	Providence, RI
126	29	23.00%	University of Wisconsin Medica	Madison, WI
40	9	22.50%	Texas A & M University System	College Station, TX

407	91	22.40%	Ohio State University College	Columbus, OH
652	141	21.60%	Harvard Medical School	Boston, MA
348	75	21.60%	Loyola University Chicago Stri	Maywood, IL
520	108	20.80%	Medical College of Wisconsin	Milwaukee, WI
533	109	20.50%	Johns Hopkins University Schoo	Baltimore, MD
133	27	20.30%	UMDNJ-Robert Wood Johnson	Piscataway, NJ
610	123	20.20%	Case Western Reserve Universit	Cleveland, OH
10	2	20.00%	Medical College of Georgia Sch	Augusta, GA
95	18	18.90%	University of Nebraska College	Omaha, NE
669	126	18.80%	Northwestern University, The F	Chicago, IL
108	20	18.50%	University of North Carolina a	Chapel Hill, NC
297	54	18.20%	Stanford University School of	Stanford, CA
274	49	17.90%	University of Virginia School	Charlottesville, VA
51	9	17.60%	University of Tennessee Health	Memphis, TN
710	125	17.60%	University of Pittsburgh Schoo	Pittsburgh, PA
240	42	17.50%	Baylor College of Medicine	Houston, TX
746	130	17.40%	New York Medical College	Valhalla, NY
161	28	17.40%	University of Utah School of M	Salt Lake City, UT
624	107	17.10%	Tufts University School of Med	Boston, MA
549	94	17.10%	New York University School of	New York, NY
76	13	17.10%	University of Missouri-Columbi	Columbia, MO
653	110	16.80%	University of Pennsylvania Sch	Philadelphia, PA
30	5	16.70%	University of Florida College	Gainesville, FL
595	99	16.60%	University of Michigan Medical	Ann Arbor, MI
386	64	16.60%	Wake Forest University School	Winston-Salem, NC
178	29	16.30%	Wayne State University School	Detroit, MI
100	16	16.00%	University of Washington Schoo	Seattle, WA
57	9	15.80%	Stony Brook University Health	Stony Brook, NY
160	25	15.60%	Michigan State University Coll	East Lansing, MI
753	113	15.00%	Tulane University School of Me	New Orleans, LA
60	9	15.00%	University of South Carolina S	Columbia, SC
148	22	14.90%	Morehouse School of Medicine	Atlanta, GA
1298	187	14.40%	Georgetown University School o	Washington, DC
243	35	14.40%	University of Colorado Health	Denver, CO
279	40	14.30%	University of Cincinnati Colle	Cincinnati, OH
84	12	14.30%	University of Texas Medical Br	Galveston, TX
1183	168	14.20%	Drexel University College of M	Philadelphia, PA
942	132	14.00%	Boston University School of Me	Boston, MA
36	5	13.90%	University of New Mexico Schoo	Albuquerque, NM

528	72	**13.60%**	Albany Medical College	Albany, NY
484	66	**13.60%**	Mount Sinai School of Medicine	New York, NY
474	63	**13.30%**	University of Rochester School	Rochester, NY
69	9	**13.00%**	University of Arkansas for Med	Little Rock, AR
511	66	**12.90%**	University of Chicago Division	Chicago, IL
250	32	**12.80%**	Mayo Medical School	Rochester, MN
125	16	**12.80%**	University of Alabama School o	Birmingham, AL
345	44	**12.80%**	Oregon Health & Science Univer	Portland, OR
613	78	**12.70%**	Emory University School of Med	Atlanta, GA
590	75	**12.70%**	Dartmouth Medical School	Hanover, NH
728	91	**12.50%**	Yale University School of Medi	New Haven, CT
16	2	**12.50%**	University of Massachusetts Me	Worcester, MA
80	10	**12.50%**	Wright State University School	Dayton, OH
843	105	**12.50%**	Saint Louis University School	St. Louis, MO
217	27	**12.40%**	David Geffen School of Medicin	Los Angeles, CA
268	33	**12.30%**	State University of New York U	Syracuse, NY
711	85	**12.00%**	Duke University School of Medi	Durham, NC
377	45	**11.90%**	University of Iowa Roy J. and	Iowa City, IA
1001	119	**11.90%**	Columbia University College of	New York, NY
662	78	**11.80%**	Pennsylvania State University	Hershey, PA
515	59	**11.50%**	University of Vermont College	Burlington, VT
725	83	**11.40%**	Temple University School of Me	Philadelphia, PA
326	37	**11.30%**	Eastern Virginia Medical Schoo	Norfolk, VA
217	24	**11.10%**	State University of New York D	Brooklyn, NY
606	67	**11.10%**	Joan & Sanford I. Weill Medica	New York, NY
250	27	**10.80%**	University of Maryland School	Baltimore, MD
940	100	**10.60%**	Albert Einstein College of Med	Bronx, NY
1144	117	**10.20%**	Washington University in St. L	St. Louis, MO
200	20	**10.00%**	University of Connecticut Scho	Farmington, CT
107	10	**9.30%**	University of California, San	La Jolla, CA
1013	91	**9.00%**	Vanderbilt University School o	Nashville, TN
116	9	**7.80%**	University of Hawaii John A. B	Honolulu, HI
26	2	**7.70%**	University of South Dakota Sch	Sioux Falls, SD
14	1	**7.10%**	University of Arizona College	Tucson, AZ
151	9	**6.00%**	University of Texas Medical Sc	San Antonio, TX

U.S. (MD) schools with the most out-of-state spots filled (2005)

Applicants	Accepted		Medical School	City, State
7915	187	2.40%	Georgetown University School o	Washington, DC
10058	174	1.70%	George Washington University S	Washington, DC
8380	168	2.00%	Drexel University College of M	Philadelphia, PA
1589	164	10.30%	Uniformed Services U of the He	Bethesda, MD
6670	150	2.20%	Jefferson Medical College of T	Philadelphia, PA
5515	147	2.70%	Chicago Medical School at Rosa	North Chicago, IL
5342	141	2.60%	Harvard Medical School	Boston, MA
8853	132	1.50%	Boston University School of Me	Boston, MA
7267	130	1.80%	New York Medical College	Valhalla, NY
5963	126	2.10%	Northwestern University, The F	Chicago, IL
4465	125	2.80%	University of Pittsburgh Schoo	Pittsburgh, PA
4213	123	2.90%	Case Western Reserve Universit	Cleveland, OH
4786	119	2.50%	Columbia University College of	New York, NY
3842	117	3.00%	Washington University in St. L	St. Louis, MO
4110	115	2.80%	Howard University College of M	Washington, DC
6602	113	1.70%	Tulane University School of Me	New Orleans, LA
4921	110	2.20%	University of Pennsylvania Sch	Philadelphia, PA
5523	109	2.00%	Johns Hopkins University Schoo	Baltimore, MD
4698	108	2.30%	Creighton University School of	Omaha, NE
5099	108	2.10%	Medical College of Wisconsin	Milwaukee, WI
7634	107	1.40%	Tufts University School of Med	Boston, MA
5252	105	2.00%	Saint Louis University School	St. Louis, MO
4898	100	2.00%	Albert Einstein College of Med	Bronx, NY
3992	99	2.50%	University of Michigan Medical	Ann Arbor, MI
6575	94	1.40%	New York University School of	New York, NY
3120	91	2.90%	Ohio State University College	Columbus, OH
4259	91	2.10%	Yale University School of Medi	New Haven, CT
4017	91	2.30%	Vanderbilt University School o	Nashville, TN
1686	89	5.30%	Loma Linda University School o	Loma Linda, CA
3253	86	2.60%	University of Illinois College	Chicago, IL
4741	85	1.80%	Duke University School of Medi	Durham, NC
6460	83	1.30%	Temple University School of Me	Philadelphia, PA
4019	81	2.00%	Virginia Commonwealth Universi	Richmond, VA
4662	78	1.70%	Pennsylvania State University	Hershey, PA
4877	78	1.60%	Emory University School of Med	Atlanta, GA
6445	75	1.20%	Loyola University Chicago Stri	Maywood, IL

4437	75	1.70%	Dartmouth Medical School	Hanover, NH
5321	72	1.40%	Albany Medical College	Albany, NY
2966	68	2.30%	Meharry Medical College	Nashville, TN
4078	67	1.60%	Joan & Sanford I. Weill Medica	New York, NY
5868	66	1.10%	University of Chicago Division	Chicago, IL
5046	66	1.30%	Mount Sinai School of Medicine	New York, NY
4247	64	1.50%	Brown Medical School	Providence, RI
5363	64	1.20%	Wake Forest University School	Winston-Salem, NC
3097	63	2.00%	University of Rochester School	Rochester, NY
5080	59	1.20%	University of Vermont College	Burlington, VT
2173	56	2.60%	University of Minnesota Medica	Minneapolis, MN
3579	54	1.50%	Stanford University School of	Stanford, CA
1872	52	2.80%	Medical University of Ohio at	Toledo, OH
2903	49	1.70%	University of Virginia School	Charlottesville, VA
2245	47	2.10%	Keck School of Medicine of the	Los Angeles, CA
2165	45	2.10%	University of Iowa Roy J. and	Iowa City, IA
3201	44	1.40%	Oregon Health & Science Univer	Portland, OR
2877	42	1.50%	Baylor College of Medicine	Houston, TX
1120	41	3.70%	West Virginia University Schoo	Morgantown, WV
2480	40	1.60%	University of Cincinnati Colle	Cincinnati, OH
717	39	5.40%	University of Texas Southweste	Dallas, TX
2669	37	1.40%	Eastern Virginia Medical Schoo	Norfolk, VA
1916	35	1.80%	University of Colorado Health	Denver, CO
1335	33	2.50%	State University of New York U	Syracuse, NY
1144	33	2.90%	University of Kansas School of	Kansas City, KS
262	32	12.20%	University of Missouri-Kansas	Kansas City, MO
2447	32	1.30%	University of Miami Leonard M.	Miami, FL
2550	32	1.30%	Mayo Medical School	Rochester, MN
1308	29	2.20%	University of Louisville Schoo	Louisville, KY
1841	29	1.60%	Wayne State University School	Detroit, MI
1973	29	1.50%	University of Wisconsin Medica	Madison, WI
620	29	4.70%	University of Kentucky College	Lexington, KY
2560	28	1.10%	University of California, San	San Francisco, CA
647	28	4.30%	University of Utah School of M	Salt Lake City, UT
2996	28	0.90%	UMDNJNew Jersey Medical Scho	Newark, NJ
2980	27	0.90%	University of Maryland School	Baltimore, MD
2567	27	1.10%	David Geffen School of Medicin	Los Angeles, CA
1816	27	1.50%	UMDNJRobert Wood Johnson	Piscataway, NJ
2140	25	1.20%	Michigan State University Coll	East Lansing, MI

1483	24	1.60%	State University of New York D	Brooklyn, NY
1116	23	2.10%	University at Buffalo State Un	Buffalo, NY
2927	22	0.80%	Rush Medical College of Rush U	Chicago, IL
1774	22	1.20%	Morehouse School of Medicine	Atlanta, GA
2252	20	0.90%	University of Connecticut Scho	Farmington, CT
2298	20	0.90%	University of North Carolina a	Chapel Hill, NC
793	18	2.30%	University of Nebraska College	Omaha, NE
620	17	2.70%	University of Oklahoma College	Oklahoma City, OK
123	17	13.80%	University of North Dakota Sch	Grand Forks, ND
1272	16	1.30%	University of Alabama School o	Birmingham, AL
2292	16	0.70%	University of Washington Schoo	Seattle, WA
558	13	2.30%	University of MissouriColumbi	Columbia, MO
435	12	2.80%	University of Texas Medical Br	Galveston, TX
618	11	1.80%	Joan C. Edwards School of Medi	Huntington, WV
716	11	1.50%	East Tennessee State Universit	Johnson City, TN
327	10	3.10%	Texas Tech University Health S	Lubbock, TX
715	10	1.40%	University of Nevada School of	Reno, NV
1794	10	0.60%	University of California, San	La Jolla, CA
1742	10	0.60%	Wright State University School	Dayton, OH
449	9	2.00%	University of South Alabama Co	Mobile, AL
368	9	2.40%	Texas A & M University System	College Station, TX
427	9	2.10%	University of Arkansas for Med	Little Rock, AR
500	9	1.80%	University of Texas Medical Sc	San Antonio, TX
1157	9	0.80%	University of Hawaii John A. D	Honolulu, HI
979	9	0.90%	University of South Carolina S	Columbia, SC
487	9	1.80%	University of Tennessee Health	Memphis, TN
839	9	1.10%	Stony Brook University Health	Stony Brook, NY
1009	8	0.80%	Medical University of South Ca	Charleston, SC
515	7	1.40%	University of South Florida Co	Tampa, FL
539	7	1.30%	University of Texas Medical Sc	Houston, TX
522	5	1.00%	Northeastern Ohio Universities	Rootstown, OH
831	5	0.60%	University of Florida College	Gainesville, FL
774	5	0.60%	University of New Mexico Schoo	Albuquerque, NM
204	5	2.50%	Louisiana State University Sch	New Orleans, LA
779	4	0.50%	University of California, Davi	Sacramento, CA
749	2	0.30%	Medical College of Georgia Sch	Augusta, GA
573	2	0.30%	University of South Dakota Sch	Sioux Falls, SD
122	2	1.60%	University of Massachusetts Me	Worcester, MA
550	2	0.40%	University of California, Irvi	Irvine, CA

| 245 | 1 | 0.40% | Louisiana State University Sch | Shreveport, LA |
| 206 | 1 | 0.50% | University of Arizona College | Tucson, AZ |

U.S. (MD) schools with the fewest number of applicants per spot (2005)

Applicants	Accepted	Applicants per spot	Medical School	City, State
123	17	7	University of North Dakota Sch	Grand Forks, ND
262	32	8	University of Missouri-Kansas	Kansas City, MO
1589	164	10	Uniformed Services U of the He	Bethesda, MD
717	39	18	University of Texas Southweste	Dallas, TX
1686	89	19	Loma Linda University School o	Loma Linda, CA
620	29	21	University of Kentucky College	Lexington, KY
647	28	23	University of Utah School of M	Salt Lake City, UT
1120	41	27	West Virginia University Schoo	Morgantown, WV
327	10	33	Texas Tech University Health S	Lubbock, TX
3842	117	33	Washington University in St. L	St. Louis, MO
4213	123	34	Case Western Reserve Universit	Cleveland, OH
3120	91	34	Ohio State University College	Columbus, OH
1144	33	35	University of Kansas School of	Kansas City, KS
4465	125	36	University of Pittsburgh Schoo	Pittsburgh, PA
4110	115	36	Howard University College of M	Washington, DC
1872	52	36	Medical University of Ohio at	Toledo, OH
435	12	36	University of Texas Medical Br	Galveston, TX
620	17	36	University of Oklahoma College	Oklahoma City, OK
5515	147	38	Chicago Medical School at Rosa	North Chicago, IL
3253	86	38	University of Illinois College	Chicago, IL
5342	141	38	Harvard Medical School	Boston, MA
2173	56	39	University of Minnesota Medica	Minneapolis, MN
4786	119	40	Columbia University College of	New York, NY
3992	99	40	University of Michigan Medical	Ann Arbor, MI
1335	33	40	State University of New York U	Syracuse, NY
204	5	41	Louisiana State University Sch	New Orleans, LA
368	9	41	Texas A & M University System	College Station, TX
7915	187	42	Georgetown University School o	Washington, DC
558	13	43	University of Missouri-Columbi	Columbia, MO
4698	108	44	Creighton University School of	Omaha, NE
2966	68	44	Meharry Medical College	Nashville, TN
793	18	44	University of Nebraska College	Omaha, NE
4017	91	44	Vanderbilt University School o	Nashville, TN
6670	150	44	Jefferson Medical College of T	Philadelphia, PA
4921	110	45	University of Pennsylvania Sch	Philadelphia, PA
1308	29	45	University of Louisville Schoo	Louisville, KY

4259	91	**47**	Yale University School of Medi	New Haven, CT
5099	108	**47**	Medical College of Wisconsin	Milwaukee, WI
5963	126	**47**	Northwestern University, The F	Chicago, IL
427	9	**47**	University of Arkansas for Med	Little Rock, AR
2245	47	**48**	Keck School of Medicine of the	Los Angeles, CA
2165	45	**48**	University of Iowa Roy J. and	Iowa City, IA
1116	23	**49**	University at Buffalo State Un	Buffalo, NY
4898	100	**49**	Albert Einstein College of Med	Bronx, NY
3097	63	**49**	University of Rochester School	Rochester, NY
4019	81	**50**	Virginia Commonwealth Universi	Richmond, VA
8380	168	**50**	Drexel University College of M	Philadelphia, PA
449	9	**50**	University of South Alabama Co	Mobile, AL
5252	105	**50**	Saint Louis University School	St. Louis, MO
5523	109	**51**	Johns Hopkins University Schoo	Baltimore, MD
487	9	**54**	University of Tennessee Health	Memphis, TN
1916	35	**55**	University of Colorado Health	Denver, CO
500	9	**56**	University of Texas Medical Sc	San Antonio, TX
4741	85	**56**	Duke University School of Medi	Durham, NC
7267	130	**56**	New York Medical College	Valhalla, NY
618	11	**56**	Joan C. Edwards School of Medi	Huntington, WV
10058	174	**58**	George Washington University S	Washington, DC
6602	113	**58**	Tulane University School of Me	New Orleans, LA
4437	75	**59**	Dartmouth Medical School	Hanover, NH
2903	49	**59**	University of Virginia School	Charlottesville, VA
4662	78	**60**	Pennsylvania State University	Hershey, PA
4078	67	**61**	Joan & Sanford I. Weill Medica	New York, NY
122	2	**61**	University of Massachusetts Me	Worcester, MA
1483	24	**62**	State University of New York D	Brooklyn, NY
2480	40	**62**	University of Cincinnati Colle	Cincinnati, OH
4877	78	**63**	Emory University School of Med	Atlanta, GA
1841	29	**63**	Wayne State University School	Detroit, MI
716	11	**65**	East Tennessee State Universit	Johnson City, TN
3579	54	**66**	Stanford University School of	Stanford, CA
4247	64	**66**	Brown Medical School	Providence, RI
8853	132	**67**	Boston University School of Me	Boston, MA
1816	27	**67**	UMDNJ-Robert Wood Johnson	Piscataway, NJ
1973	29	**68**	University of Wisconsin Medica	Madison, WI
2877	42	**69**	Baylor College of Medicine	Houston, TX
6575	94	**70**	New York University School of	New York, NY

7634	107	71	Tufts University School of Med	Boston, MA
715	10	72	University of Nevada School of	Reno, NV
2669	37	72	Eastern Virginia Medical Schoo	Norfolk, VA
3201	44	73	Oregon Health & Science Univer	Portland, OR
515	7	74	University of South Florida Co	Tampa, FL
5321	72	74	Albany Medical College	Albany, NY
5046	66	76	Mount Sinai School of Medicine	New York, NY
2447	32	76	University of Miami Leonard M.	Miami, FL
539	7	77	University of Texas Medical Sc	Houston, TX
6460	83	78	Temple University School of Me	Philadelphia, PA
1272	16	80	University of Alabama School o	Birmingham, AL
2550	32	80	Mayo Medical School	Rochester, MN
1774	22	81	Morehouse School of Medicine	Atlanta, GA
5363	64	84	Wake Forest University School	Winston-Salem, NC
2140	25	86	Michigan State University Coll	East Lansing, MI
6445	75	86	Loyola University Chicago Stri	Maywood, IL
5080	59	86	University of Vermont College	Burlington, VT
5868	66	89	University of Chicago Division	Chicago, IL
2560	28	91	University of California, San	San Francisco, CA
839	9	93	Stony Brook University Health	Stony Brook, NY
2567	27	95	David Geffen School of Medicin	Los Angeles, CA
522	5	104	Northeastern Ohio Universities	Rootstown, OH
2996	28	107	UMDNJ-New Jersey Medical Sch	Newark, NJ
979	9	109	University of South Carolina S	Columbia, SC
2980	27	110	University of Maryland School	Baltimore, MD
2252	20	113	University of Connecticut Scho	Farmington, CT
2298	20	115	University of North Carolina a	Chapel Hill, NC
1009	8	126	Medical University of South Ca	Charleston, SC
1157	9	129	University of Hawaii John A. B	Honolulu, HI
2927	22	133	Rush Medical College of Rush U	Chicago, IL
2292	16	143	University of Washington Schoo	Seattle, WA
774	5	155	University of New Mexico Schoo	Albuquerque, NM
831	5	166	University of Florida College	Gainesville, FL
1742	10	174	Wright State University School	Dayton, OH
1794	10	179	University of California, San	La Jolla, CA
779	4	195	University of California, Davi	Sacramento, CA
206	1	206	University of Arizona College	Tucson, AZ
245	1	245	Louisiana State University Sch	Shreveport, LA
550	2	275	University of California, Irvi	Irvine, CA

| 573 | 2 | **287** | University of South Dakota Sch | Sioux Falls, SD |
| 749 | 2 | **375** | Medical College of Georgia Sch | Augusta, GA |

Success Stories

Chris's story

I initially wanted to be a marine biologist, but started to fulfill the premed requirements after seeing the effect a heart transplant had on my fiancée's father's health. It was really eye opening for me and I wanted to be like the doctors who were able to do that kind of miracle. It might sound corny, but sometimes clichés are true.

I took the MCAT the first time in 1994, in April of my sophomore year. I received the scores on the first day of my honeymoon. My in-laws called and told me. I was so uninformed I didn't know if I'd done well or badly. There was no excuse for that. If I had really wanted to be a doctor, I should have talked to the premed advising office, found out how important the test was, found out what scores were competitive, and taken practice tests. I did okay despite that—I got a 31 composite with a bio score of 9. I retook it the next year, because I had been teaching SAT for the Princeton Review and they'd given me the opportunity to take the MCAT instructor course. I didn't take full advantage, but the course helped me score 32 that time, with all my sub scores in the double digits.

I went to college on scholarships and financial aid. I had no idea how I was going to pay for medical school. I should have gone to the premed office and asked the question because I think I would have found that financial aid wasn't hard to come by, especially for someone like me who had essentially no income, but I didn't. Instead I cut my hair and went to the ROTC detachment in late spring of my junior year and asked if they would send me to medical school if I got admitted. They were enthusiastic that they would and scheduled me to go to summer field training that year to get started.

So, when it came time to apply, I was an Air Force ROTC cadet. My GPA wasn't really competitive for medical school at around 3.25. The Air Force offered me a pilot slot. So when I didn't get into medical school, I took it. It seemed exciting, I would get a break from school, and I'd earn a decent paycheck much sooner.

This turned out to be a lucky decision. My wife was diagnosed with idiopathic cardiomyopathy the next fall. Because I was an Air Force officer, her health care was completely covered, which it likely wouldn't have been if I'd pursued my initial course of going to medical school. I spent my weekdays learning to fly and my weekends with my wife in the cardiac intensive care unit an hour and a half down the road. She received a transplant, but had to be relisted a couple of years later, after her donor heart slowly failed. My first assignment as a pilot was at the same base I'd trained at, which helped us, since she was able to see the same transplant doctors who were familiar with her case. She received a second transplant and did very well after spending time in a wheelchair due to initial problems with overall myopathy caused by her steroid dose. We spent years in and out of the hospital and I got to see the medical system from the patient perspective. My interest in medicine didn't wane, despite my career as a pilot. I began to research what it would take to try to apply as an Air Force officer.

My next assignment was as a cargo pilot. I enjoyed it, but always felt that I'd made a mistake in not continuing with my dream of becoming a physician. The Air Force personnel center let me know that I was unlikely to get permission to change my career, since pilots were in high demand. Since I was a combat-experienced instructor pilot, I was valuable to them, especially considering they'd paid to train me. I requested permission to apply anyway. During a mission in the Washington DC area, I went to visit the director of admissions at the Uniformed Services University. She was incredibly helpful, making an appointment to see me and evaluating my qualifications. She said that I would be a competitive applicant, considering my life experiences, if I was able to score in the same range on the MCAT as I had as an undergrad. I had some positive feedback and I had a goal. I also learned that admissions committees can have a human face. I don't think most are that helpful, but you don't know until you try and as long as you're courteous and professional, I think you're unlikely to hurt your chances.

I returned home after the trip was over and called the Princeton Review to see if I could buy their materials because there was no way I could take a class given my flying schedule. They don't sell course materials to anyone not taking the course, but they were very helpful and I decided to sign up for the course anyway and attend when I could. I managed to make more class sessions than I thought and I studied on my own when I was away from home flying. My goal was to score what I had before, but I exceeded that by the third of five diagnostics. I changed my goal to scoring a 35 and beat that by the final diagnostic. I scored a 36 on the real thing, beating my best undergrad performance by four points. The prep course definitely helped, but I think my military experience really gave me the discipline I needed. I was over eight years removed from my science education, so I should have scored lower, but hard work mattered more. I can't emphasize intense, dedicated preparation for the MCAT. I think that was the turning point for my application.

I shadowed a flight surgeon at my local clinic for a week, which was valuable to see patient contact from a doctor's perspective and to specifically evaluate the most common specialty for Air Force doctors. I also met a Navy doctor on SDN that invited me to shadow him aboard ship during sick call. He had gone through a similar path, attending med school after a career in the military, so he was incredibly helpful. Both of these doctors became mentors and friends, eventually writing me letters of recommendation. Since I wasn't in college anymore, I didn't feel I could get letters from professors, so these really helped. I also volunteered with the Red Cross at Madigan Army Hospital. I helped in the MRI section and gained some valuable experience.

The Air Force denied me permission to apply for the 2005 entering class. My wife passed away that fall, so that denial was less significant than what was happening in my personal life. I concentrated on work, on learning to live without my wife of ten years, and tried again in 2005 for the 2006 entering class. I applied to twenty schools, a mix of allopathic, osteopathic, and Texas schools, which meant I had to complete three primary applications. I submitted my applications the first week of June, on advice from my premed committee. I had already requested the colleges I had attended send transcripts in May. I interviewed with the premed committee of my alma mater, an option I didn't think was possible, but which the committee enthusiastically allowed me to do once I asked. I completed somewhere around fifteen secondaries, having been rejected by one school pre-secondary and some of the others not requiring a secondary. My first interview invitation was from UT San Antonio. I loved the experience and the school. My second was at the Uniformed Services University, which was my first choice. With nine years of military experience, I really wanted to continue my service, students there are paid a full salary, and the education is specialized to prepare students to be military doctors. My military background really helped me at all the interviews I attended and I didn't feel that any schools held my nontraditional background against me. I had so much more to talk about in interviews. They were stressful, mostly because of how important they were to me, but I had tools to deal with the stress that I didn't have ten years before as a traditional applicant.

I received word of my acceptance to USUHS on October 15. I was accepted to UTHSCSA soon afterwards. I received an interview to Baylor, one of my extreme reach schools, later in the fall and found I'd been accepted there in the spring. I chose to attend USUHS due to my intentions to serve in the military. It was amazingly hard to withdraw from the other two because I'd spent the entire process praying for one acceptance and they were both high quality schools that I would have loved to attend, but I am happy to be scheduled to start at USUHS in August 2006!

So, my story really shows initially how not to get accepted into medical school. My GPA was around a 3.28 and my science GPA was lower. I had really superficial extracurricular activities, very little volunteering, and I couldn't show that I really knew what a doctor's life was like since I only had a few hours of shadowing. I was continually striving to overcome my early mistakes, but how I did is a lesson in how to apply successfully. I devoted myself 100 percent to preparing for the MCAT and did well. I made sure

I had medical and volunteer experience. I had the good fortune to meet some incredible doctors who took the time to get to know me in real depth, so they were able to write more than a superficial letter. I applied extremely early, made sure my transcripts were in early, and submitted my secondaries early. I did my best to submit a quality personal statement. I had good editors work on it and I really do believe that it made a significant difference, even though some people undervalue it. Every single factor is important, especially when one factor is already below average. I got in despite my GPA and despite not having a hard science class in ten years. Never give up, but it takes more than a positive attitude to get in. It takes a lot of hard work, constant attention to every detail, and a little luck.

David's story

I have taken a highly circuitous route to becoming an anesthesiologist/ICU physician. I wouldn't recommend my path to anyone nor would I, in retrospect, wanted to have done it any other way. My self-inflicted trials and tribulations not only make me a better, more humanistic physician; but also make me a better husband, father, and person—the latter aspects being far more important, yet supportive, than my goals as a physician. I know that I am more fully prepared and able to handle the stressors of my chosen profession secondary to my acquired maturity and wonderful support mechanism, my family: wife – Wendy, daughter #1 – Dillon, and daughter #2 – as-yet-to-be-named.

After having been an honors student throughout my entire public school education with minimal effort, the higher intensity of college coupled with total freedom proved a wee bit more of a challenge than I was personally prepared for—from the standpoint of maturity and discipline. I had to drop out of school in the fall of 1987 to avoid expulsion for grades. My 90+ credit hour cumulative GPA was circa 1.2 and I was failing every class I was enrolled in at the time.

For obvious reasons, I was convinced that I would never be able to achieve my dream of becoming a physician. Whatever my chosen profession was to be, I knew I had to amend my excessive debt situation, incurred from way too much partying, before I could ever even reattempt school. So, I worked a plethora of jobs ranging from sales associate to bouncer/bartender. When I initially returned to college, I took classes part time and worked two full-time jobs (salesman and bouncer/bartender) for two semesters.

One of my many jobs was a cardiac monitor technician. Here, I met and befriended a professor at the University of Arkansas's medical school, who taught cardiovascular physiology. We chatted at length about my history, grades, and whatnot. He and I contrived a "recovery" plan. He was not too optimistic about my prospects for redemption and success. As a matter of fact, he termed it as "an ice cube's chance in hell." The plan: First, go back to school to get a licensed, patient care type profession. I chose to enter respiratory care and it turned out to be a wonderful experience! Second, after a few years of experience, return to the undergrad world to get a BS of some sort and really kick butt on the grades. Third, apply to medical school and hope for success.

We formulated this plan in 1989. I became a respiratory therapist in 1990. In 1996, I was able to begin my BS in neurosciences at the University of Texas at Dallas. I graduated, *magna cum laude*, from UTD in May of 1999 with my BS in Neuroscience.

Even though my UTD GPA was 3.88, with a 4.0 in my major, AMCAS and AACOMAS required a complete accounting of my transcripts—drastically decreasing my cumulative and science GPAs. This spanned fifteen years and 260+ college hours...and it brought my net GPA down to a whopping 2.7 and 2.9 for the science GPA! My MCAT scores were verbal 8, physical science 11, writing sample Q, biology 10, total score 29R. That is not stellar, but not too shabby either!

I applied to all of the Texas schools, nineteen other allopathic programs, and five osteopathic schools. I ended up netting three interviews and two acceptances. Funny thing is, I still have a few schools that I NEVER heard from: UT-Houston, Finch University, Des Moines COM, and St. Louis U. I guess they eventually figured it out?

During my time in Texas, I worked with some top-notch physicians at Cook Children's Medical Center. Many of the docs were very helpful and were free with guidance. One of them was especially helpful and essentially took me under his wing. For that I will be eternally grateful. Once I finally got in, of course, I purchased a token of my appreciation. When I gave it to him, his response was that the greatest way I could show my appreciation to him would be to teach others what I had learned and what he had taught me. He also told me that when he was a premed, an older physician had done for him what he had done for me. The teaching of others was also his obligation. Now that is a charge I bear with great pleasure and the impetus behind OldPreMeds, the two BBSs that I moderate, and my extensive involvement at KCOM.

During medical school, at the end of second quarter, I came down with pneumonia, was hospitalized for four days, and missed almost two weeks of class. I received visits and calls from many classmates, faculty, and the dean! I cannot even describe how accommodating my professors were in helping me get caught up. I assumed that my illness was going to force me to repeat my first year...nowhere near the truth!

When I received that "fat envelope" on April 14, 1999, it was the culmination of over fifteen years of hard work, dedication, and discipline. Of course, my previous lacking in those qualities is why it took fifteen years to get there. Now that I am less than ten months from becoming an attending in anesthesiology/critical care, I can reflect upon my lengthy journey—my life. I love my profession and I actually look forward to going to work. However, my family was, is, and will remain my utmost priority. I wouldn't trade a single moment...not even the painful parts. You see, I believe the underpinning of my success has been my ability to keep my priorities straight and recognize that "physician" is just a part, albeit a very important part, of who I am; but there is a much broader, deeper person that is "me" and I strive to nurture that person as I grow as a physician. I used to sit back in class and wonder if these "kids," who did it all right from the starting gates, can even comprehend the extreme honor that has been bestowed upon them to be allowed to sit in that chair. Somehow, I doubt it.

Medical Student Answers

Beware that all of these answers are biased opinions from current medical students who successfully were admitted to medical school.

Read them accordingly and realize that these represent answers from a wide variety of individuals with different ambitions, goals, attitudes and personalities. The previous chapters of this book cover all of these topics more objectively from a standpoint of what is best for most applicants. The following answers have only been edited for major spelling errors to preserve the original answer as much as possible and are actual answers from students.

The authors of this book are not responsible for the following information or the advice and opinions expressed.

Why medicine? What is your story?

Although I was interested in medicine since my early teenage years, I took a circuitous route to arrive at this destination. Being a science major and doing research in college helped prepare me academically, but the later experiences—living in East Africa, doing public health research in Alaska, and working as a social worker for several years—helped solidify my decision and prepared me for what's to come. I'll be 28 when I start school in August 2007, and feel completely ready!

Student at Arizona College of Osteopathic Medicine of Midwestern University (AZCOM) (DO)

I always knew that I would go back to graduate school at some point. I was a French teacher and was getting a little bored of always teaching the same thing. Some of my colleagues made the jump from theoretical linguistics into medicine, via ENT and neurology. I gave it some thought, and decided to do the same.

Student at University of Vermont College of Medicine (MD)

I want a career that is exciting, inspiring, and challenging, and I think that medicine is all three. In years when I wasn't focusing on medicine, I found myself bored and wasting my time, and I hated that. Now I feel that I am committed to a worthy goal and working toward something important and that means a lot to me. Also I wanted to find a career where I wouldn't be working behind a desk all day and I could talk with and meet many people.

Student at New York Medical College (MD)

I attended UCLA my freshmen year of college in '01 but transferred back "home" to the University of Utah for my final 3 years, which let me ski to my little heart's content. And now after four years of college, I find myself in flat but pretty Wisconsin.

Student at Medical College of Wisconsin (MD)

I chose podiatry because I really enjoy the hours that will be associated with it. Also because it incorporates many aspects of medicine which includes dermatology, neurology, and surgery. The reason I got interested into podiatry was because as a child I had many foot problems and had to see the podiatrist on many occasions. Then later in life one of my friends entered the field before I did and really got me interested in the profession.

Student at College of Podiatric Medicine and Surgery (Podiatry)

I'm smart enough and dedicated enough to make a great doctor, and I want to make a ton of money.

Student at Medical College of Wisconsin (MD)

There is a long history of doctors in my family so I guess you could say it is in my blood to be a doctor. In high school, I began to learn about science and saw the applications of medicine in real-world situations. It was then that I decided that I wanted to be an agent of positive change in people's lives.

Student at University of Miami Leonard M. Miller School of Medicine (MD)

I went into medicine for the same reason everyone else goes into medicine: fame, fortune, and fun. But you can't say that during the medical school interview so most applicants take the cookie-cutter approach and say they want to be a doc cause they enjoy the sciences and, most importantly, because they want to help people. I probably went into medicine for the same reasons.

Student at Medical College of Wisconsin (MD)

I knew coming out of high school that I wanted to go into medicine. The problem was how to pay for school—my family is not well off. I decided to join the Army Reserve as a pharmacy specialist and field medic with the hope that the Army would help pay for school and that I could find a decent job that would support me through school. After a year in the Reserves, I served two years as a missionary in Texas for my church. After the mission, I married my wife and we moved to Arizona where I found it difficult to work full time and go to school. I ended up starting a business with the hope that it would support us financially and allow time for school—it only half worked. The money was great but there was no time for anything other than work as the business grew from just my partner and I working to a full-time staff of 35–40 employees. After 6 years, my partner felt like he wanted the chance to run the business by himself and offered to buy me out—I said yes and retired at the ripe old age of 30. The buyout gave us enough money to live on for about 8 years, so we did some planning and thought about our future and I decided that I really did want to become a physician. I had only completed two semesters of undergrad, so I enrolled at the U of Arizona and completed my degree. When it came time to apply for med school, a friend in Tucson recommended MCW. I was impressed by how well they ran the application process/business side of the school and when I got the offer, I accepted (after my wife told me I could). Our family really likes it here in Wisconsin and the school is excellent.

Student at Medical College of Wisconsin (MD)

Ever since I can remember, I have wanted to be a pediatrician. My mom works as an RN in the nursery of a hospital and I have always loved science. Those were initially the two driving forces for me to start on the premed pathway. During my freshman year of college, I was in an accident and broke my right leg. All of the experiences from being rushed to the emergency room to almost not being able to walk again really confirmed my desire to become a doctor and help others as my doctors helped me.

Student at Lake Erie College of Osteopathic Medicine (LECOM) (DO)

I love Hospitals, I love science… Put the two together and you get DOCTOR!! I am also a very helping person by nature so being a doctor will fill that void.

Student at TUCOM-Nevada Campus (DO)

Medicine is a career where science is combined with helping others in a way that is exciting, challenging, and rewarding. As a physician, I am able to teach, do research, and work with patients. No other career allows me to do all of this.

Student at Johns Hopkins University School of Medicine (MD)

I am not one who has always known that they wanted to go to medical school. A series of experiences throughout my life has indirectly led me to medical school and here is the short version. Throughout both junior high and high school, I was exposed to a lot of genetics in several different science classes. The genetics fascinated me and I was determined that I wanted to get a PhD and then run my own human genetics lab. Sometime during undergraduate, as I got more into the science classes and labs, I decided that the bench research was not for me. My next idea was that I wanted to become a clinical geneticist, which obviously involves going to medical school. This is the first thought that I had given to going to medical school. I then got involved in volunteering and shadowing that exposed me to the medical field. Through these experiences, I came to the conclusion that I definitely wanted to become a physician, although I decided that clinical genetics is probably not the specialty for me.

Student at Medical College of Wisconsin (MD)

I have been a registered nurse for 8 years. I have always wanted to be a doctor. I went to nursing school because I supported my husband while he went to law school. I continued to take classes required for med school while working full time. It took several years to complete the pre-reqs because I had to take them one at a time. When I was 30 years old, I was finally ready to apply. I was fortunate that I was also accepted in my first application cycle.

Student at Morehouse School of Medicine (MD)

I don't know why medicine. I guess b/c I've always been in the top 10 in my class. So, people always assumed I'd do something in the medical field.

Student at College of Podiatric Medicine and Surgery (Podiatry)

Medicine gives me the honor and privilege of serving humanity. I bring with me the empathy, passion, and motivation to help my fellow man. Yes, it sounds cliché but I have spent many years trying to get to this point, and it was that drive to serve mankind that keeps me on course now.

Student at Ohio State University College of Medicine and Public Health (MD)

I chose medicine because isn't that every mom and dad's dream for their little kid? Hahaha...in all seriousness now...I specifically want to pursue a career in academic medicine. It all started in my engineering undergrad when I got exposed to several different research projects. I decided I liked doing research, but also decided that I didn't want to do a traditional engineering field. After doing a research gig in biomed engineering in a research hospital, I decided that I loved that atmosphere so much (the whole research, practice, and teaching bit) that I wanted to stay in it. I thrive off of good stress and good puzzles to solve, so here goes!

Student at University of Mississippi School of Medicine (MD)

I've always wanted to help people, since I was very young + had intense interest in the medical sciences + enjoyed the diversity and the continued education medicine provided. After volunteering in hospitals and conducting cardiovascular research, I decided to definitely pursue medicine.

Student at Chicago Medical School at Rosalind Franklin U-Med & Sci (MD)

I chose medicine because I was raised around it. It's my passion and I could not picture myself doing anything but being in the medical field. It's something that will always keep me challenged and a job that you will always see something new.

Student at University of Miami Leonard M. Miller School of Medicine (MD)

The reason I want to be a physician is so that I can wear one of those lights that surgeons put on their heads…yeah I really like those and so that's what I want to do…that and sigmoidoscopies!!! Medicine snuck up behind me and stole me from dentistry. I can't explain what drove me to medicine but I can say that I love the science and practical parts of medicine. Plus, now even though I have to call my brother "Major," he has to call me "Doctor."

Student at Medical College of Wisconsin (MD)

I can remember wanting to become a doctor since the age of 12, after I seriously injured my knee sliding over a sprinkler. At the time, I also wanted to become a professional basketball, football, and baseball player. My athletic skills never really materialized, but my desire to go into medicine remained a part of my life. I became confident in my decision to pursue medicine as I studied subjects like physiology and anatomy and saw their real life applications in my clinical experiences.

Student at Medical College of Wisconsin (MD)

It is a well-respected field that will give me the opportunity to greatly impact the lives of others in ways that would otherwise not be possible.

Student at Medical College of Wisconsin (MD)

I started my first year of college as an art/photography major, and enjoyed the work. I hated science. Still, I felt that cliché sense of emptiness with school—that I couldn't figure out what or why I would do anything with the degree I was working toward. I switched colleges for personal reasons, and after a month or two decided to pursue medicine. The final spark came from a really bad medical computer game, but it had always been in the back of my mind...I was already somewhat involved in Emergency Medical Services; my dad had been an EMT for nearly 25 years. After taking additional science courses and spending more time in EMS, I decided that this was where I wanted to be. Since then I have (and still do) strongly debate with myself whether I'd be happier in medical school or as a paramedic on the streets, but I think that this will provide me with more of a challenge and be more rewarding to myself and the people I treat in the end.

Student at Medical College of Wisconsin (MD)

Several years ago, I became interested in EMS. Eventually, I decided to take the EMT-Basic class and volunteer for my local squad. EMS quickly became my passion. I soon started working part-time for a full-time 911 System, in addition to my full-time job. I also took the EMT-Intermediate class. After a couple of years of EMS, and becoming increasingly unhappy with my full-time career of teaching, I began investigating medical careers. Initially, I planned to pursue certification as an EMT-Paramedic. For various reasons, that didn't work out. I also considered nursing school. One day I made an off-the-cuff comment about how if I could do college over again, I would do what was needed to get into medical school. My boyfriend (now husband) took me seriously and encouraged me to investigate what it would take.

Student at Ohio State University College of Medicine and Public Health (MD)

I was around medicine a lot as a child, suffering from fairly serious asthma and an orthopedic problem, both of which required continual monitoring and doctor's appointments. My mother is also an RN and my father a social worker, so I learned early the value of helping others in your work. I guess these experiences along with a natural interest in science and a need for a challenging career path made medicine a good fit for me.

Student at Medical College of Wisconsin (MD)

I decided to go into medicine because I believe it to be one the most rewarding roles that a person can hold. A physician is a confidant, a friend, ally, teacher, and learner. Perhaps no other calling allows someone to have the opportunity and responsibility to help people in such a broad spectrum of mental, physical, and emotional difficulties encountered in life. Over the years I have found myself having and gaining the qualities that I believe all physicians should maintain and utilize: those of empathy, sympathy, care, compassion, perseverance, confidence, and an endless desire to help others and to learn…and let's face it, the ever-changing fields of medicine provide some of the most interesting and difficult intellectual challenges we can face today.

Student at Medical College of Wisconsin (MD)

My mother is a nurse of 28 years. She is one of my biggest influences and introduced me to the medical field. And I had an incredible interest in the body, how it works and what happens when it does not. I also feel it is my "calling."

Student at Philadelphia College of Osteopathic Medicine (PCOM) (DO)

I chose medicine because I want to give of myself to help someone better themselves whether it be physically, mentally, emotionally, or spiritually.

Student at West Virginia School of Osteopathic Medicine (WVSOM) (DO)

Curiosity for science. Need to help others. Serve my Savior. My mother is a family practice nurse practitioner. From day one, all I ever knew of a maternal profession, I learned in stories from the ER where she worked. I grew up wanting to do just that, and still do today.

Student at Medical College of Wisconsin (MD)

I started out in computer programming some years ago, after completing college for the first time and worked in programming for about 4.5 years total. With time, work became monotonous, less challenging, and less exciting. I was in my own cubicle within the basement and stared at my computer screen all day. Although the job was pretty decent overall, this was not what I had envisioned for my life and I could not see myself doing this for another 40 years. I wanted people contact, more interaction and involvement. I am an "immediate gratification" type of a person and I like to be able to see the difference I am making. All things considered, I had chosen the wrong profession, although I was good at programming. After many long deliberations with my wife, we decided I needed to quit my job and return to school. Initially, I wasn't sure whether medicine or law would be a better fit for me, so I researched and talked with professionals of both professions, finally settling on medicine. When I started taking the Biology courses at Idaho State University, I was fascinated and quickly embraced the sciences. I also started shadowing physicians and volunteering in a clinic, both of which heightened my excitement and verified my decision. Especially shadowing and the clinical volunteer work convinced me completely that medicine was what I wanted to pursue. I think medicine offers what I was lacking in my prior career and provides plenty of challenges, intellectual stimulation, people contact and interaction, opportunities to help people and seeing the difference I am making.

Student at Medical College of Wisconsin (MD)

Are you in any special circumstances? Anything unique?

Nothing particularly special, except that I'm slightly older than most matriculants; but I believe this has definitely worked to my advantage, at least in the application process.

Student at Arizona College of Osteopathic Medicine of Midwestern University (AZCOM) (DO)

During my premed years, I went through a divorce. I am a single mom with two children. This has never made me think twice about going to medical school in the first place.

Student at University of Vermont College of Medicine (MD)

I wasn't interested in medicine until the end of my sophomore year of college. Other than that not really...

Student at New York Medical College (MD)

I'm 40 years old now and driven like never before.

Student at Des Moines University -- College of Osteopathic Medicine (DMU/COM) (DO)

Only that I will be married when I start school in August of 2007.

Student at College of Podiatric Medicine and Surgery (Podiatry)

Nope...just a regular Joe trying to live his dream.

Student at University of Texas Medical School at Houston (MD)

I was admitted to the Medical Scholars Program, a 7-year BS/MD program offered to sophomores at the University of Miami. I have not taken the MCAT and do not believe that I need a minimum score on the MCAT since the requirements for the program changed after I enrolled at the University.

Student at University of Miami Leonard M. Miller School of Medicine (MD)

No special circumstances—unless you consider being older (32 when applying), being married (13 years this year), having 3 girls (6, 9, and 10 years old), 2 dogs (a lab mix and a newfie puppy), 1 cat (my wife's), 1 rat (pretty complacent sitting in its cage all day), 20 million guppies (increasing daily), and a successful previous career as unique.

Student at Medical College of Wisconsin (MD)

I come from a very bad place. Anyone that knew me back in Junior high and high school would have thought I'd be dead or in prison.

Student at TUCOM-Nevada Campus (DO)

Nah…I'm just your average half-Asian southern girl. I also like to count things.

Student at University of Mississippi School of Medicine (MD), class of 2010.

I applied for only MD-PhD programs because I worked in a research lab for 5 years before applying to medical school. During my senior year in high school, I was selected to participate in a special research program. Participating in research at the age of 18 was the beginning of my journey in becoming a physician-scientist.

Student at Johns Hopkins University School of Medicine (MD)

For the most part my situation is not unique. The only thing that is somewhat different is that I am married and am somewhat older than the typical medical student. I waited out two years for my wife to finish pharmacy school. We both thought that it would be best for her to finish pharmacy school before I started medical school.

Student at Medical College of Wisconsin (MD)

I have been an ER and critical care nurse for 8 years. I think my exposure to the medical field will be a nice foundation for starting medical school.

Student at Morehouse School of Medicine (MD)

I took 2 years off after undergrad to "grow up." Just before I entered school, I got engaged. I am now married and expecting my first child in September.

Student at College of Podiatric Medicine and Surgery (Podiatry)

I am first-generation. I carry the blessing and burden of being the first in my family to attend and graduate college, not to mention move on to graduate and medical school. Living below the poverty line most of my life has taught me to appreciate the blessings of my struggle and to see the lessons that each obstacle has provided me.

Student at Ohio State University College of Medicine and Public Health (MD)

I think that what makes me different from a lot of premed students in Miami is the fact that there are not many women neurosurgeons in south Florida.

Student at University of Miami Leonard M. Miller School of Medicine (MD)

I've lived in 4 different countries and seen so much. I personally suffered from Grave's disease and was very sick for a few years. Nevertheless, I still persevered and here I am.

Student at Chicago Medical School at Rosalind Franklin U-Med & Science (MD)

I am married to my better half, and have two kids.

Student at Medical College of Wisconsin (MD)

Nothing really that special. I am married with a little boy born during the first semester of medical school. That made things a little interesting.

Student at Medical College of Wisconsin (MD)

I did not major in a biological science in undergrad. I chose to major in management science (business) in order to broaden my education and to prepare myself to one day run my own clinic if I should choose to open one.

Student at Medical College of Wisconsin (MD)

I'm a chewy abnormal center with a sweet normal shell.

Student at Medical College of Wisconsin (MD)

I do not think so...

Student at Medical College of Wisconsin (MD)

I am one of the older students in my class. There are 7 or 8 students (out of a class of 210) who are older than me. I am also one of several students in my class who are pursuing medicine as a second career. I taught high school Spanish for 10 years before deciding to try for medical school.

Student at Ohio State University College of Medicine and Public Health (MD)

I am engaged to be married.

Student at Medical College of Wisconsin (MD)

Not really, other than on a 4-year Army scholarship, which is super sweet.

Student at Philadelphia College of Osteopathic Medicine (PCOM) (DO)

I can't say that I am in any special circumstances now. When I was coming up, I was home schooled part of the way and attended a very small Baptist high school. At the time, some people thought that I might not get the "proper" education with home schooling and a Christian school. But, I guess my accomplishments speak for themselves.

Student at West Virginia School of Osteopathic Medicine (WVSOM) (DO)

Went on a 2-year church mission to a foreign land after my freshman year at UCLA. Came back and transferred to BYU because it was a lot cheaper. Got Married, graduated in Neuroscience, moved to Wisconsin, deferred med school for a year while doing research in Pulmonary Hypertension, had a kid, then started school.

Student at Medical College of Wisconsin (MD)

None exactly.

Student at Medical College of Wisconsin (MD)

I received my acceptances to medical school as a reapplicant, so I have a somewhat unique outlook on the application process from that angle.

Student at Medical College of Wisconsin (MD)

I was born and raised in Germany until age 18 and came to the U.S. as a high school exchange student. While on the exchange, I met my future wife and immigrated to the U.S. permanently in 1995. Medicine is my second career. I am married with 5 children, ages nine to three (2 boys, 3 girls).

Student at Medical College of Wisconsin (MD)

What was the hardest part in preparing for med school?

The application process, studying for the MCAT, and trying to maintain my grades.
Student at PCOM-Georgia Campus (DO)

Staying dedicated when all of my friends were out partying.
Student at College of Podiatric Medicine and Surgery (Podiatry)

For me, the hardest part was preparing for the MCAT entirely on my own. Living in such an isolated area, I had no peers to commiserate with or tutors/prep courses in the area; I was also working full time. It definitely built character, and now I'm used to getting home at night after working for 8–10 hours and hitting the books for an additional 3–4.
Student at Arizona College of Osteopathic Medicine of Midwestern University (AZCOM) (DO)

Definitely taking care of the kids alone while going to school for 16 credits/semester (all hard science/math classes) and working night shift. To this day, I don't know how I survived this. I took the MCAT in April 2003, 26 days after my divorce was final.
Student at University of Vermont College of Medicine (MD)

Getting in
Student at New York Medical College (MD)

Affording the plane tickets to interviews
Student at Des Moines University — College of Osteopathic Medicine (DMU/COM) (DO)

Three things. The MCAT for sure because of the preparation (it's like taking an extra 15 hours in college) and the mind-numbing 9 hours of total test time. Next one is the application itself. Gathering information and countless personal statements make this task tedious. But the hardest part is the waiting. You wait for months before the MCAT scores come out. Another few months before you hear if you got an interview. And then another few months before you find out if you got in, if you're in the waiting list, or if you have to do it all over again. The application process is like a roller coaster ride with peaks and valleys.

Student at University of Texas Medical School at Houston (MD)

The interview. Everyone has good grades and MCAT scores or they wouldn't bother applying. Get some clinical experience and volunteer work on your resume if you want serious consideration.

Student at Medical College of Wisconsin (MD)

Right now I am studying for the MCAT and that is pretty tough. Although I did not need to take the MCAT before I applied to medical school, I definitely would consider that to be very difficult. Having the mental toughness to do well in school while pursuing extracurricular activities is very challenging. Time management is key.

Student at University of Miami Leonard M. Miller School of Medicine (MD)

Sorry to have to say it, but school is a piece of cake compared with running your own business. I had so much time for my family and hobbies while I completed my undergraduate degree that it always felt like I was on vacation. After a year of medical school, it still feels that way. If anything was hard about the process, it was not knowing if we were going to have to sell our house and move—and if we were moving, where we were going.

Student at Medical College of Wisconsin (MD)

Seeking out the necessary clinical experiences and studying for the MCAT.

Student at Lake Erie College of Osteopathic Medicine (LECOM) (DO)

Studying for the MCAT while not losing focus on the current semester

Student at TUCOM-Nevada (DO)

Being around all the rabid pretentious premed kids. Thank goodness for engineering school. It's going to be hard adjusting to the med school environment. Please forgive me (if you're in my class) if I'm a bit anal retentive or weird for the first month or so.

Student at University of Mississippi School of Medicine (MD)

The hardest part for me was preparing for the volume of material taught in medical school. While in college, a topic may be covered over a week. In medical school, the same topic may be covered in less than an hour. Medical students must do tons of reading and studying on their own to acquire and master the topics.

Student at Johns Hopkins University School of Medicine (MD)

The hardest part in preparing for medical school for me was the MCAT. Standardized tests have always been my enemy and I knew that the one thing that would potentially stop me from getting into medical school was the MCAT. Preparing for the MCAT as well as taking the test itself was very stressful for me.

Student at Medical College of Wisconsin (MD)

The length of time required to complete my pre-reqs. Oh, and studying for and taking the MCAT BEAST!!

Student at Morehouse School of Medicine (MD)

Organic Chem. :-) I didn't think anything was really hard. But if I had to choose one thing, I would say the MCATs. I chose to take them cold turkey.

Student at College of Podiatric Medicine and Surgery (Podiatry)

Getting volunteering and shadowing experience.

Student at Medical College of Wisconsin (MD)

Being humbled and having to step back to re-learn in order to move forward. My post-bac program did an excellent job of that.

Student at Ohio State University College of Medicine and Public Health (MD)

All the waiting...waiting for MCAT scores, secondaries, and decisions from schools. It is a long process!

Student at Joan & Sanford I. Weill Medical College of Cornell University (MD)

I would have to say the verbal section on the MCAT (since English is NOT my first language)

Student at Chicago Medical School at Rosalind Franklin U-Med & Science (MD)

The hardest part in preparing for medical school is the pressure. You always hear people say how extremely hard it is and how competitive it is, so when it comes time for you to be ready, you're never really sure if you are or not.

Student at University of Miami Leonard M. Miller School of Medicine (MD)

I hated waiting and trudging through all that O-chem and chemistry to get to where I wanted to be. It was necessary at the time and I accepted the importance it played in my entry to med school, however, it seemed like I couldn't do what I really wanted to...you know rectal exams, inserting foleys that sort of thing.

Student at Medical College of Wisconsin (MD)

The hardest part for me was finding the motivation and time to do all the extracurriculars that I felt I needed to do in order to be competitive.

Student at Medical College of Wisconsin (MD)

Choosing activities that would set me apart from other applicants, choosing which schools to apply to, and paying for trips to interviews

Student at Medical College of Wisconsin (MD)

Mostly getting the motivation to get all the applications/essays/forms finished in good time. Also, the overall stress of "wondering" about what will happen was a pain in the rear, especially while trying to finish undergrad.

Student at Medical College of Wisconsin (MD)

Being patient. I was always looking forward to the next step, whether that was the MCAT, or applying, or interviewing. I think it is hard to get through all the hurdles while still being patient enough to allow everything to sort itself out.

Student at Medical College of Wisconsin (MD)

For me, the hardest part was quitting my job and going back to school full time. I also had to get over my math and science phobia, since those were the courses I needed to take for medical school.

Student at Ohio State University College of Medicine and Public Health (MD)

Figuring out who you are and whether or not you have the true desire to take on this profession that will have a major part in defining you as a person.

Student at Medical College of Wisconsin (MD)

To be honest, the application process was the hardest thing for me. After that, I was quite relieved and just ready to begin!

Student at Philadelphia College of Osteopathic Medicine (PCOM) (DO)

One, the isolation that my major required. I went to a really small undergraduate university and there were very few Biology majors at my school. Moreover, being cooped up in a science lab with only the professor and maybe some other student got sorta discouraging. Secondly, the MCAT had to be the toughest part of it all. There is so much you have to know for the test, and you can never feel like you know enough.

Student at West Virginia School of Osteopathic Medicine (WVSOM) (DO)

The toughest part was coming to grips with the fact that this application process is all a game… a very expensive game if you pay for all those blasted secondary applications. It's a big scam if you ask me. But I think all the hoop jumping prepares a person to become a physician because now that I'm 3 years into medical school, I am realizing that the hoop jumping never ends.

Student at Medical College of Wisconsin (MD)

That stinking MCAT prep work, but it pays off.

Student at Medical College of Wisconsin (MD)

Knowing exactly what the process entailed. I really had only a vague understanding of the application process even months into my first application cycle. Websites like this one really help out in understanding where you stand and what you are up against.

Student at Medical College of Wisconsin (MD)

Choosing which schools I was most interested in and narrowing down my search. Also, the secondary applications were much more time consuming than I had thought they'd be.

Student at Medical College of Wisconsin (MD)

I think that the hardest part is the MCAT. The stress, the studying, the remembering what you studied from a year ago, the waiting for the scores. Just work harder than I did and you should be fine.

Student at Kansas City University of Medicine and Biosciences (KCUMB) (DO)

To me, trying to do all the extracurricular activities and attending school full time besides spending time with family was hard. Moreover, we had decided that I would complete my BS degree in 3 years (I started over at zero credits since none of my credits from my first degree transferred). To do this, I had to take a very heavy class load and take courses each summer as well. To still have some family time, I could not work and our finances suffered.

Student at Medical College of Wisconsin (MD)

How much did you work while going through premed?

During my premed years, I worked as a Nursing Assistant close to my rural hometown in Minnesota. I would work about 15–20 hours per week during school and full time during the summers. Within my 5 years of being a CNA, I worked in Nursing Homes, Assistant Living, and in a Hospital.

Student at Scholl College of Podiatric Medicine (Podiatry)

As an undergrad, I generally worked only during the summers. I was very lucky in that respect. I did research in a neurosurgery department at a teaching hospital in Philadelphia, and actually got paid to do it. I also did some teaching assistant gigs during the school year, which weren't particularly time consuming, so it was pretty cushy. Since busting into the "real world," I've been breaking my back to make ends meet (social workers make a laughable salary). I've had part-time music gigs that help, however, and teach violin lessons as well. Overall, I'd say I work about 50–60 hours a week.

Student at Arizona College of Osteopathic Medicine of Midwestern University (AZCOM) (DO)

I worked A LOT! At one point, after graduation, I was working 3 jobs at the same time when my kids were with their dad! I was a full-time tech in a research lab, doing work on ion channels. Then I would take a quick nap before working on Labor and Delivery as an aide (aka secretary, aka housekeeper) during the night shift. Then I would squeeze in another 24 hours as aide in a nursing home. Pfew! While in school, I worked on campus as a lab tech, preparing the labs for my classmates. I also worked as an aide on L&D.

Student at University of Vermont College of Medicine (MD)

Work like a job? Made Pitas at the Pita Pit, usually worked once a week… Sold Beer at Broncos and Rockies games in Denver during breaks.

Student at New York Medical College (MD)

I did not work during the school year because school was my job. In the summer, I worked in hospice and developed a very good bedside manner.

Student at College of Podiatric Medicine and Surgery (Podiatry)

Owner of construction business. Less than 20 hpw.

Student at Des Moines University — College of Osteopathic Medicine (DMU/COM) (DO)

I tutored Physiology during the last two years of college. Three nights a week for about 1 hour each. And yes even on nights I had an MCAT prep course, I still taught later that night.

Student at University of Texas Medical School at Houston (MD)

Did some teaching assistant jobs and homework grading... usually 5–10 hours per week.

Student at Medical College of Wisconsin (MD)

I worked as an Emergency Medical Technician throughout undergraduate school (see clinical experience). I worked full time when I could handle it, but I worked at least twenty hours a week.

Student at Medical College of Wisconsin (MD)

I did not work at a job as a premed student.

Student at University of Miami Leonard M. Miller School of Medicine (MD)

The first year I worked full time (graveyards or second shift) as a pharmacy tech. I did not have to work when I went back to complete my degree.

Student at Medical College of Wisconsin (MD)

I worked about 8–10 hours a week at the college library during the school year and 25–30 hours a week during the summer at Eckerd Pharmacy.

Student at Lake Erie College of Osteopathic Medicine (LECOM) (DO)

First 2.5 years of college I worked 35 hrs a week with a 2-hour commute daily. Last 2.5 years I worked 20 hours a week as a tutor in the sciences.

Student at TUCOM-Nevada Campus (DO)

I worked in the college library 5 hours a week. I also worked in a research lab during the summers and my vacations. In addition to the above, I also worked at Taco Bell, retail stores, and started small businesses to gain experience.

Student at Johns Hopkins University School of Medicine (MD)

I really worked a lot during my premed years. I started as a clinical research assistant doing drug studies on sleep disorders patients and grew that into being a full-time sleep medicine technologist and working additional part-time jobs in lab management and drug study consulting.

Student at University of Mississippi School of Medicine (MD)

I worked the entire time throughout undergraduate school and worked between 12–24 hours a week. I had three different jobs during this time. The first was as a night auditor at a local hotel. This job was difficult because the shifts were at night and I went to school twice a week on no sleep. During my time at this job, I worked 24 hours a week. My next job was as a unit clerk in an emergency room. This job was great in that I got a lot of good clinical exposure and I got to know several doctors quite well. I worked about 12 hours a week at this job. My last job was as a unit clerk in an urgent care. This job was not as exciting as the emergency room job, but it was still good clinical exposure. I worked about 16 hours a week at this job.

Student at Medical College of Wisconsin (MD)

Registered nurse, several different states and locations for 8 years.
Student at Morehouse School of Medicine (MD)

I worked in admissions at my undergrad but that was only 8–10 hours per week. I also worked in the summer.
Student at College of Podiatric Medicine and Surgery (Podiatry)

I worked a lot because I had to contribute to my family's needs as well as my premed education. I worked mostly in food service, helping and tending to the needs of others. But I also volunteered with inner-city students as mentor and a tutor.
Student at Ohio State University College of Medicine and Public Health (MD)

I had a job freshman year as a lab assistant in a coal combustion lab. Summer after freshman year I still worked in that lab and took classes part time, after sophomore year I worked for the government in an environmental engineering lab, and last summer I did a biomed engineering research job. I also play piano at a church and have played a few gigs for the theater dept. at my school.
Student at University of Mississippi School of Medicine (MD)

I made the mistake of working in my third year of undergrad and my GPA plummeted.
- I worked in the summers for pharm companies, private tutoring, research etc
- after undergrad I did research in lower back pain (took some time off) + tutored + worked 1 to 1 with psych patients.
Student at Chicago Medical School at Rosalind Franklin U-Med & Sci (MD)

I generally worked 10–20 hours per week. I have tutored, worked in the cafeteria, was a peer health educator, caregiver for Alzheimer's patients, researcher, etc.
Student at Joan & Sanford I. Weill Medical College of Cornell University (MD)

I worked as little as possible while accruing as much debt as possible. This is not a recommendation but a lamentation: I was in Hawaii, there were beaches and parties everywhere, and I showed up in style on my motorcycle. Just like Aesop's grasshopper, I played my summer away. Fortunately, I found a good job after and paid off all that debt.

Student at Medical College of Wisconsin (MD)

I worked about 10–15 hours a week during the school year and full-time during the summer building fences. In addition, I taught two labs a week for the biology department during the last two years of college. I was also involved in research for about 10 hours a week during two of those semesters.

Student at Medical College of Wisconsin (MD)

For the first three years of undergrad, I would work random full-time jobs during my summers and part-time teaching/tutoring jobs during the school year. During the summer before my senior year, I began working full time as an EMT for a private ambulance company where I continued to work full time throughout my senior year and the year in between undergrad and med school.

Student at Medical College of Wisconsin (MD)

While I was in undergrad, I worked on average 20–24 hours a week. I worked as a department assistant in a hardware store during my first and second year. My third year I worked third shift as a lab tech assistant for 6 months and then as a pharmacy technician in a hospital.

Student at Medical College of Wisconsin (MD)

I worked part time for my hometown volunteer emergency medical services as an EMT, mostly during the summer and vacations. Throughout the school year, I worked weekends with a private ambulance service as an EMT, doing 911 calls and inter-facility transport. I was also a tutor at the UWGB writing center for a few hours a week.

Student at Medical College of Wisconsin (MD)

I worked as a teaching assistant during my junior year and the summer following my junior year. I taught for both the chemistry department and the biology department. I was a TA for both organic chemistry and analytical labs and I also lead a discussion section for a human physiology class.

Student at Medical College of Wisconsin (MD)

I worked part time as an EMT about 20 hours a week for a private ambulance service. I also tutored Spanish a couple hours a week. My husband and I also lived on the family farm, and I spent a couple of hours a day (on average) doing chores and helping around the farm.

Student at Ohio State University College of Medicine and Public Health (MD)

I tutored approximately 20 hours per week as a group and individual tutor in various subjects such as physiology, chemistry, psychology, and general biology. I also worked every summer in addition to taking classes.

Student at Medical College of Wisconsin (MD)

I took one year off from undergrad and worked in the Durable Medical Equipment field. This was actually awesome preparation for medical school as I was constantly exposed to patients, paperwork, and therapists/doctors. I did this for one year.

Student at Philadelphia College of Osteopathic Medicine (PCOM) (DO)

My first two years, I worked as a lab technician and at a retail store. The lab technician job allowed me to get my studying done before I went to work at my retail job. I averaged about 35–40 hrs of work a week my first two years. My last two years, I was an RA assistant, so I was able to cut back on working off campus a little bit. I got a job my last year at the campus information desk working about 20 hrs a week. I was able to get quite a bit of homework done with that job.

Student at West Virginia School of Osteopathic Medicine (WVSOM) (DO)

Taught a physiology lab my sophomore, junior, and senior year of college (~10 hours/wk). Did some research so I could put it on my app. But it was all so long ago, I can't remember much more than that. Whatever you do, don't spread yourself out too thin with extracurriculars. Do several things that you like and devote yourself to it. Then when you interview, you can really talk about it. Get good grades, but don't kill yourself for a 4.0 because there is more to life than the inside of a library. And trust me, when you get to med school, you'll be spending plenty of time inside a library.

Student at Medical College of Wisconsin (MD)

I worked 20 hours or less a week at a snowboarding shop. I made jack...

Student at Medical College of Wisconsin (MD)

I worked an average of 12–15 hours/week during the semester, and worked full time over the summers. My part-time jobs included being a lab assistant in a hematology lab at a vet hospital, caring for mentally ill and mentally disabled adults in a group home setting (also full time for two summers), and working in an evolutionary biology lab (also full time for 2 years following undergrad).

Student at Medical College of Wisconsin (MD)

I worked various jobs (tutoring, research, grading, etc.) throughout my 4 years. My summer jobs and internships were close to full time but I only worked approximately 5 hrs a week during the school year.

Student at Medical College of Wisconsin (MD)

I completed my BS degree in 3 years and took 24 credits my first semester back at school, then dropped down to 18 and a little less than that the semester I prepared for the MCAT and when I went on interviews. I had little time to work and so I didn't during the first 2 years until the MCAT was out of the way. Then, I worked part time (about 10 hours per week) during the semesters and full time during school breaks.

Student at Medical College of Wisconsin (MD)

What did you do for MCAT preparation?

I took a Princeton prep course, which was about $1,200. It was really helpful considering most of the courses were freshman level. The verbal section was the most helpful because the only way you can practice for that is by reading passages. Tutors offered great test taking tips. However, the real preparation was taking practice tests to build up stamina and work on speed. The biggest thing I learned is that the MCAT is a massive English proficiency test that tests nothing about your scientific or medical aptitude. Believe me when I tell you that all the answers are there in the test itself…you just have to figure out how to eliminate wrong ones. I seriously think anyone who hasn't taken a science course will do well. Of course taking those premed courses won't hurt.

27 MCAT.

Student at University of Texas Medical School at Houston (MD)

I needed to travel to take the test, which added the expense of transportation and a hotel visit. This is important: it takes practically forever (seems that way at least) to get your scores after the test, so don't put off taking the test until the last minute! I know some academic advisors will caution you to wait until you have taken all of the related course work (e.g., physics, organic, biochem) before taking the test. Well… ideally you would take those courses as a sophomore and junior to free up your senior year for interviewing. Even if you haven't taken the courses, you will probably delay entrance to medical school by a year if you don't take the MCAT early enough. Don't assume that the medical school will cut you any slack for either low scores or missing course work; they won't. Applications are competitive. Practice Makes Perfect… My recommendation? Take the April test a year and a half before you plan to enter school. Unless your scores are marvelous, take the August test too. That way, if you have a summer or early fall interview you can say that you are retaking the test… shows a self-improvement goal if nothing else. The August test seems more laid-back to me. Also, I think your scores are likely to look better because the test has a lot of procrastinators or poor planners who weren't there in April, making you look better in comparison. Remember, your scores are given in relation to that of other test-takers. DO NOT wait until August the year before you plan to attend and certainly don't wait until April the spring before classes start. Your scores will take too long to arrive and the classes may be full before you get reviewed. Take a Class or Not? There are several excellent courses you can take to prepare for the MCAT. Among them are the Kaplan Review, Princeton Review, and Berkeley Review. The AAMC says that taking a review course has no statistical impact on your scores... I disagree with them and I'll tell you why: the reviews don't just go over the course material, they teach to the test, meaning that you focus on test-taking strategies and review only the information that may be on the exam. That said, I don't recommend everyone take a review course (I didn't). Many students tell me they aren't taking the review because of the cost involved. Wake up call! Medical school costs thousands to a hundred thousand dollars! Don't skimp on preparation, either for the test or for the interview! If you think the review will help you, then plan for the cost. As I said, not everyone will benefit from taking a review course, but I do believe everyone will benefit from studying the text materials used for the review course (get a "used" copy for cheap). You will get practice tests and a focused, concise study guide. Using the review texts is much more helpful than randomly scanning your biology, chemistry, and physics texts. The possible writing sample topics may be viewed online at the MCAT website. Obviously you shouldn't practice all of them, but do look them over and practice this part of the test, timed, for a few topics. Neatness counts! The Test Day... The big day has finally arrived! Ideally, you want to get a good night's sleep the night before (uh huh...). No matter what, try to relax. Really tense people might find studying relaxing; otherwise turn your brain off and take it easy. Make sure you locate the test center before test day. Eat breakfast! Get to the test center bright and early with pencils, pens, and erasers in hand. Food and drinks aren't allowed in the test room, but hard candy may take the edge off, especially if you have butterflies. Do not bring a calculator or anything with an alarm. Be considerate... no cell phones, pagers, etc. Don't berate yourself if you have trouble with a section. Just shrug it off and move on. It may be helpful to bring a lunch, especially if traffic is a concern. You don't want to be late for the afternoon fun and games! If you are like me, your brain will be pretty fried after the test. You'll get out around 5 pm. If travel is required, like mine was, plan to stay with a friend or get a hotel room - plan wisely.

30 MCAT.

Student at University of Texas Southwestern Medical Center at Dallas Southwestern Medical School (MD)

Studied from an MCAT prep book on my own... went through the whole thing and took a few practice tests... didn't practice any of the essays but I should have.

31 MCAT.

Student at Medical College of Wisconsin (MD)

If the test is foreign to you, then practice, practice, practice. And then practice some more. The prep course was a waste of time for me, but the course materials (practice tests and books) were very helpful.

Unknown MCAT.

Student at Medical College of Wisconsin (MD)

Right now I am preparing with the Columbia Review every day at the University of Miami.

Unknown MCAT.

Student at University of Miami Leonard M. Miller School of Medicine (MD)

Getting a good score on the MCAT really depends on timing. For me, my timing sucked! I had just returned to school. It had been 8 years since I had taken the basic chem/bio courses and I had only taken one of the substantive courses from my major. I was very unprepared. The only thing that saved me was taking a lot of practice tests. For a few months before the actual test, I would spend each Saturday in the library and go through a practice test.

30 MCAT.

Student at Medical College of Wisconsin (MD)

I received a scholarship to take a Kaplan MCAT prep course for free. I took that during the 2 months prior to the exam. It was a lot of work and I could not really keep up with it. Honestly I can't remember how much I studied per week. I just know that being it was summer time, I was not very motivated and did not study every day. I regret not studying more and not taking the MCAT in April instead of August. But there was no way I could have studied for the April test with my involvement in Circle K and my academic studies.

25 MCAT.

Student at Lake Erie College of Osteopathic Medicine (LECOM) (DO)

Kaplan class. I had a horrible teacher though, she only read straight from the book and offered us no other help.

Unknown MCAT.

Student at TUCOM-Nevada Campus (DO)

I mainly used the Kaplan review course; however, I didn't go through tons of questions. If I had to do it again, going through questions is the key.

30 MCAT.

Student at Johns Hopkins University School of Medicine (MD)

Kaplan Course, but not worth the money. The course is expensive, but does help with time management and provides somewhat accurate sample tests.

21 MCAT.

Student at PCOM-Georgia Campus (DO)

I used the Kaplan course book and studied independently, 8 hours a day for two weeks. I think taking the course probably would have benefited me more, but I got into a great school that I think I will be able to make a significant contribution at.

29 MCAT.

Student at University of Mississippi School of Medicine (MD)

For my MCAT preparation I took the Kaplan course. Many people have said that they thought it was a waste of time and money, but for me it was great. As I mentioned before, standardized tests are not my strong point and so I felt I needed all the help that I could get. In the Kaplan course, you take several full-length practice tests that are very similar to the real MCAT. This was very helpful to me. Also, I am not a very disciplined unless I have a set schedule and deadlines to keep me on track and the Kaplan course provided me that set study schedule.

30 MCAT.

Student at Medical College of Wisconsin (MD)

I took the MCAT twice. April and August '05. I took a Kaplan prep course for the first MCAT. I wasn't so happy with my score. The second time I took the MCAT, I studied on my own and did better.

27 MCAT.

Student at Morehouse School of Medicine (MD)

Nothing.

24 MCAT.

Student at College of Podiatric Medicine and Surgery (Podiatry)

Took the MCAT twice. Once while I was in school and once while I was out for a few years. The hardest part was having to answer questions on material that I hadn't seen in 5–6 years. I studied mostly for two weeks with old tests direct from MCAT website and with a Princeton review book. My only problem with that was I did not have any of my undergrad books for a reference so many things were a little unclear when I took the test.

27 MCAT.

Student at Medical College of Wisconsin (MD)

I took a Kaplan prep course where I was living. It lasted about 3 months and really kept me on task.

MCAT score unknown.

Student at College of Podiatric Medicine and Surgery (Podiatry)

I got Kaplan books and parked myself in the library or at my desk after work every day for 3–4 hours. On weekends, it'd be more like 6–8 each day. This went on for about three months total. If there had been a prep course available in my area, I would have taken it.

24 MCAT.

Student at Arizona College of Osteopathic Medicine of Midwestern University (AZCOM) (DO)

I did tons of questions. I tried to put my hands on as many questions as I could. I bought the Kaplan review book but I can't say that it helped me as much answering questions.

MCAT score unknown.

Student at University of Vermont College of Medicine (MD)

Kaplan, studied, a lot.

MCAT score unknown.

Student at New York Medical College (MD)

Well I took the MCAT four times. The first two times I was ignorant of the scope of the exam and did poorly. The third time I took a Kaplan course and still did not get into medical school. The last time I did a post-bac program in the Midwest and here I am a rising M1.

29 MCAT.

Student at Ohio State University College of Medicine and Public Health (MD)

First time I didn't study. I took 2 practice tests. I did well. Second time I took 3 practice tests. I did about the same.

27 MCAT.

Student at University of Mississippi School of Medicine (MD)

Princeton (great review), 2–3 months was sufficient, although the verbal was hard for me, I redid the test a few times ONLY to improve my verbal.

31 MCAT.

Student at Chicago Medical School at Rosalind Franklin U-Med & Sci (MD)

I was lucky enough to be able to take the Kaplan course. I studied a lot, but balanced it with my regular school load. I probably put about 20–25 hours per week including class time. It was really helpful for me to take a lot of practice tests because when it came time for the real thing, it just felt normal.

36 MCAT.

Student at Joan & Sanford I. Weill Medical College of Cornell University (MD)

I just took tests. That was the key: practice, practice, practice.

28 MCAT.

Student at Medical College of Wisconsin (MD)

I took the KAPLAN course because I was busy with school, work, research, and family and I knew I wouldn't discipline myself to study on my own. I don't think the class itself really helped me but I think the five practice tests they make you take did. If you're disciplined at studying, I would just get the books and do it on your own.

30 MCAT.

Student at Medical College of Wisconsin (MD)

All I did for the MCAT was bought an MCAT review book and took as many practice exams as I could. My commitment to preparing was less than inspiring.

30 MCAT.

Student at Medical College of Wisconsin (MD)

I took the Kaplan prep class during the spring of my junior year and then I took the test that April. The class cost over $1,000 but that is just a drop in the bucket compared to what you will be spending on interviews and tuition. I feel like it truly prepared me for the test which was proven by my strong performance and the fact that I only had to take the test once. The full-length practice tests were extremely helpful, as a whole I would strongly recommend taking the course.

32 MCAT.

Student at Medical College of Wisconsin (MD)

My preparation for the MCAT was minimal. I purchased the Examkrackers MCAT kit, but only went through about 5% of it. Overall, I probably spent about 5 hours TOTAL studying/preparing for the MCAT. I didn't do any practice exams. My lack of prep was mostly because I'm a procrastinator, and the actual MCAT came before my motivation did. Had I prepared more, I'm sure I would have done better. But I'm a minimalist like that. Side note: I actually sold the Examkrackers books on eBay USED for more than I paid NEW. Shop around, folks.

27 MCAT.

Student at Medical College of Wisconsin (MD)

I did not take any of the name brand test preparation classes. I took something of an informal one...I think that the best test preparation is recognizing your strengths and weaknesses. I cannot say how much traditional prep classes help, but I would highly recommend taking as many full-length practice tests as you can get access to. These tests will be great indicators of content and length and allow you to get used to the timing.

33 MCAT.

Student at Medical College of Wisconsin (MD)

I didn't do much actual MCAT prep. I finished organic chemistry (summer) on a Monday, and took the MCAT on that Saturday. I spent a little bit of time going through the Kaplan book and did one full-length AAMC practice test from the website. I think I was able to get away with so little prep because I had taken all of the pre-reqs in the 12 months prior to the test.

31 MCAT.

Student at Ohio State University College of Medicine and Public Health (MD)

I bought the Kaplan MCAT book the August prior to the test and went through it once in total. I only had time for about an hour per week during the school year and some extended studying over that spring break. I also took a practice test in the book and online.

33 MCAT.

Student at Medical College of Wisconsin (MD)

I bought a Kaplan review book and went through that several months in advance. I ended up taking that beast twice and still didn't get the score I wanted to. But, I am in my second year of medical school and have proven myself otherwise so this test is not the only thing they look at.

24 MCAT.

Student at Philadelphia College of Osteopathic Medicine (PCOM) (DO)

For my first MCAT, I took a Kaplan classroom course. It was a big waste of time because I didn't put enough outside studying time into it. I was taking Orgo II and Physics II at the time, so those two classes got the vast majority of my studying time. For my second MCAT, I purchased Audio Osmosis and listened to those CDs around the clock. I also purchased a bunch of practice tests. If I wasn't listening to the CDs, I was doing practice tests. I went up four points on my second MCAT score.

23 MCAT.

Student at West Virginia School of Osteopathic Medicine (WVSOM) (DO)

Took a BYU class that was on Saturdays for several weeks. It got me to study, but the April score yielded a 28, little lower than what I was shooting for. The testing conditions also involved some extenuating circumstances such as a water leak over my head dripping onto my test during the verbal reasoning portion which I attribute to my 8 score on the verbal. Studied on my own for a few months, took it in August, made sure to sit in a dry area, and scored a 31. I had friends spend tons of cash for the Kaplan course. But in my honest opinion the only reason Kaplan MIGHT work is because you spend so much money on it, you feel motivated/obligated to study. Save yourself the grand or however absurd amount of money it is these days, buy the books for a lot less (Kaplan does have good review materials), and use the leftover money for a vacation to some exotic location. We did a cruise to Alaska. A much better use of the money.

31 MCAT.

Student at Medical College of Wisconsin (MD)

Kaplan preview…too expensive, but worth it because it only took one try.

29 MCAT.

Student at Medical College of Wisconsin (MD)

I took a Kaplan course but did not study as much as they told us we needed to. I had already seen most of the material covered so that may have helped. I found the most helpful thing for me to do was take past exams.

35 MCAT.

Student at Medical College of Wisconsin (MD)

I took the August MCAT in 2002. My first advice would be to avoid the August MCAT at all costs. It really puts you behind on submitting your applications to schools, and I found that the earlier the applicant submitted, the better. I spent the 2–3 months during the summer prior to the MCAT preparing for the test. I had purchased two books to review material for the test: a comprehensive review of the material and a book with practice tests and questions for each section. I did not opt for taking a review course due to monetary concerns and my personal learning style, which is geared toward teaching myself material. I probably spent about 6–8 hours/week during the better part of that summer reviewing for the MCAT, and amped up studying the week prior to the test to about 6 hours/day. In retrospect, I may have studied harder, and would have probably spent more time on the biology section of the test, which (being a Bio major) I really ignored. I found that taking 2–3 practice tests in environments as close to those found at testing centers was useful, and also gave me an idea of where I might score. If I were to retake the test,

I probably would have taken one of these practice tests every month leading up to the exam. All told, I feel like my preparation was adequate, and I thought my score reflected my capabilities pretty well. (33R-10 Bio, 11 Physical, 12 Verbal)

33 MCAT.

Student at Medical College of Wisconsin (MD)

I took the Kaplan course at Idaho State University. Bad choice! The course was too new to be efficient. I could have bought the Kaplan MCAT study guide book at Barnes and Noble for a whole lot cheaper, and had better study time. The only thing that I liked about the Kaplan course it that you take, I think, 7 full-length MCATs. That helped me build up my stamina for the real deal. Basically, when it all boiled down, I didn't put enough time into studying for the MCAT. One of my friends studied 10–15 hours a week for MCAT prep, I probably put in 3–5 hours a week, and my score shows that. Luckily, I was accepted into a school anyways.

21 MCAT.

Student at Kansas City University of Medicine and Biosciences (KCUMB) (DO)

I bought the most current Kaplan Comprehensive Review book (about $50) and worked through it, studying and memorizing the key concepts again. I also worked all of the calculation and other examples and made sure I could do all of those (esp. all the Chemistry, Physics calculations). I memorized some of the formulas you need for the MCAT. Also, I purchased a package of 6 practice tests. These were the "real" practice MCAT tests on paper, so I could try them under testing conditions, which I did on 4 different Saturdays at the library. These tests were the best. I would highly recommend these. They gave me a real sense of what questions to expect and I learned how to pace myself. I got a good feel for which topics are "hot" as well. Tests put out by other test prep companies are not the same. Kaplan and other prep tests are much harder than the real test to scare you into taking their courses and so they can show that you have improved (that's what I think anyway).

28 MCAT.

Student at Medical College of Wisconsin (MD)

How much did you shadow physicians?

Shadowed a podiatrist in Vestal, NY. Attended weeklong internship at OCPM where I scrubbed in on a number of cool surgeries.
Student at Scholl College of Podiatric Medicine (Podiatry).

I shadow physicians as much as possible.
Student at University of Texas Southwestern Medical Center at Dallas Southwestern Medical School (MD), class of 2009.

None.
Student at Medical College of Wisconsin (MD), class of 2010.

I shadowed a respected cardiothoracic surgeon at Doctors Hospital several times as well as an Interventional Radiologist at a nearby Hospital. On a trip to Peru during Winter break, I shadowed an internist, a gynecologist, witnessed several gynecological surgeries, and interacted with medical students during their rounds. I also visited a Psychiatric Hospital in Peru, shadowed a psychiatrist, and interacted with several patients.
Student at University of Miami Leonard M. Miller School of Medicine (MD)

Fortunately, I have a few friends that are finishing or recently finished their residencies and I was able to shadow them. If you get a chance to shadow a surgical intern on trauma call, do it! I also had a few connections with physicians that had treated my 9-year-old daughter. She has a genetic disorder, which required close medical supervision for many years. Her pediatrician was invaluable in helping me decide to return to school.
Student at Medical College of Wisconsin (MD)

During the summer before my senior year of high school, I was involved in the Health Careers Opportunity Program at SUNY Stony Brook. For a week we got to follow around various health professionals such as a respiratory therapist, physical therapist, and emergency room doctor.

During the summer before my junior year of college, I volunteered in an emergency room at a hospital. This was quite minimal though as I found that emergency medicine wasn't for me. During this past winter, I followed around my mom in the nursery for a couple of hours and then an osteopathic pediatrician for a day.

Student at Lake Erie College of Osteopathic Medicine (LECOM) (DO)

Total of 100 hours. Shadowed a DO (family practice) and an MD (chief of anesthesiology at parkland Dallas).

Student at TUCOM-Nevada Campus (DO).

I didn't shadow one physician. I worked with scientists and physician-scientists in the lab.

Student at Johns Hopkins University School of Medicine (MD)

I shadowed a neurologist/neuroradiologist/sleep medicine specialist for 6–8 hours a week for 6 months. Lots of great experience and connections.

Student at University of Mississippi School of Medicine (MD)

I did not spend tons of hours on shadowing because I feel that it is the shadowing experience itself that is important and not the number of hours that matters. Total I spent about 40 hours shadowing several different physicians. First, I was able to watch two different surgeries. One surgery was a nasal surgery for sleep apnea done by a maxillofacial surgeon. The other was a revision of a total knee replacement done by an orthopedic surgeon. Next, I shadowed two different emergency room physicians at the emergency room that I worked at. Finally, I shadowed two different family practice physicians in their clinics and on hospital rounds.

Student at Medical College of Wisconsin (MD)

I shadowed 2 different podiatrists in the area in two very different settings to get a total feel of what it was like to be a podiatrist.

Student at College of Podiatric Medicine and Surgery (Podiatry)

Besides working side by side with various physicians, I shadowed many as well. Such as an Anesthesiologist, Primary Care, and two different Podiatrists.

Student at Scholl College of Podiatric Medicine (Podiatry)

I did not technically "shadow" any physicians, but spent a gazillion hours in clinical settings, research labs, and as a patient myself!

Student at Arizona College of Osteopathic Medicine of Midwestern University (AZCOM) (DO)

Not much shadowing...I was more a lab rat.

Student at University of Vermont College of Medicine (MD)

A few times, like a few days following guys around, plus for my EMT class we had to work like 20 hours in an ER.

Student at New York Medical College (MD)

50 hours dental 30 hours podiatry.

Student at Des Moines University — College of Osteopathic Medicine (DMU/COM) (DO)

No official shadowing. Working with them on my job has been shadowing enough so far.

Student at Morehouse School of Medicine (MD)

None...I've seen how they act while I was working at the hospital though.

Student at University of Texas Medical School at Houston (MD)

I shadowed a family practitioner (DO) for 1 month or about 60 hours. I also shadowed an internal med physician (10 hours) and a podiatrist (20 hours).

Student at College of Podiatric Medicine and Surgery (Podiatry)

I have only shadowed one physician for a total of about 10 hours. It was really informative and he was wonderful to let me watch, but our schedules didn't really work.

Student at Joan & Sanford I. Weill Medical College of Cornell University (MD)

I shadowed a pediatrician who owned his own practice.

Student at Ohio State University College of Medicine and Public Health (MD)

I only shadowed one doctor for one day. Last year I saw some Bolivian surgeries. Last summer I went to the morgue for "showings" once a week with all the interesting pathologists.

Student at University of Mississippi School of Medicine (MD)

I volunteered at a peds clinic + breast cancer clinic, but I didn't actually "shadow a physician."

Student at Chicago Medical School at Rosalind Franklin U-Med & Sci (MD)

I had to scratch, pull hair, kick, and use dirty words to get every hour of shadow time I got. I just kept after it until I ended up spending 9 hours in an OR in our community hospital. That was AWESOME!

Student at Medical College of Wisconsin (MD)

I spent a total of about four days shadowing orthopedic surgeons. Half of the time I was in the office and the other half I was in surgery. I also spent another day shadowing a family medicine resident.

Student at Medical College of Wisconsin (MD)

During my senior year, I shadowed a family med doc for about 30 hours. I was not able to arrange this until about halfway through my interviews.
Student at Medical College of Wisconsin (MD)

I shadowed a DO at an Urgent Care center near my house for a handful of times, which totaled to about 50 hours. Although not very exciting, this activity showed that I was interested in the field and gave me more to talk about during interviews.

Student at Medical College of Wisconsin (MD)

I clocked over 50 hours of shadowing the year before I started medical school. Every single hour was worth it. I felt that it gave me an advantage during the application process and school itself. It gave me a much broader sense of what being a doctor entailed. One of the most important things you can do in my opinion is to shadow as much as you can. Also, try to shadow physicians in different fields. This will keep your shadowing experience interesting and also give you a more global perspective on medicine. Physicians I shadowed: 2 Family Practice 1 Anesthesiologist 1 General Surgeon 1 Pediatric Oncologist.

Student at Medical College of Wisconsin (MD)

I shadowed an internal medicine MD several times throughout undergrad, and also spent some time shadowing in the emergency department.

Student at Medical College of Wisconsin (MD)

I shadowed a general surgeon covering both his office visits and in the OR approximately once a week over a summer.

Student at Medical College of Wisconsin (MD)

I didn't do any formal shadowing. Through my various EMS jobs, I had the opportunity to talk with physicians in different Emergency Departments.

Student at Ohio State University College of Medicine and Public Health (MD)

I had the unique opportunity to be involved in two preceptorships at Marshfield Hospitals and Clinics during the winter breaks in my junior and senior year. In total, I was with 19 specialists in 20 days. This was a very helpful factor in my realization that I love medicine.

Student at Medical College of Wisconsin (MD)

I shadowed doctors on breaks during college and that was enough for me. I did it in my hometown. The one guy was a vascular surgeon and then I shadowed a couple of internists. It was a good experience overall.

Student at Philadelphia College of Osteopathic Medicine (PCOM) (DO)

The summer between my junior and senior year, I volunteered at my local emergency room two days a week. Among many things, I was able to shadow the doctors quite a bit. Near the end of my senior year, I shadowed a Family Practice DO for nearly a month. It was a fantastic shadowing experience.

Student at West Virginia School of Osteopathic Medicine (WVSOM) (DO)

Since my little brother is going through the whole hoop jumping premed thing right now, I have a lot to say about getting in to medical school (if you have not already noticed). I believe that shadowing is extremely important. How else can you know what a doctor does all day? I feel that several full days of shadowing is far more beneficial for the applicant than is months and months of volunteering at a hospital being a nurse's slave/ phone answerer/ greeter/ or hospital information provider. I've been there. Volunteering gives you little contact with the MDs and the contact you do have is but a slice in time. Shadow docs in different fields for full days. You'll have a blast, it takes less of your time, and you'll have plenty of sweet experiences to talk about on the interviewing trail.

Student at Medical College of Wisconsin (MD)

I shadowed three physicians before I entered medical school in a number of settings (clinic and hospital). VERY IMPORTANT to do as medical school is very difficult and you have to have a lot of motivation.

Student at Medical College of Wisconsin (MD)

I shadowed minimally during one of my summer internships but did not do it on a regular basis.

Student at Medical College of Wisconsin (MD)

I treated shadowing as a mere formality in my application, and wasn't sure I agreed with the idea that it was valuable for everyone to do. I simply shadowed two different family doctors for 5 hours each. I believe that this helped my application at least a little bit, because I was able to talk in my interviews about what I learned through the experience.

Student at Medical College of Wisconsin (MD)

I first shadowed a doctor by turning in an application for a 3-day undergraduate internship to shadow a family practitioner through University of Washington's WWAMI program. I was fired up afterwards and even more excited to get the applications. I should have shadowed more before taking my MCAT, maybe it would have motivated me to study more. Think about that all of you premeds that haven't taken the MCAT yet. Then, a year later I applied through the same WWAMI program to do a 2-week family practice internship of 8–10 hours a day at the Pocatello Family Medicine residency program. I loved it, plus I received $500 for being accepted for the internship! The only regret that I have about shadowing is that I should have done more hours and shadowed outside of family practice also.

Student at Kansas City University of Medicine and Biosciences (KCUMB) (DO)

In total, I spent 3 weeks, or about 135 hours, shadowing in 3 different offices. I spent one week with an ENT (ear-nose-throat), one week with an orthopedic surgeon, and one week in an urgent care facility, following different physicians. I shadowed from Monday through Friday, 8 am until 5 pm (or a little later) and went on call with the ENT for a couple of nights. I followed both the ENT and orthopedic surgeon into surgery, on rounds and in the office. Great experiences—they made me choose medicine for sure. I would recommend lots of shadowing.

Student at Medical College of Wisconsin (MD)

How much did you volunteer?

EMT-Basic. 3 years volunteering with Emergency Medical Services.
Student at Scholl College of Podiatric Medicine (Podiatry).

None.
Student at Medical College of Wisconsin (MD)

None.
Student at Medical College of Wisconsin (MD)

I volunteered in the emergency room at a nearby Hospital every week during the summer for a few hours.
Student at University of Miami Leonard M. Miller School of Medicine (MD)

Other than volunteer service for my church, the majority of my volunteering time went to a health care clinic on the Arizona/Mexico border that catered to special needs children from Mexico. I translated for pediatricians and helped out where I could. The clinic was run one day a month. I volunteered for almost a year before we moved.
Student at Medical College of Wisconsin (MD)

I was extremely involved in a community service organization called Circle K (related to Key Club and Kiwanis). I volunteered about 250 hours with Circle K at a soup kitchen, elementary/middle schools, a nursing home, an emergency shelter, and various other events. I volunteered about 20 hours in the emergency room of a hospital.
Student at Lake Erie College of Osteopathic Medicine (LECOM) (DO)

Didn't do much volunteering.
Student at TUCOM-Nevada Campus (DO)

I coordinated the Red Cross blood drives at my college along with two other students. I volunteered for muscular dystrophy summer camps as a counselor.

Student at Johns Hopkins University School of Medicine (MD)

For volunteer work I volunteered at a local hospital in the cardiopulmonary department for a year. For one semester, I helped with the cardiopulmonary rehabilitation program. This involved mostly talking with the patients in the program and taking their blood pressures. The second semester I did more inpatient stuff, doing some filing and helping the respiratory therapists with their rounds. Total this involved about two hours a week for the school year.

Student at Medical College of Wisconsin (MD)

I have not been a volunteer.

Student at Morehouse School of Medicine (MD)

I played sports in college so I didn't have a lot of time to volunteer. I did work in a soup kitchen, and helped build a house for Habitat for Humanity.

Student at College of Podiatric Medicine and Surgery (Podiatry)

I volunteered a lot, mostly for the Boys and Girls Club. I also had my fair share of missions trips and recruitment fairs.

Student at University of Mississippi School of Medicine (MD)

Peds clinic - breast cancer clinic - charity work etc. etc. etc....

Student at Chicago Medical School at Rosalind Franklin U Med & Sci (MD)

I volunteered whenever I could in hospitals. I speak Spanish fluently so that gave me an inside edge. Then, I would use my secret weapon to watch the docs, talk to their head nurse, make friends, ho'll get you in

Student at Medical College of Wisconsin (MD)

I spent two years in Germany as a missionary for my church and each week I was involved in various service projects within the community. Throughout college, I volunteered a few hours a week at a pediatric rehabilitation center. I also briefly volunteered in the sterilization unit of a hospital.

Student at Medical College of Wisconsin (MD)

I volunteered for Habitat for Humanity many times at my college, which was building a house.

Student at College of Podiatric Medicine and Surgery (Podiatry)

I volunteered for the American Cancer Society, where I was able to sit on the board in my rural community and help construct dafidil days and relay for life. Also, I volunteered for honor societies at Minnesota State University.

Student at Scholl College of Podiatric Medicine (Podiatry)

I volunteered over 1,000 hours in a hospital during my teenage years. In high school and college, I tutored elementary school students and GED candidates. I've been a CPR/First Aid instructor for the Red Cross for several years as well.

Student at Arizona College of Osteopathic Medicine of Midwestern University (AZCOM) (DO)

as an EMT like 4 hours a week on average

Student at New York Medical College (MD)

Averaged about 4 hours per week for one semester

Student at Des Moines University — College of Osteopathic Medicine (DMU/COM) (DO)

I had been active in volunteering throughout college through various campus groups I was in. I spent three of my Spring Breaks on service projects, two of which were with Habitat for Humanity. I really did not do any medically related volunteering.

Student at Medical College of Wisconsin (MD)

I volunteered in a local emergency room during my year off of school. I would go in for just a few hours at a time about once a week totaling to about 100 hours. Most of the work I did was not very attractive but it did give me many opportunities to speak with docs about how I should go about applying, what they liked about medicine, etc.

Student at Medical College of Wisconsin (MD)

I volunteered at Children's Hospital of Wisconsin for almost two years before I started school. I worked on the pediatric oncology unit for a year, security for 6 months, and Pediatric E.R. for 6 months.

Student at Medical College of Wisconsin (MD)

I volunteered with my hometown EMS service mostly during the summer, but occasionally during the school year on weekends or during other vacations.

Student at Medical College of Wisconsin (MD)

I volunteered in the Emergency Department at the Veteran's Administration Hospital in Salt Lake City between four and six hours a week over the course of my sophomore year of college.

Student at Medical College of Wisconsin (MD)

I didn't really do any volunteering during the year prior to applying, because my school and work schedule didn't allow me a lot of extra time. Before going back to school, I volunteered for my local fire department (a couple of hours a week) and my local EMS squad (on call 40+ hours a week). I also volunteered with my local Friends of the Library.

Student at Ohio State University College of Medicine and Public Health (MD)

I volunteered between 3 and 6 hours per week my senior year at the local hospital. My duties ranged from escorting patients to various locations in the hospital to delivering medical records to their respective departments.

Student at Medical College of Wisconsin (MD)

I really didn't do a whole lot of volunteer work except through some Christian organizations at my undergraduate college.

Student at Philadelphia College of Osteopathic Medicine (PCOM) (DO)

I find volunteer work great for the philanthropist, but the goal here is Physician, not Mother Theresa. Do it if you enjoy it and it makes you feel warm and fuzzy inside. Do NOT do it to pad the resume. Your time is better spent shadowing doctors.

Student at Medical College of Wisconsin (MD)

Quite a bit everywhere I could. Medical and Non-medically related. I didn't feel as though it was a chore, but more an extension of what I wanted to eventually do.

Student at Medical College of Wisconsin (MD)

I volunteered at a local emergency room for approximately 4–5 months an average of 4 hours a week. I thought that my time spent volunteering was below average for premeds, but the necessity of my working in a paid job for many hours and my ability to extract meaningful lessons from my volunteer experience made up for it.

Student at Medical College of Wisconsin (MD)

I volunteered various places. I spent 4 hrs/week in the Duke Cancer Clinic just talking with patients (nothing clinical really) and also taught basic first-aid principles to first graders at an inner-city grade school.

Student at Medical College of Wisconsin (MD)

I volunteered at the Pocatello Free Clinic for about 45 hours total. At the clinic, I was able to screen patients, take patient histories, take blood pressure, and other miscellaneous duties. It was fun and great to interact with both patients and physicians while being involved myself. I volunteered at the soup kitchen a couple of times and at a few other miscellaneous events. Also, I spent several years in my church teaching and working with youth and other volunteer work. Additionally, I coached my 2 boys in soccer for a season.

Student at Medical College of Wisconsin (MD)

What clinical exposure did you have?

None.
Student at Medical College of Wisconsin (MD)

I worked as an Emergency Medical Technician on an ambulance for nearly two years and in a hospital emergency department for three and a half years.
Student at Medical College of Wisconsin (MD)

Just physician shadowing.
Student at University of Miami Leonard M. Miller School of Medicine (MD)

With the Army, I was trained as a field medic (basically EMT/paramedic level) and a pharmacy technician. For my reserve drills, we would spend the weekend in the VA hospital working with the nurses.
Student at Medical College of Wisconsin (MD)

I followed/assisted health professionals around for a week in high school such as a respiratory therapist, physical therapist, and emergency room doctor for a total of 30 hours. I volunteered in an emergency room for 20 hours. I shadowed an RN in the nursery for 3 hours and an osteopathic pediatrician for 5 hours.
Student at Lake Erie College of Osteopathic Medicine (LECOM) (DO)

I didn't have hospital experience; however, I worked with children with muscular dystrophy.
Student at Johns Hopkins University School of Medicine (MD)

With my background in sleep medicine, I was able to be a clinical assistant once a week for 6 months. It was volunteer experience, but I was able to take histories and work with the attending to make a differential, order tests, and plan treatment. Great fun, and it sealed the deal for me becoming a physician. I also have 4 years of sleep medicine technology experience in direct patient care and lab supervision.

Student at University of Mississippi School of Medicine (MD)

I feel that I had quite a bit of clinical exposure. I had the shadowing and the volunteer work that I listed before. In addition, two of the jobs that I had were in clinical settings. As listed before, I worked as a unit clerk in both an emergency room and an urgent care. In addition to the exposure to the clinical environment at these jobs, I was able to get to know several physicians quite well.

Student at Medical College of Wisconsin (MD)

My most significant "clinical" experience was working as a caregiver to Alzheimer's and dementia patients. It was by far the best job I have ever had. I worked full time during the summer, and part time during school. It made me really interested in pursuing geriatrics, but of course, I have no idea where I will actually end up.

Student at Joan & Sanford I. Weill Medical College of Cornell University (MD), class of 2010.

I worked as an ER tech during nursing school, and I have been a registered nurse for 8 years. I have worked in large teaching hospitals and small community hospitals in ER and ICU.

Student at Morehouse School of Medicine (MD)

Only when I job shadowed.

Student at College of Podiatric Medicine and Surgery (Podiatry)

I saw a few surgeries in Bolivia. That kind of freaked me out.

Student at University of Mississippi School of Medicine (MD)

Peds clinic, breast cancer clinic, helping patients fill out charts, talking to them about various treatment options and their concerns. I also worked with a schizophrenic patient on a one-to-one basis, which taught me A LOT about her condition.

Student at Chicago Medical School at Rosalind Franklin U-Med & Sci (MD)

Only shadowing.

Student at Medical College of Wisconsin (MD)

My clinical experiences consisted of volunteering in a pediatric rehab center and shadowing physicians.

Student at Medical College of Wisconsin (MD)

Most of my clinical exposure, besides my 30 hours of shadowing, came through having a parent who was/is a physician. Growing up in that environment exposes you to many sides of clinical practice that you can't see while in the office. Not that that really impresses any med schools.

Student at Medical College of Wisconsin (MD)

I worked at the Mayo Clinic as an intern and had the opportunity to experience many surgeries first hand.

Student at College of Podiatric Medicine and Surgery (Podiatry)

Besides working 5 years as a Nursing Assistant, I worked 2 years as a Medical Technologist at the Mayo Clinic, Rochester. The clinical exposure I received was huge. Such as working with doctors, nurses, and patients in the ICU, ER, OR, Peds, OBGYN, and PACU. I would perform a wide array of stat clinical tests as well as draw blood (arterial or venous) and read ventilators for the physicians. I was part of the CODE team to help revive a patient. Also, I would be on call for liver, cardiac, and lung transplants, where I would have to operate the OR lab. A great portion of my work involved being called down to a patient to draw an arterial blood gas and run an ABG test to get the results to the physicians. Through this experience, I learned a great deal of how to palpate a patient's extremity to feel for veins, nerves, tendon, and arteries. In addition, I learned how important it is to have fast and accurate test results while treating a patient.

Student at Scholl College of Podiatric Medicine (Podiatry)

I worked with geriatric and pediatric patients in the hospital; on the geriatrics ward, I assisted in bathing, feeding, and changing patients. On the peds ward, I coordinated playroom activities. While working in a neurosurgery lab in college, I spent many hours in the operating room to observe hippocampectomies (very intricate, delicate process) and collect tissue for use in our research.

- I did a public health fellowship with the CDC in Alaska and traveled to several remote villages for clinical research activities.

- I've been working with mentally ill children and adults for over three years, coordinating social and medical services.

Student at Arizona College of Osteopathic Medicine of Midwestern University (AZCOM) (DO)

EMT. I was really good at taking Vitals and dressing Trauma wounds

Student at New York Medical College (MD)

None

Student at Des Moines University -- College of Osteopathic Medicine (DMU/COM) (DO)

My most significant clinical exposure was the two years I spent working as an EMT for a private ambulance service. My company ran private transports as well as 911 calls along with the fire dept.'s paramedics. This job taught me a great deal about the field of medicine. Through this experience, I met countless interesting nurses, docs, paramedics, etc., who all had an impact on my decision to enter the field of medicine.

Student at Medical College of Wisconsin (MD)

I had several clinical exposures. I worked as a lab tech assistant at West Allis Memorial Hospital for 6 months. After that, I was a pharmacy/IV/ Chemotherapy IV technician at St. Luke's Medical Center for almost 5 years. These comprised most of my hospital experience. All of my clinical experience came from shadowing.

Student at Medical College of Wisconsin (MD)

I have been a rural emergency medical technician-basic since 2002 and an I.V. tech since 2004. With both ambulance services that I worked for, I was usually the primary pre-hospital care provider for patients, making the medical decisions and actions necessary for those patients' well-being.

Student at Medical College of Wisconsin (MD)

Both my shadowing and volunteer experiences exposed me to a variety of situations in clinical medicine. I also was a certified HIV counselor for the Student Health office at the University of Utah my senior year.

Student at Medical College of Wisconsin (MD)

My clinical experience was all EMS related. I had about 6 years of EMS experience (emergency and non-emergency transports) prior to applying.

Student at Ohio State University College of Medicine and Public Health (MD)

Besides what I mentioned under shadowing experience, I currently hold a job as an ER registration clerk on third shift. By working in a hospital, you get a whole new perspective that you can hardly get by just volunteering.

Student at West Virginia School of Osteopathic Medicine (WVSOM) (DO)

Only shadowing.

Student at Medical College of Wisconsin (MD)

I had exposure when I shadowed and I also went on a medical missions trip in the summer of 2002 to Romania. We basically "played" doctor and saw many patients during 10 days. It was a life-changing experience.

Student at Philadelphia College of Osteopathic Medicine (PCOM) (DO)

Refer to the shadowing question.

Student at Medical College of Wisconsin (MD)

I worked as a PCA in the Dean Health System in Madison, Wisconsin, for two years rooming patients and helping with outpatient surgeries. This is an excellent program for anyone interested in medical school because they train you for free, and you get excellent clinical experience.

Student at Medical College of Wisconsin (MD)

My clinical exposure was limited to my volunteering in an emergency room and my very limited shadowing experiences. See those sections for more info.

Student at Medical College of Wisconsin (MD)

I worked at a hospital for one of my summer internships doing outcomes research where I was allowed to do some shadowing and attend rounds. I also volunteered at a cancer clinic regularly.

Student at Medical College of Wisconsin (MD)

I shadowed physicians for 3 weeks and volunteered at the Pocatello Free Clinic for 45 hours. See my responses under Shadowing and Volunteer work for details. That's about it.

Student at Medical College of Wisconsin (MD)

Do you have any leadership experience?

Resident Assistant for 1 year.

Student at Scholl College of Podiatric Medicine (Podiatry).

None.

Student at Medical College of Wisconsin (MD)

By way of leadership experience, I mentioned some church missionary positions that I held. That was all.

Student at Medical College of Wisconsin (MD)

I started my own premedical website.

Student at University of Miami Leonard M. Miller School of Medicine (MD)

Running my business provided plenty of leadership experience. Serving in the Army and as a missionary for my church provided additional experiences.

Student at Medical College of Wisconsin (MD)

I have tons of leadership experience, mostly with Circle K. Here are the positions I held throughout my undergraduate career. -Circle K *New York District Secretary (Twice) *New York District Conventions and Conferences Committee Chair *New York District Kiwanis Family Committee Chair (Twice) *New York District Marketing Committee Chair *New York District Sunshine Committee Chair *Club President *Club Treasurer -Premed Society *Vice President *Treasurer -Beta Beta Beta Biological Honor Society *Executive Committee Member

Student at Lake Erie College of Osteopathic Medicine (LECOM) (DO)

I organized and coordinated the blood drives while in college.

Student at Johns Hopkins University School of Medicine (MD)

VP of College of Science and Math Ambassadors (1yr) Chair of Tours for College of Science and Math Ambassadors (1yr) Relay for Life (fundraiser) Team Captain (3mo) Developed new information for Peer Health Educators (1yr)

Student at Joan & Sanford I. Weill Medical College of Cornell University (MD)

I had a few different leadership positions. For one semester I was the student representative on the campus planning committee which made decisions regarding campus planning and maintenance. Another semester I was on the election board which involved running the elections for the student government. Also, one semester I was the vice president of Golden Key International Honor Society at my university and then the following year I was the president. In my leadership positions with Golden Key, I was involved with planning activities such as service projects and running the yearly induction ceremony.

Student at Medical College of Wisconsin (MD)

SGA Varsity Soccer Team Varsity Wrestling Team Presidential Scholar.

Student at College of Podiatric Medicine and Surgery (Podiatry)

I was a captain of my hockey team in high school, an athlete in college, and a tutor for individuals and groups of up to 30 people in my undergrad.

Student at Medical College of Wisconsin (MD)

President of local AIChE student chapter, vice president of engineering student body, Wesley Foundation leadership team, etc., etc.

Student at University of Mississippi School of Medicine (MD)

WOW where do I start LOL... - President of several undergrad clubs - organized many educational seminars for undergrad students - organized students to make sandwiches and feed homeless people etc., etc., etc.

Student at Chicago Medical School at Rosalind Franklin U-Med & Sci (MD)

I served as an LDS missionary in Mexico. I oversaw the work in 3 cities as a "zone leader" for 10 months.
Student at Medical College of Wisconsin (MD)

I have had several leadership positions in my local church congregation.
Student at Medical College of Wisconsin (MD)

I was on several boards in undergrad but nothing serious. Mostly just resume builders.
Student at Medical College of Wisconsin (MD)

Only unofficially, being in charge of EMS crews on 911 calls.
Student at Medical College of Wisconsin (MD)

I was president of Residence Hall, a delegate at a leadership conference for my university, and also President of Mortar Board of my school. I also taught anatomy lab.
Student at College of Podiatric Medicine and Surgery (Podiatry)

I been supervising over 30 mental health direct care workers at a social services agency for the past year; this is probably the most hands-on leadership experience I've had.
Student at Arizona College of Osteopathic Medicine of Midwestern University (AZCOM) (DO)

Leading myself to the library and back. In high school I was editor in chief of newspaper
Student at New York Medical College (MD)

Coaching, teaching 4 years
Student at Des Moines University -- College of Osteopathic Medicine (DMU/COM) (DO)

I was an Editor and officer for the Student Health Advisory Committee at the University of Utah.

Student at Medical College of Wisconsin (MD)

I served as Captain for the EMS squad and held several different offices for different organizations that I was a part of.

Student at Ohio State University College of Medicine and Public Health (MD)

During college I had some leadership roles in different clubs and in various functions.

Student at Philadelphia College of Osteopathic Medicine (PCOM) (DO)

Various committees and camp counseling opportunities I found online. Just go searching, there is a lot of stuff for an individual who wants to volunteer all over the world.

Student at Medical College of Wisconsin (MD)

Nope. Overrated in my opinion...as Karl Rove has shown, people in leadership roles can be manipulated quite readily from the sidelines ;-)

Student at Medical College of Wisconsin (MD)

Not much.

Student at Medical College of Wisconsin (MD)

From prior employment, I had some mentor type of responsibilities for some time. Also, through my church service, I had held some leadership positions as Ward Mission Leader for 3 years in the Church of Jesus Christ of Latter-Day Saints and teaching youth.

Student at Medical College of Wisconsin (MD)

What suggestions do you have for the personal statement?

Make it entertaining and very personal. It is a personal statement and it should reflect what you are as a person. Imagine how many essays these people read and if yours is not close to being lively, they won't remember it. *Lord of the Rings* was 3 hours long but people still watched it because it was engaging. Tell a story or two about why you chose medicine. Don't bog them down about "it's a dream or a calling." They know that. They want concrete examples or proofs to show you are dedicated and sure about your decision. Make sure your statement flows and doesn't jump around to avoid confusing your reader. Lastly, be true to yourself…listen to your heart. This part of the application is what makes you more than an MCAT grade or GPA.

Student at University of Texas Medical School at Houston (MD)

Mine was a pile of crap. Have someone give you advice on making yours better.

Student at Medical College of Wisconsin (MD)

I would be unique, but not too pretentious. Sell yourself, but don't brag too much. Be honest.

Student at Medical College of Wisconsin (MD)

I actually just finished my personal statement for my radiology residency. Comparing it to the personal statement I had for medical school makes me laugh. For medical school, I tried to be creative, give it flare, so as to stand out. For radiology, they look more for short and straightforward personal statements. The personal statement is important, so don't brush it off. Have a bunch of people who know you read it. Give it to premed professors and MDs to read and critique. The best personal statement is one that DOES NOT stand out for better or for worse. You don't want your application flagged for being too strange. Rarely has a personal statement gotten someone into med school. Conversely, many great candidates have lost opportunities because of personal statements that were just too off the wall. Remember your audience, they are doctors, not actors.

Student at Medical College of Wisconsin (MD)

Same old stuff: Think it out. Write a draft. Rewrite it. Have a few people that know something about grammar and the English language review it.

Student at Medical College of Wisconsin (MD)

Write it from the heart. Include the one thing that truly pushed you to pursue medicine. For me, breaking my leg really pushed me forward. It encouraged me to help others more through volunteering and to never give up on my dream of helping others as a doctor just as I was helped. My doctor helped me walk again. I want to be such a support system for children one day.

Student at Lake Erie College of Osteopathic Medicine (LECOM) (DO)

Be honest. Use your personal experiences to illustrate your points, which will make your essay unique. For instance, the statement "I enjoy working with people" is generic. However, if you use a personal experience to explain how you enjoy working with people, then you'll have a story that helps to distinguish you from other applicants.

Student at Johns Hopkins University School of Medicine (MD)

I don't know that I have any good suggestions for the personal statement because I feel that I am a very poor writer. The only thing that I can say is to try and write something that will make you stand out from the rest of the crowd. Try to think of a unique and entertaining story from your life and work that into your personal statement.

Student at Medical College of Wisconsin (MD)

Start early. Many, many, many rough drafts. Do not give a canned statement for why you want to be a doctor. Tell something interesting and unique about yourself and tie it in to medicine.

Student at Morehouse School of Medicine (MD)

Be honest.

Student at College of Podiatric Medicine and Surgery (Podiatry)

Start early, and don't give it to everyone you know to help you with editing. I gave mine out to too many people, and got different suggestions from all of them. It was way too much. I recommend giving it to a couple people that know you very well, and someone with amazing grammar.

Student at Joan & Sanford I. Weill Medical College of Cornell University (MD)

SELL, SELL, SELL yourself. Unfortunately that is what the personal statement is. Think of it as a job application with more personal and abstract questions. If they don't like what they read, chances are you won't get an interview. Be honest and original. Some of the questions they like to ask are: What type of hardships have you overcome? Why do you want to be a doctor? Things of that nature. Many of the interviewers have been doing this for years and they know when someone is being a cookie cutter. Make it personal for you and very apparent how and why this was such a hardship for you.

Student at Medical College of Wisconsin (MD)

Be honest to yourself and to those who will read it.

Student at Medical College of Wisconsin (MD)

Don't be a cheese. And don't talk about how your mom's aunt's brother's cousin's twice-removed dog that had cancer moved you to want to become a doctor because you did not have the "skills required" to remove the tumor yourself. Talk about why you are a nerd, or why you like cooking or something.

Student at University of Mississippi School of Medicine (MD)

BE HONEST - Make it interesting, Admission Committees see tons of personal statements and yours HAS to stand out. - THE FIRST few sentences are crucial, perhaps start with an interesting quote - I think I did mine chronologically, to make it easier for the Admission Committees.

Student at Chicago Medical School at Rosalind Franklin U-Med & Sci (MD)

Everybody says what they think admissions committees WANT to hear...even I did that sometimes. If you really want to impress them, write why you really want to be a doc. That'll stick out like a sore thumb in a stack of 5,000 essays. Does anybody really go into medicine JUST to help people? I don't think so and neither did the guy who interviewed me.

Student at Medical College of Wisconsin (MD)

I simply tried to write the personal statement so that it reflected my personality without making it sound too casual.

Student at Medical College of Wisconsin (MD)

Be honest. Play to your strengths. Put some actual voice in your statement...something that is just you.

Student at Medical College of Wisconsin (MD)

Try to use one specific instance that really changed the way you thought about medicine and intertwine that throughout your whole paper.

Student at College of Podiatric Medicine and Surgery (Podiatry)

Go to your local university's writing workshop, or at least a good writer you know, to have them critique it for grammatical accuracy and basic structure. You don't want a lot of "fluff" in there because you have limited space. You want to grab them in the beginning; don't start out with "I have always wanted to be a doctor." Actually, don't put that in ANYWHERE. They read that sentence all the time. Tell them something different, something unique about you.

Student at Arizona College of Osteopathic Medicine of Midwestern University (AZCOM) (DO)

Make it interesting somehow!

Student at New York Medical College (MD)

Work hard.

Student at Des Moines University -- College of Osteopathic Medicine (DMU/COM) (DO)

Just be honest. It will probably take a few drafts but eventually you will end up with something that you truly think represents who you are.

Student at Medical College of Wisconsin (MD)

That's a personal question you must ask yourself, by looking deep inside. Practically speaking, have other people look it over. Preferably a writing center/tutor at your school. Don't rush it. And start it well in advance, as that is what delayed my initial AMCAS about a month more than I would have preferred.

Student at Medical College of Wisconsin (MD)

Do not simply repeat your resume. If the question asks why medicine, answer the question, do not repeat your activities section from your AMCAS.

Student at Medical College of Wisconsin (MD)

Avoid clichés. Also - don't get discouraged if you read some of the books out there on "How to Write a Personal Statement." Don't embellish on your experiences too much. Telling a story is fine, but don't be overly dramatic. Be prepared to be asked about your personal statement at interviews.

Student at Ohio State University College of Medicine and Public Health (MD)

Don't sugarcoat things. Allow your real "voice" to be heard and try to be somewhat creative so that those who are reading the statements are not bored. Be adventurous and don't be afraid to gloat about yourself.

Student at Philadelphia College of Osteopathic Medicine (PCOM) (DO)

Get a number of really good writers/editors to help you with the statement. Their advice is usually worth more than gold.

Student at Medical College of Wisconsin (MD)

It is absolutely necessary to treat this as one of the most important parts of your application. It may not make or break you, but it will certainly influence how your interviewers approach you going into the interviews, and gives you a chance to show aspects of your personality that are impossible to convey through your stats. Spend at least a month writing the PS and have as many people (medical and otherwise) as you can go over it carefully.

Student at Medical College of Wisconsin (MD)

Write about something you really can put some character into...not what you think admissions committees want to hear.

Student at Medical College of Wisconsin (MD)

Try to tell your story. Don't worry about what other people have written about. Be sure to tell your own story. Write down a quick list of events in your life from the beginning, including all the main events leading you to medicine. Think of any other interesting characteristics you have. Make a list of the three most important strengths or traits that define you and try to incorporate them in your statement. Include stories and explain through examples how you are instead of stating "I am good looking, very smart, charming, incredible, the best thing since the invention of the telephone..." Show through example and story instead of just stating your characteristics. Give an example of a situation that shows how you care about people instead of saying you care about people, for example.

Student at Medical College of Wisconsin (MD)

What suggestions do you have for the secondary applications?

Most were pretty basic. If you're lucky you can even reuse essays for multiple schools.

Student at Medical College of Wisconsin (MD)

Pain in the butt. These can cost $40 – $100 a piece. Be certain about what you want and how much you are willing to spend. And…keep jumping through the hoops, it will be good practice for the rest of your life.

Student at Medical College of Wisconsin (MD)

Secondary apps are a scam and a way for some schools to get your money in exchange for a rejection letter. They are tedious and some require more essays. Just grin and bear it as you jump through more hoops.

Student at Medical College of Wisconsin (MD)

Just get through it and get on to the interviews.

Student at Medical College of Wisconsin (MD)

Put as much effort into the essays as you can. As much as the personal statement on the primary application if you can. I wish I had put more effort into mine.

Student at Lake Erie College of Osteopathic Medicine (LECOM) (DO)

Wash, rinse, and repeat. Most of the questions can be answered from your personal statement in your main application. Heck, almost all of the secondaries I had had similar themes for their questions (e.g., would you like to work in a rural community, what do you think being a doctor means). Get them done early though and space them out. I was burnt out doing applications after applications for 2 months. Oh, watch those deadlines.

Student at University of Texas Medical School at Houston (MD)

Recycle answers! I had a list of answers on my computer and I recycled them to fit the questions.

Student at Johns Hopkins University School of Medicine (MD)

Like everyone else says...do them as soon as you can!

Student at Joan & Sanford I. Weill Medical College of Cornell University (MD)

The only advice that I have for secondary applications is to get them back as soon as possible. I made it my goal to have my secondary applications in the mail within two days of receiving them. This seemed to work very well for me in that I got an interview invitation from almost every school that requested a secondary application from me.

Student at Medical College of Wisconsin (MD)

EARLY!!!EARLY!!!EARLY!!! Did I mention EARLY?!

Student at Morehouse School of Medicine (MD)

Finish them as quickly as possible and get them in.

Student at Ohio State University College of Medicine and Public Health (MD)

Prepare to do quite a few essays.

Student at Medical College of Wisconsin (MD)

Decide for real what schools you want/don't want. I wasted too much money on schools that I knew I wasn't going to go to.

Student at University of Mississippi School of Medicine (MD)

GET THEM IN FAST!!!!!!!!!! Even FedEx them!

Student at Chicago Medical School at Rosalind Franklin U-Med & Sci (MD)

I would just suggest finishing them as soon as you get them.

Student at Medical College of Wisconsin (MD)

They are less than fun. Just be diligent and get them back in as soon as you can. Stay on the people who are providing your recommendation.

Student at Medical College of Wisconsin (MD)

Finish them as quickly as possible. In general, the sooner you get them turned in the better your odds at an interview.

Student at Medical College of Wisconsin (MD)

Did not have to fill any out.

Student at College of Podiatric Medicine and Surgery (Podiatry)

Most schools will ask similar questions on their secondaries: why medicine, why our school, tell us about yourself. Don't re-hash your personal statement; give them something new to chew over. It's your chance to tell them everything about yourself that you think is relevant. Take advantage of that. And get them done as soon as humanly possible!

Student at Arizona College of Osteopathic Medicine of Midwestern University (AZCOM) (DO)

Proofread, name specific things about school you like

Student at New York Medical College (MD)

Fill them out quickly, make sure they have everything they need.

Student at Des Moines University -- College of Osteopathic Medicine (DMU/COM) (DO)

Do exactly what the directions tell you to do. Follow deadlines to a T. The major thing is to make it complete as possible in the shortest amount of time as possible. The faster you get your application in the faster you will get an interview. If you wait too late, you may be interviewing as an alternate and not next year's class.

Student at Medical College of Wisconsin (MD)

Stay on top of those mothers. Feel free to reuse essays, just make sure you change the name of the school if you use it in the essay. I'm sure UConn would be thrilled to hear that you can think of no better place to study medicine than Tulane.

Student at Medical College of Wisconsin (MD)

Turn around your applications as fast as you can, many schools having a rolling admissions policy and the faster you get your application in the earlier you will hear about interviews.

Student at Medical College of Wisconsin (MD)

Don't blow it off. It deserves as much if not more attention than the primary. Do your best!

Student at Philadelphia College of Osteopathic Medicine (PCOM) (DO)

Get them done early!!!!!

Student at Medical College of Wisconsin (MD)

Fill them out carefully but quickly, remember time is of the essence as many schools have rolling admissions. Make sure to use any additional essays required to present unique aspects of yourself that have not been covered elsewhere in your application. Strive to give them as complete a picture of yourself as possible.

Student at Medical College of Wisconsin (MD)

They take a long time so narrow down your search as early in the process as possible.

Student at Medical College of Wisconsin (MD)

Turn them around as fast as you can. Same as your application and all materials in general. Fast response is key. I would respond to all schools since you really don't know at that point who will interview you and who will not. Maybe only leave out a school or two that really doesn't feel right and you really don't want to attend.

Student at Medical College of Wisconsin (MD)

What suggestions do you have for the interview?

Be prepared for the numerous types of questions you might be asked. Also come with questions of your own, even if you legitimately don't have any.

Student at Medical College of Wisconsin (MD)

Be yourself. Smile. At least think about your responses to the big questions, "Why a doctor?" "Why our school?" "What makes you so special?" etc.

Student at Medical College of Wisconsin (MD)

Be yourself. Remember, the interview is for you to see if you will be a good fit at their institution so be prepared to ask good questions about the school. Most of my interviews were low stress and they just wanted to know if I had personality. You'd be amazed at the number of premeds out there who are just social misfits.

Student at Medical College of Wisconsin (MD)

RELAX. The interviewer does not want you to fail (I think). It is imperative that you prepare well in advance for the interview. Go to the interview feedback section on www.studentdoctor.net, Download the questions for the medical school you will be interviewing at, and have mock interviews with friends and family. Dress sharply.

Student at University of Miami Leonard M. Miller School of Medicine (MD)

Be yourself. They should know that you are pretty well qualified—but they don't know how you conduct yourself. Let them see a little bit of your personality and what you have to offer the school.

Student at Medical College of Wisconsin (MD)

Really prepare for the interview using the questions on SDN (www. studentdoctor.net). I didn't discover this site until a few days before my first interview. I would have been so much better prepared if I had known about that sooner and if I had done mock interviews.

Student at Lake Erie College of Osteopathic Medicine (LECOM) (DO)

You've heard this often so I'll say it again...be yourself BUT don't be an idiot. Be professional and courteous. And at least practice your responses or try to figure yourself out. I had a list of my strengths and weaknesses as well as responses to common questions. It's a 30-minute interview so be clear, quick, and don't forget to show your enthusiasm.

Student at University of Texas Medical School at Houston (MD)

Practice delivering concise answers.
Wear a nice suit.
Maintain eye contact.
Smile and relax.
Use "sound bites."
Have a discussion with your interviewers.
Prepare a list of questions to ask.

Student at Johns Hopkins University School of Medicine (MD)

Just be yourself. Check on SDN (www.studentdoctor.net) for information on interviews from students that have already been to the school, that way there's less surprises. Try to figure out what you want in a school. Make lists after visiting every school about likes/dislikes. For me, they started blending together after a while...

Student at Joan & Sanford I. Weill Medical College of Cornell University (MD)

I went to eleven different medical school interviews, so I feel that I had quite a bit of experience. I know that it sounds trite, but all you can really do is try to be calm and relaxed and then just be yourself. After the first few interviews, I became much more relaxed and after that the interviews went very well for me.

Student at Medical College of Wisconsin (MD)

It is normal to be nervous, but be yourself. Try to find something interesting about your interviewer and ask them about it. Try to also talk about things other than medicine.

Student at Morehouse School of Medicine (MD)

Relax, they wouldn't ask you to interview if you didn't have a chance. Be honest, if you try too hard to impress they will see through your bull. Dress for success, this should be obvious.

Student at College of Podiatric Medicine and Surgery (Podiatry).

Be relaxed and confident. Honesty and tact is the best policy. Don't be discouraged if one interview doesn't go as well as you would have hoped. Remember that the short duration of the interview cannot give a true perspective of who you are but rather how you present yourself. Oh…and smile. Interviewing is the most fun of the whole process.

Student at Medical College of Wisconsin (MD)

Be yourself! And look presentable. Talk confidently. Do not apologize for anything and stand up for yourself. Give a good firm handshake. For some reason, everyone loved my handshake and they all commented about it. It set things off to a good start. And ultra-pointy girly shoes help too.

Student at University of Mississippi School of Medicine (MD)

BE ON TIME - BE POLITE - BE RESPECTFUL - BE INTERESTED - BE HONEST - Practice a mock interview with your family and friends several times, and get feedback. Try to stay over with a med student host and ask them for advice/mock interview.

Student at Chicago Medical School at Rosalind Franklin U-Med & Sci (MD)

Same as previous…I spent 20 minutes of a 30-minute interview talking about ice fishing. Just so happened that she, my interviewer, and I were into that. Don't pretend you are somebody else. Interviewers see right through it.

Student at Medical College of Wisconsin (MD)

Just be yourself and be honest in your answers.

Student at Medical College of Wisconsin (MD)

Review your personal statement and visit Student Doctor Network for interview feedback from the school you will be interviewing from.

Student at College of Podiatric Medicine and Surgery (Podiatry)

It's okay to be nervous, but also try to relax as much as possible. They may ask you some tough questions, but they are trying to see how you think on your feet, not necessarily expecting a perfect answer (because let's face it, there's no real "perfect" answer to anything). Smile. Be gracious. Be approachable and open, and most of all, be honest. I was asked about my physical sciences MCAT score at least 239,487 times; my answer? "I've always struggled with Newtonian mechanics. I took too much time on those questions, and didn't end up finishing." It's the simple truth. It's okay to admit your weaknesses! That shows you are humble and realistic about yourself. You also have to be able to admit your strengths, though, and be confident in those.

Student at Arizona College of Osteopathic Medicine of Midwestern University (AZCOM) (DO)

Tell them that you want to go to their school and getting into their school is your top priority

Student at New York Medical College (MD)

Just be yourself

Student at Des Moines University -- College of Osteopathic Medicine (DMU/COM) (DO)

Relax. Think of who you are and what you want beforehand. Be honest. Don't be afraid to take a moment or two to think about a question while in the interview. It can be ok to say "I don't know."

Student at Medical College of Wisconsin (MD)

Do a little research on the school and city that it is in beforehand, they might ask you what you like about their school in particular.

Student at Medical College of Wisconsin (MD)

BE HONEST!!!! If you have gotten this far, you must sell yourself. Do not be argumentative, and answer questions to the best of your ability. Most times they really don't care what your answer is, but how you will respond. Don't try to impress them with who you know or how good you are. The biggest application killer is conceit or self-centeredness. That is a key sign to them that you are not a team player. Your patient not only relies on you, but all the staff under you.

Student at Medical College of Wisconsin (MD)

Again, be yourself. I think one of the most important things in making a good impression is a firm handshake with a genuine smile while looking the interviewer in the eyes. Maintain eye contact, even if it makes you very uncomfortable. I'm not a huge fan of sustained eye contact, but I forced myself to lock eyes and probably came off as a little creepy, but I was 2 for 2 with my interviews, so take that for what it's worth. If an interviewer becomes very conversational, asking random non-medical stuff, don't feel the need to relate your answers to medicine. Just have a good conversation. AND SMILE, DAMMIT!!!!

Student at Medical College of Wisconsin (MD)

Try to be aware of some of the questions the school asks, although I did not know about them at the time, resources like this site or student doctor can be helpful…just remember the school is aware of the sites as well and they do read what students say.

Student at Medical College of Wisconsin (MD)

Arrive early. Be yourself. Research the school by checking out their website and the Interview Feedback on SDN. Even if you don't have questions about the school, have some handy to ask your interviewer. Be prepared to discuss ethical issues. Keep in mind that, in most cases, they are not looking for a specific answer. They are looking to see that you can express and back up your opinion clearly. Try not and be too "absolute" as it may be preferable to demonstrate that you are open to discussion and other viewpoints.

Student at Ohio State University College of Medicine and Public Health (MD)

Be yourself. Allow yourself to be nervous and don't freak out that you are nervous. Ask the interviewers questions; be interested in what they do too.

Student at Philadelphia College of Osteopathic Medicine (PCOM) (DO)

Relax and try to be yourself. Yoga and meditative thought work for me... and pray.

Student at Medical College of Wisconsin (MD)

Relax! Really, the horror stories you have heard about interviewers being jerks are few and far between, and even if you are put in this situation (I was!) you simply have to maintain a professional demeanor and come out the other side having not freaked out on your interviewer. Interviews are mostly about making sure you have at least minimal social skills, so be prepared for some small talk. Also, have an idea going in of what aspects of your application you would like to highlight, explain, or downplay (e.g., poor grades in certain subjects). Also objectively look at your application and determine at least one weakness, personality-wise or scholastic that you can talk about, and explain how this can be converted to an advantage or has already been addressed. They eat that stuff up!

Student at Medical College of Wisconsin (MD)

Be yourself!

Student at Medical College of Wisconsin (MD)

If you get an early interview at your first choice school, TAKE IT!! I know a few friends that were accepted to their school of choice and saved a couple to a few thousand dollars from canceling the rest of their interviews. I didn't know which school I wanted to go to, so I had to spend the few thousand dollars, but when I had my interview at KCUMB it just fit me, the atmosphere, the city, my peers. When you are at an interview, just take a deep breath and look around. You've accomplished one of your goals!! You are one step closer to the big journey. Then, take another big breath and try to relax and enjoy the day. Make sure you have done all of your preparation beforehand. I suggest that you ask and answer questions to yourself in the mirror (do this alone so people don't think you are Schizo :). This helps to have some sentences formed in your head so you don't stumble over your own words during the interview. ALSO, once you are in the interview, don't practically cut off the questioner by blurting your response like it was some regurgitated speech! Practice talking about yourself, why you want to go into medicine, ethic questions, then let it flow once at the interview.

Some schools do the interviews first, then tour the campus, some vice versa, so be ready.

Student at Kansas City University of Medicine and Biosciences (KCUMB) (DO)

Dress professionally, be on time. Try to get the earliest possible interview day – you'll have much better chances to get in that way. Especially if you have done everything else early (MCAT, application submission, secondary returned) you will have the opportunity to interview early. Take the first interview day you can. Review the basic questions and learn how to handle ethical questions. You may also want to review interview feedback and some questions students were asked on the Student Doctor Network.

Student at Medical College of Wisconsin (MD)

Describe your premed schedule, typical day, and week

Classes MWF and labs TR. Material was difficult but I managed to study less than most other premed student with similar results.

Student at Medical College of Wisconsin (MD)

Too long ago to remember. My best advice though is to enjoy your undergrad years and the time you have to play.

Student at Medical College of Wisconsin (MD)

Go to class for maybe 1/4 of the day, sleep for 1/4 of the day, study for almost 1/2 the day and talk to my girlfriend. During the week I would usually conduct research for a few hours a week. I went out with my girlfriend once a week on the weekends.

Student at University of Miami Leonard M. Miller School of Medicine (MD)

Typical undergrad school schedule (up to 18–20 credit hours). The rest of the time spent with the family and working on the house. Plenty of time to relax.

Student at Medical College of Wisconsin (MD)

I attended all of my classes, which usually lasted until about 2, 3, or 4 during my first 2 years. I got out earlier the last two years, but during those years, I did have to fit in time for research, Circle K, and work at the library. I remember not really doing the required reading for my classes until it was time to write a paper or study for a test. Of course, I am sure I will have to keep up in med school though! I really had plenty of free time to devote to Circle K and my boyfriend. I rarely did homework on the weekends until Sunday night. And I pulled a 3.85.

Student at Lake Erie College of Osteopathic Medicine (LECOM) (DO)

I had a fairly standard premed schedule with chemistry, biology, calculus, and English (humanities) during the first year. The second year consisted of physics and organic chemistry.

Student at Johns Hopkins University School of Medicine (MD)

I did not have a typical day or week during undergraduate school. I did not have a regular study schedule. Some days I would not study at all and other days I would study all day long.

Student at Medical College of Wisconsin (MD)

Class from 8 - 3 Practice from 3 - 6 Study/Relax/Work 7-10

Student at College of Podiatric Medicine and Surgery (Podiatry)

I went to school full time and worked 24 hours a week.

Student at Medical College of Wisconsin (MD)

I took the required courses for medical school and others that I was interested in or that I thought might help me in the future. Abbreviated list of courses taken: zoology, physiology, anatomy, genetics, microbiology, cell biology, cancer biology, general chem., organic chem., quantitative chem., biochem., philosophy of science, psych., physiological psych., mythology in literature, speech, computing, sociology, medical terminology, clinical lab science, stats., calculus, all the general courses (GDRs), etc.

Student at Medical College of Wisconsin (MD)

Eh...usually freaking out (hahaha) and cramming in all my engineering homework before deadlines. Right now I'm trying to balance a senior design project, honors thesis, job, and undone Latin assignments. I reserve Tues and Thurs mornings for breakfast at a local bakery with my girlfriends. A good way to unwind and consume large amounts of caffeine.

Student at University of Mississippi School of Medicine (MD)

I never had a "typical" day or week, some days I studied 14 hours straight, others I slept most of the day. The key is to know what makes you successful and to try to keep a balanced life!

Student at Chicago Medical School at Rosalind Franklin U-Med & Sci (MD)

Study at least one hour a day, then, the day before the ole physics test, study hard from 7 pm to 7 am and go in at 8 am and take the test. Binge and Purge baby. You may not be able to walk straight the next day but you'll get that A.

Student at Medical College of Wisconsin (MD)

In a typical day, I attended a couple of lectures in the morning, spent an hour or two volunteering around lunch, went to work building fences for a few hours in the afternoon, and then spent the evening with my wife. I was a procrastinator so I generally didn't study on a regular basis but crammed the night before a test.

Student at Medical College of Wisconsin (MD)

Umm…it was pretty normal. As a BTS major, I only took the required premed classes so for the most part I only had one lab a week. I study for a couple of hours a day then try to have some fun with the roommates.

Student at Medical College of Wisconsin (MD)

Have class in the morning until noonish. Study in the afternoon and then have most nights free to hang out with friends.

Student at College of Podiatric Medicine and Surgery (Podiatry)

I've been out of school for nearly six years. But I did take 12 credits this past summer (just for kicks?) while I was working full-time and part-time jobs and starting the application process. I'd study a couple hours each night, and revise an essay or two, but always left room for some exercise and quality time with my "family" (fiancé and two cats). It's all about balancing your load, or you'll collapse under the weight of it.

Student at Arizona College of Osteopathic Medicine of Midwestern University (AZCOM) (DO)

Study class sleep x5 sleep drink sleep study
Student at New York Medical College (MD)

During the school year: 14–16 credit hours per semester. I worked 20 – 35 hours per week to pay the bills.
Student at Medical College of Wisconsin (MD)

12 hour days with school, volunteer, shadowing, kids
Student at Des Moines University -- College of Osteopathic Medicine (DMU/COM) (DO)

Pretty variable, but I was usually in class from 9 or 10am until 2pm, occasionally 5pm on days with lab. Studied usually no more than a couple hours a day, and that's pushing it.
Student at Medical College of Wisconsin (MD)

It was normally pretty busy, as a chemistry major, I had lots of labs between physics and chemistry especially. I also took Spanish and some non-required courses like anatomy and physiology for "enjoyment" and preparation for medical school.
Student at Medical College of Wisconsin (MD)

First quarter: about 8 hours of class and 4 hours of lab per week (Gen Chem w/lab and Trig). Second quarter: 16 hours of class and 12 hours of lab per week (Gen Chem II w/lab, Bio I w/lab, Pre-calc, Physics I w/lab) Third quarter: 16 hours of class and 16 hours of lab per week (Gen Chem III w/lab, Bio II w/lab, Calculus, Physics II w/lab) Summer: HELL!!! Organic Chemistry lecture 9 – 12 M-F, and lab 1-5 M,W,Th for 8 weeks. Fourth quarter: 12 hours of class, 7 hours of lab per week (Physics III w/lab, Biochem, Microbiology w/lab)
Student at Ohio State University College of Medicine and Public Health (MD)

When I was in college, I had 8 o'clock classes all of the time and went most of the day. Then I would study a bit after that and try to be active in other activities. I didn't kill myself though because I knew that once I got to medical school I would be studying pretty much all of the time.

Student at Philadelphia College of Osteopathic Medicine (PCOM) (DO)

I am a fairly non-stop individual. I don't like to be bored so most of my time was filled with outdoors adventure stuff, studying, and work. I am still trying not to forget those I love in the world. Their company is priceless.

Student at Medical College of Wisconsin (MD)

I always took approximately 15 credits (12 credits was full time at my university) and worked an average of 12–15 hours/week. I usually studied outside of class between 2–3 hours per day, much more just prior to tests.

Student at Medical College of Wisconsin (MD)

I was a biomedical engineer so I had a lot of labs in undergrad (mostly electrical engineering) and design courses. I did not have to take many courses outside of my major to fulfill premed requirements.

Student at Medical College of Wisconsin (MD)

My schedule was a bit odd since I completed my BS degree in Zoology in 3 years instead of 4. Also, I have a large family, so I tried to spend some time with them. Overall, I tried to spend 8 am until 5 pm at school or in the library studying and then again from about 8 pm until 10 pm or 11 pm. The time from 6 pm (I also had to drive one hour each way to school and back) until 8 pm I tried to be home with the family. However, during my first semester, when I took 24 credits, I saw my family less than that. Also, before tests I saw them less than that in most of the other semesters with the exception of the two semesters following the MCAT and med school application. The first two years I did not work, but took a heavy load (18 credits) and maintained a GPA above 3.95. The last year,

I took it a little easier, but worked part time as well, so I worked some of the hours that I spent studying before. Overall, my last year was pretty relaxing and I spent more time with family as well. I always took my Sundays off to relax and managed to take some Saturdays off as well.

Student at Medical College of Wisconsin (MD)

Did you do any other extracurricular activities?

I AM A CREATIVE WRITER, I DO SPOKEN WORD POETRY. I AM ALSO AN ARTIST.

Student at University of Texas Southwestern Medical Center at Dallas Southwestern Medical School (MD)

None.

Student at Medical College of Wisconsin (MD)

Worked as a physiology lab instructor, did research, volunteered at church, had my own band called the Sea Monkeys.

Student at Medical College of Wisconsin (MD)

Aside from volunteering, I was a member of several Premed clubs. I love basketball!

Student at University of Miami Leonard M. Miller School of Medicine (MD)

In Tucson, I would go mountain biking with some friends every Saturday morning. Running a few times a week. Basketball Thursday nights. Church on Sunday and usually Tuesday/Wednesday nights. Family time in between.

Student at Medical College of Wisconsin (MD)

Circle K (all 4 years, many leadership positions, 250 service hours) - Premed Society (all 4 years, held leadership positions) -Beta Beta Beta Biological Honor Society (all 4 years, held leadership position) -Red Cross (last semester) -Community Service Network (2 semesters) -Phi Kappa Phi Honor Society -Oracle Honor Society

Student at Lake Erie College of Osteopathic Medicine (LECOM) (DO)

College Rugby (10 hours a week).
Salt Water Aquarium Business (10–20 hours a week).
My entrepreneurial drive later developed a publishing company.

Student at Johns Hopkins University School of Medicine (MD)

In addition to the extracurricular activities I have mentioned, I also got involved in some of the honor societies that I was a member of, particularly Mortar Board. Mostly I got involved in some of the community service projects that they had which involved activities will local elementary schools. In addition to these activities, I was involved in non-school activities to keep myself sane. I took piano lessons from a concert pianist throughout undergraduate school. I was also on several different indoor soccer teams and tried to go water-skiing as much as possible.

Student at Medical College of Wisconsin (MD)

I love to fish as often as possible. It is a great stress reliever for me.

Student at Morehouse School of Medicine (MD)

Varsity Wrestling Varsity Soccer SGA Founder of the Blue Crew, student athletic supporters :-) Worked on Festivus, a large spring bash at BC.

Student at College of Podiatric Medicine and Surgery (Podiatry)

Weightlifting, movies, volunteering, and work, work, work.

Student at Medical College of Wisconsin (MD)

I exercised, went to sporting events, watched a lot of movies and sports on TV, went out on the town with buddies, met and spent time with my fiancée, read, slept, etc. Remember to live a well-rounded lifestyle no matter what educational undertaking you may be in.

Student at Medical College of Wisconsin (MD)

I don't do as much now as I did before, but I do all the "typical" things I believe an average student would do. Just have a schedule.

Student at University of Mississippi School of Medicine (MD)

Aerobics - Chess - Swimming - Movies/hanging out with friends.

Student at Chicago Medical School at Rosalind Franklin U-Med & Sci (MD)

I love to fish: fly fishing, ice fishing, boat fishing. I can't wait to go to Wisconsin. I also like to play with my son and take my wife out to eat. I am a novel junkie: I read everything from John Grisham to Stephen King to Tess Gerritson to Shannon Drake (lesser known vampire novels) NO romance.

Student at Medical College of Wisconsin (MD)

I played on a few intramural sports teams.

Student at Medical College of Wisconsin (MD)

Football for two years. Omicron Delta Kappa leadership fraternity two years. Resident Assistant one year. Studied abroad on Semester at Sea Spring '05. Habitat for Humanity.

Student at Medical College of Wisconsin (MD)

Yes, I played intramural football, basketball, and was involved in church group activities.

Student at College of Podiatric Medicine and Surgery (Podiatry)

The main extracurricular activity in my life has been playing the violin and viola (for the past 20 years). I've played in semiprofessional symphonies and world music groups, and so a lot of time has been devoted to that, as well as teaching students. I've also been writing for ages and do some freelance work when I can. I did all the typical premed activities in college (volunteering, EMT certification, science clubs, etc.) and had a great time with those.

Student at Arizona College of Osteopathic Medicine of Midwestern University (AZCOM) (DO)

Played in band, worked in student-run EMS agency

Student at New York Medical College (MD)

Bike, hike, geocache

Student at Des Moines University — College of Osteopathic Medicine (DMU/COM) (DO)

Team-based improvisational comedy at ComedyCity Green Bay...performing comedy in front of large audiences. Occasional photographer/digital artist Amateur juggler. Computer/websiting stuff I taught a semester-long principles of biology lab (TA), doing all the setup/lecturing/cleanup/grading stuff that goes along with it. Randomly breaking out into song (I didn't list that on AMCAS)

Student at Medical College of Wisconsin (MD)

I was a member of the Student Health Advisory Committee at the University of Utah for two years. SHAC helped/s to organize the annual health fair, we also performed HIV screenings and counseling. I also skied a lot but that is probably of little interest as far as med school apps go.

Student at Medical College of Wisconsin (MD)

During my premed stint, I didn't do a lot of extracurriculars. As a teacher, I advised and coached numerous activities.

Student at Ohio State University College of Medicine and Public Health (MD)

I participate in numerous medical school clubs in various ways. It is good to join clubs mainly for community service opportunities and just being with people who share the same interests as you.

Student at Philadelphia College of Osteopathic Medicine (PCOM) (DO)

I played on the football team at school for a year until I had to leave with injuries. After that, a conflict resolution group, a freshman orientation group, and a mentoring group took up most of my sophomore year. A lot of running, biking, and swimming to round it off. Sculpting as well.

Student at Medical College of Wisconsin (MD)

My biggest extracurricular activity was playing bass guitar in a local indie rock band, which took up an average of 5–10 hours per week. We had weekly rehearsals, writing sessions, and also tried to play at least one show per month. Other than that, I played in a few intramural leagues for various sports.

Student at Medical College of Wisconsin (MD)

I raced on the ski team, which was a short season so didn't take up too much time except for in the winter.

Student at Medical College of Wisconsin (MD)

Research for a semester, volunteered 45 hours, shadowed 135 hours, church service, worked at Domino's Pizza as a driver, volunteer soccer coach, soup kitchen, miscellaneous service activities, mowing lawns, shoveling snow, lawn raking, etc., for some older people.

Student at Medical College of Wisconsin (MD)

How did you choose your med school?

They accepted me and I liked the facilities and location.
Student at Medical College of Wisconsin (MD)

My undergrad had a file of all the places premeds applied to and where graduates actually ended up. I applied based on location and then based on where kids from my school got accepted. That's how I ended up in Milwaukee. Love it here too!
Student at Medical College of Wisconsin (MD)

Medical Scholars program at the University of Miami Miller School of Medicine. I graduate college in 3 years, don't have to worry about applying to medical schools, get to stay in Miami. I love it here and think the school is magnificent. For me, it was a no-brainer.
Student at University of Miami Leonard M. Miller School of Medicine (MD)

Our first choice was based on location—if Arizona had offered me a spot, we would have stayed in Tucson. We looked at other schools based on the advice of friends that had attended the schools as well as the location.
Student at Medical College of Wisconsin (MD)

It was the only one I got into!
Student at Lake Erie College of Osteopathic Medicine (LECOM) (DO)

The school chose me, plain and simple. It turned out perfectly because I don't think there are any other places in Texas that can compare to a school in the middle of the Texas Medical Center.
Student at University of Texas Medical School at Houston (MD)

Hopkins was going through change in their curriculum in 1993. The school was transitioning from an 8-hour a day lecture-based format to a less didactic and more interactive format. With this new format of teaching and the name associated with the school, I felt it was a good investment for the future. In the end, it paid off because it helped me acquire an ophthalmology residency at one of the top 5 programs.

Student at Johns Hopkins University School of Medicine (MD)

I love the flexible schedule, emphasis on problem-based learning, and wanted an adventure. This school is in NYC, and I have barely even been out to the East Coast before. Very hard choice between my state school, but in the end, I just followed my gut (and my fiancé's too!).

Student at Joan & Sanford I. Weill Medical College of Cornell University (MD)

I mostly chose my medical school by how I felt about the school while at the interview. At some schools I just did not like the atmosphere and the feeling of the school. At other schools, like Medical College of Wisconsin, I just really liked the general atmosphere of the school and the medical students that I met throughout the interview day.

Student at Medical College of Wisconsin (MD)

I wanted to remain in Georgia, so a lot of it had to do with location. Also, the school's mission statement influenced my decision.

Student at Morehouse School of Medicine (MD)

Curriculum, board pass rate, overall comfort of the school/atmosphere, reputation, residency placement, location, cost of living, scholarship.

Student at College of Podiatric Medicine and Surgery (Podiatry)

It was in town. I wanted to stay here.

Student at Medical College of Wisconsin (MD)

I went on my gut instinct. I got the best feeling at MCW and was most impressed with the people and opportunities here. This was my first choice and I was accepted here one week after interviewing. Surprisingly, MCW handily defeated UW-Madison on my list and I am from Madison.

Student at Medical College of Wisconsin (MD)

I chose UMC because that's the only school that accepted me! Haha... but seriously...I'm glad it worked out that way. I'm very comfortable with the area, I'll be semi-close to home, and I believe it will be a good match for me in the long run.

Student at University of Mississippi School of Medicine (MD)

I chose my medical school because I love Miami. I love Florida and the University of Miami has a great medical school. I also did my undergrad at the university of Miami and could not picture myself anywhere else but being a Miller alumni and a cane.

Student at University of Miami Leonard M. Miller School of Medicine (MD)

I was REALLY impressed with the facilities at RFUMS-CMS and the match list was GREAT! The board scores are also above the national average. In addition, as a Canadian student, they DID NOT require an escrow account (have $200,000 grand in your bank account) as many other schools do. I did have a choice for other schools, but am REALLY glad I came here, the people are great. Our dean is really friendly and even has lunches with students every week. The facilities in the anatomy lab are great and the histo labs are all online!!!

Student at Chicago Medical School at Rosalind Franklin U-Med & Sci (MD)

My first priority is my family so I chose schools that gave me access to suburban areas with good schools. For example G.W. would not be a good school for me, so I didn't apply. MCW, Creighton, UofU, Loyola, all good schools.

Student at Medical College of Wisconsin (MD),

I think that the biggest factor for me and my wife was having family close by.

Student at Medical College of Wisconsin (MD)

I picked DMU because it has awesome first pass rate on boards, excellent residencies, the campus is really new, and the school is located in the Midwest.

Student at College of Podiatric Medicine and Surgery (Podiatry)

Several factors contributed to my decision to attend school in Arizona: 1) Location: my fiance and I wanted to be in a place where we'd be able to get out and hike or camp once in a blue moon; we love the outdoors. 2) Clinical rotations: when I'm married, I don't want to have to go to different rotation sites all over the country every 4–8 weeks. I wanted the option to do my rotations in the area (even if I end up choosing not to); I also wanted a diverse patient population, which describes Arizona to a T. 3) Preparation for boards: I wanted a school that was known for preparing its students exceptionally well for Steps I and II. AZCOM has the highest pass rate of all DO schools for Step I. 4) The overall "feel" of the school: I just liked the laid-back atmosphere of AZCOM. I also liked the fact that there are allied health programs affiliated with the school; no doctor is an island, after all.

Student at Arizona College of Osteopathic Medicine of Midwestern University (AZCOM) (DO)

Being an out-of-state student, University of North Texas was the hardest osteopathic medical school to get into, it was also the least expensive for an out-of-state student. When I went there for the interview, I really enjoyed my experience.

Student at Univ of North Texas Health Science Center at Fort Worth/Texas College of Osteopathic Medicine at Ft Worth (UNTHSC/TCOM) (DO)

Acceptance.

Student at New York Medical College (MD)

If you're lucky enough to be able to choose your school, you have to pick the school that feels most comfortable. It has to be a good fit all around.

Student at Medical College of Wisconsin (MD)

Des Moines, Scholl, best around

Student at Des Moines University — College of Osteopathic Medicine (DMU/COM) (DO)

MCW was the school that made me feel like they actually were interested in me beyond being an applicant and actually wanted me to come here. I was impressed by the area, the facilities, and the people. When all was said and done, MCW had moved to #1 on my list.

Student at Medical College of Wisconsin (MD)

The overall atmosphere at MCW, plus the nicer hospital facilities nearby, gave me a very good impression. I chose MCW over Madison mostly because I thought MCW would be a better place to prepare for emergency medicine. Also, I did not like the thought of being shipped all over the state for 3rd and 4th year rotations through Madison. I also thought the general aspects of living (location, commuting, food, people) was better in the Milwaukee/Wauwatosa area.

Student at Medical College of Wisconsin (MD)

Ohio State and MUO were probably my two top choices after interviewing. Ohio State won out due to location (being able to live with my husband).

Student at Ohio State University College of Medicine and Public Health (MD)

Through recommendations from my premed advisor at Grove City College. And also based upon my realistic chances of getting into medical schools in Pennsylvania.

Student at Philadelphia College of Osteopathic Medicine (PCOM) (DO)

It was the closest to family.

Student at Medical College of Wisconsin (MD)

I gained acceptances to three schools, which were also my top three choices due to geographic considerations. Ultimately, I felt comfortable at all three schools and chose the one where my wife would be closest to her family (to offer her another support system while I am in school) and where we would not be forced to move after two years—the University of Minnesota-Duluth does not offer years 3 and 4 in Duluth at this time…you have to move to the Twin Cities.

Student at Medical College of Wisconsin (MD)

I am from Milwaukee so I wanted to come back home and be near my family. I also really liked the program at Medical College of Wisconsin and liked that it was solely a medical school and that the faculty was here for us and not for undergrads.

Student at Medical College of Wisconsin (MD)

I interviewed at four schools and Medical College of Wisconsin was simply the best for me. I had a great interview day, connected with the interviewers, and loved the whole experience. I also received an offer there by October 15th, which enabled me to cancel all the other interviews I had. Some of the other interviews were good as well and I received some additional offers, but things at MCW just felt totally right. I knew I had found the right place.

Student at Medical College of Wisconsin (MD)

Did you take any extra course work in preparation for med school?

None.

Student at Medical College of Wisconsin (MD)

Nothing more than what was required of my major (Neuroscience). You'll learn the stuff when you get there. Undergrad is a time to get a broad education of stuff you are interested in and stuff you won't get to see in medical school. You can learn all the biochem you want in first year of med school only to forget 99% of it because all of it except the pathologies related to certain metabolic disorders do not apply to medicine. So forget that undergrad pharmacology class and take a guitar class or something.

Student at Medical College of Wisconsin (MD)

No.

Student at University of Miami Leonard M. Miller School of Medicine (MD)

I minored in Anthropology—mostly cultural anthropology. I would recommend it to everyone. It really helps broaden your perspective about people and the way they view the world.

Student at Medical College of Wisconsin (MD)

I simply took the required prep courses such as Organic Chem, Gen Chem, Physics, and Bio. I did take Microbiology and Biochemistry because I thought med schools might like those advanced courses. I was a Biology major.

Student at Lake Erie College of Osteopathic Medicine (LECOM) (DO)

I took the basic requirements for med school (e.g., Bio, Chem, Org)...you know the stuff that really didn't matter. There were upper-level classes that were required for my major like anatomy, physiology, and biochem. I also took electives that pretty much ended in –ology (immunology, virology, histology). The thing is the entire undergraduate material will be covered in about two weeks. That's what I've heard from most people so my advice is, take the class to gain some exposure and because you like it.

Student at University of Texas Medical School at Houston (MD)

No. I just took biochemistry, genetics, and other advanced biology courses during college. Reed College also requires a written thesis to graduate. This helped prepare me for medical and graduate school.

Student at Johns Hopkins University School of Medicine (MD)

I completed a Master's in health administration...basically a health care oriented MBA. I would highly recommend a few business/finance courses at least for each and every premed.

Student at University of Mississippi School of Medicine (MD)

The only extra course work that I took to specifically prepare for medical school was biochemistry. By the time I got to medical school, I felt that I had forgotten most of it, but at least I had already heard a lot of the material they taught in medical school biochemistry. I felt like this helped me to pick up the material faster than those students who had never heard the material before. In general, I feel that whatever extra course work you can take in undergraduate school will help you during medical school.

Student at Medical College of Wisconsin (MD)

Just the required work for med school and my degree.

Student at College of Podiatric Medicine and Surgery (Podiatry)

None.

Student at Medical College of Wisconsin (MD)

Just undergrad.

Student at Medical College of Wisconsin (MD)

Took the standard required courses plus biochem. No genetics or anything else like that for me. Might bite me in the butt one day.

Student at University of Mississippi School of Medicine (MD)

My undergrad education was enough, double specialist in tox and pharm + human bio major

Student at Chicago Medical School at Rosalind Franklin U-Med & Sci (MD)

Nah…just prepped for the MCAT

Student at Medical College of Wisconsin (MD)

My major was biology and that gave me a pretty solid background in most of the major courses during the first two years of medical school. In addition to the courses in my major, I took physiology, anatomy, and human dissection classes.

Student at Medical College of Wisconsin (MD)

No.

Student at Medical College of Wisconsin (MD)

Nope just took the required courses.

Student at College of Podiatric Medicine and Surgery (Podiatry)

I took some upper-level science courses as a neuroscience major, but I doubt these will be particularly helpful in medical school…maybe for the first day or so! I think the most important part of my education in undergrad was learning how to properly study.

Student at Arizona College of Osteopathic Medicine of Midwestern University (AZCOM) (DO)

Nope. Try to take anatomy and biochem before med school though.

Student at New York Medical College (MD)

Take biochem! Endocrinology was also helpful.

Student at Medical College of Wisconsin (MD)

Yes, about 60 credits worth.

Student at Des Moines University — College of Osteopathic Medicine (DMU/COM) (DO)

Since I took all the basic pre-reqs through my biology major and chemistry minor (big mistake on the chem minor), I pretty much had everything I needed. However, I did go above and beyond by taking classes in immunology, biochemistry, physiology lab, and neurobiology, and thus far they have all proven to be very helpful. Still, don't go overboard on science classes…take some courses that interest you and will be fun. I took Latin, electronic imaging, etc.

Student at Medical College of Wisconsin (MD)

I did do extra course work, but often times these courses either interested me or were required for graduation.

Student at Medical College of Wisconsin (MD)

Biochemistry and Microbiology were really my only "extra" courses.

Student at Ohio State University College of Medicine and Public Health (MD)

Nope.

Student at Philadelphia College of Osteopathic Medicine (PCOM) (DO)

None.

Student at Medical College of Wisconsin (MD)

I was lucky enough to qualify for a scholarship offered to University employees during my 2 years "off" from school, so I took several classes to pinpoint my interests and try to get comfortable heading into medical school. I took several graduate level genetics courses, an undergrad-level anatomy course—complete with prosections, an introductory course to pharmacology, and was certified as an EMT-Basic.

Student at Medical College of Wisconsin (MD)

Yes, I have taken some courses in preparation for med school. Part of my Zoology degree included 2 semesters of Anatomy and Physiology, Cell Biology, Genetics and many other courses. However, I purposely took 2 semesters of Human Physiology with the Pharmacy students and 1 semester of Human Pathophysiology with the Physician's Assistant students at my undergrad institution. These were not required, but highly recommended in preparation for med school.

Student at Medical College of Wisconsin (MD)

Any open-ended advice?

YOU BETTER BE SURE YOU WANT THIS. Getting prepared takes a long time. The application phase itself is very stressful. There are times when I asked myself if I was good enough and I probably felt the lowest in my life during that one year. But keep your head up. If you want it, then you will do anything to get in. Keep in mind that the hardship doesn't end during the application. The real tough part comes when you get accepted. From your date of matriculation, starts a life-long process which will surely test every amount of intellect and character within yourself.

Student at University of Texas Medical School at Houston (MD)

A place to prepare... A place to get scared... Worth it in the end!

Student at University of Texas Southwestern Medical Center at Dallas Southwestern Medical School (MD)

Don't aim too high when you're applying to schools or you'll end up just wasting a lot of money and then reapplying the following year.

Student at Medical College of Wisconsin (MD)

If your whole academic career is "focus on the light on the end of the tunnel," you might be in for a long and tiring journey only to find that the light was a train. Enjoy the journey, not just because it's a long one, but because it's a fun process. Hoop jumping can be fun! So enjoy the journey and that will make the destination that much more satisfying.

Student at Medical College of Wisconsin (MD)

If you are sure you want to be a doctor, then congratulations. This is a wonderful, rewarding field. Study hard but don't get burned out. Have fun as well. The most important thing I have learned is that you need to stand out. Start EARLY ON (pref. freshman yr) volunteering, doing research, shadowing. Find something you enjoy that you think most others will not have on their application. Best of luck to all of you! Feel free to ask me any questions and I will gladly respond.

Student at University of Miami Leonard M. Miller School of Medicine (MD)

Good luck!

Student at Medical College of Wisconsin (MD)

Apply EARLY! Take the MCAT in April not August. If you get a low MCAT score, don't be afraid to apply to DO schools. Take interviews SERIOUSLY! Get lots of clinical experience!

Student at Lake Erie College of Osteopathic Medicine (LECOM) (DO)

Just relax! It's going to be hard work and take some dedication and discipline, but don't be so focused on MED SCHOOL MED SCHOOL that you miss out on the fun times that college can offer. And try not to be "that kid" that annoys everyone for old tests and notes and don't brag to the whole world if a prof "helps" you out with grades at the end. Be humble.

Student at University of Mississippi School of Medicine (MD)

Although physicians are paid well, do not be lured into medicine for the money. Medicare, for instance, is cutting physician reimbursements by 4–5% yearly for the next 5 years. Malpractice insurance is expensive. There are many stresses associated with the "high income."
Physicians will continue to make a good income, however, my advice is to: Do what you love and the money will be icing on the cake… do what you hate and the money becomes the shackle that binds you to the thing you despise.

Student at Johns Hopkins University School of Medicine (MD)

I probably can't give you any advice that you've not already heard about medical school. *Student at West Virginia School of Osteopathic Medicine (WVSOM) (DO)*

I cannot emphasize this point enough. Apply as early as you can and get the secondary applications back as soon as possible.

Student at Medical College of Wisconsin (MD)

Don't give up if this is your goal!!! Apply EARLY!

Student at Morehouse School of Medicine (MD)

Always set goals for yourself. And remember everything works out in the end.

Student at College of Podiatric Medicine and Surgery (Podiatry)

Just be yourself. On paper and in person. If you don't get in the first time, Med schools love persistence so try again. If you know what school you really want to go to, apply for early admission. Your chances of getting in may be better if they see that you are committed only to them. For instance, at MCW if you apply for early admission I don't think you can apply anywhere else until the process is over. So by doing so you may be severely limiting yourself with other schools depending on when you hear back. It really is a double-edged sword. A resident once told me if you apply to too many schools, you appear needy and desperate. If you apply to only one or two (not in your area or for early admission), you may look cocky. I don't know if that is true or not, but 7–12 seems to be a nice magic number. Hope that helps. Good luck.

Student at Medical College of Wisconsin (MD)

Work and play hard, always have a goal to work toward, be happy, honest, thoughtful, and enjoy the ride.

Student at Medical College of Wisconsin (MD)

Talk to current med students and get them to look over your application + APPLY EARLY!!!

Student at Chicago Medical School at Rosalind Franklin U-Med & Sci (MD)

If you want to be a doc, its all or none…you're either balls to the wall or you're not…either you'll get in (no matter what) or you won't. Make up your mind and the go for it. If I can make it, so can you.

Student at Medical College of Wisconsin (MD),

Start gathering all info needed for applications early. If you can download secondary apps prior to receiving them in the mail do it and send them out ASAP. The faster you get everything done, the better chance you have of being accepted. Get all your letters of recommendation well before applying. You don't want to keep your applications waiting to process due to a recommendation that hasn't arrived.

Student at PCOM-Georgia Campus (DO)

If you really stick with it, you can achieve it. This might mean retaking classes or the MCAT and watching friends out in the work place making money, but if you really want it, hard work pays off and dreams do come true!

Student at College of Podiatric Medicine and Surgery (Podiatry)

I think it should be mandatory for premeds to take at least two years off after college to start the med school process. That time off in the "real world" was invaluable for me, and certainly for others.

Student at Arizona College of Osteopathic Medicine of Midwestern University (AZCOM) (DO)

Don't give up! And don't listen to advice you don't want to hear!!!

Student at University of Vermont College of Medicine (MD)

Be honest, true, and make sure you do what you want to.

Student at Des Moines University — College of Osteopathic Medicine (DMU/COM) (DO)

I think that applying as early as possible is one of the biggest factors for getting interviews and ultimately getting in. Get your primary application ready the month before you are able to send it and then send it as soon as it becomes available. I would complete each secondary as soon as you receive them.

Student at Medical College of Wisconsin (MD)

Always have a backup plan…I had one and knowing that there something else I could do that I would find fulfilling if I were not accepted really took a lot of pressure off during the whole process. I thought all the practice exams were a heck of a lot harder than the MCAT. Apply to MCW! It's a great place!

Student at Medical College of Wisconsin (MD)

Don't lose yourself by trying to meet some other standards. Meet the general requirements, but beyond that, make standards for yourself. Learn to remain calm and accept failure and success equally. There's no point in getting worked up over something you can't change. Just learn to make the best of it. And don't give in to hate. That leads to the Dark Side.

Student at Medical College of Wisconsin (MD)

Be patient and have some faith in yourself. The entire application process is difficult and has a lot of ups and downs, but in the end if you want to go to medical school, you will find a way to make it there.

Student at Medical College of Wisconsin (MD)

SHADOW!! I was asked at every interview about shadowing and how I knew what a physician's job and life was like. Also, your volunteering doesn't have to be medically related if you have other clinical and/or research experience. Volunteer for something that you truly enjoy, not for something that you think will "look good."

Student at Ohio State University College of Medicine and Public Health (MD)

No matter what, don't give up. If medicine is your dream, you can make it happen. The route may be longer than anticipated, and you may find that the process forces you to look at yourself and your accomplishments and truly evaluate your shortcomings, but it is worth it in the end.

Student at Medical College of Wisconsin (MD)

Don't give up—ever. If this is what you want to do with your life, you will give it your BEST effort which means not giving up. Enjoy the process, as hellish as it may get at some points, and grow from it. Realize that this is all a lesson in being humble and serving your patients first.

Student at Philadelphia College of Osteopathic Medicine (PCOM) (DO)

Apply early, the earlier you do…the better chance you'll get in at most schools. They take the largest pool in the first few months!!

Student at Medical College of Wisconsin (MD)

Read as much as you can on how to get into medical school. The more you find out, the better. Also, meet with your premed advisor as soon as possible. Meet and speak with some successful applicants. Also, there are many things to complete outside of the classroom and many people have no clue. You need to get shadowing, research, etc., out of the way as soon as possible and you will want to take the April MCAT in your junior year. Also, make sure you do everything in the application process early and in a timely manner—it really pays off! Good Luck!

Student at Medical College of Wisconsin (MD)

INDEX

Please contact Mill City Press
for bulk discounts or any orders

•

Phone: 612-455-2290 ext 202

Fax 612-455-2297

Email: sales@millcitypress.net

Website http://www.millcitypress.net

Printed in the United States
100479LV00002B/46/A

9 781934 248171